K9 EXPLOSIVE AND MINE DETECTION

Other titles in the *K9 Professional Training Series*
K9 Aggression Control, 2nd ed.
K9 Behavior Basics, 2nd ed.
K9 Decoys and Aggression, 2nd ed.
K9 Drug Detection
K9 Investigation Errors
K9 Personal Protection, 2nd ed.
K9 Scent Training
K9 Schutzhund Training, 2nd ed.
K9 Search and Rescue, 2nd ed.

Other K9 titles from Dog Training Press
K9 Complete Care
K9 Explosive Detection
K9 Officer's Manual
K9 Professional Tracking
K9 Scent Detection
K9 Suspect Discrimination
K9 Working Breeds
Police Officer's Guide to K9 Searches

K9 EXPLOSIVE AND MINE DETECTION

A Manual for Training and Operations

Dr. Resi Gerritsen
Ruud Haak

K9 Professional Training Series

An imprint of
Brush Education Inc.

Copyright © 2017 Resi Gerritsen and Ruud Haak

17 18 19 20 21 5 4 3 2 1

Thank you for buying this book and for not copying, scanning, or distributing any part of it without permission. By respecting the spirit as well as the letter of copyright, you support authors and publishers, allowing them to continue to create and distribute the books you value.

Excerpts from this publication may be reproduced under licence from Access Copyright, or with the express written permission of Brush Education Inc., or under licence from a collective management organization in your territory. All rights are otherwise reserved, and no part of this publication may be reproduced, stored in a retrieval system, or transmitted in any form or by any means, electronic, mechanical, photocopying, digital copying, scanning, recording, or otherwise, except as specifically authorized.

Brush Education Inc.
www.brusheducation.ca
contact@brusheducation.ca

Cover Design: John Luckhurst; Cover images: Dog Training Center Oosterhout and Shutterstock/Boonroong
Interior Design: Carol Dragich, Dragich Design
Illustrations: Chao Yu, Vancouver

Printed and manufactured in Canada

Library and Archives Canada Cataloguing in Publication
Gerritsen, Resi, author
K9 explosive and mine detection : a manual for training and operations / Resi Gerritsen, Ruud Haak.

Includes bibliographical references.
Issued in print and electronic formats.
ISBN 978-1-55059-690-8 (softcover).—ISBN 978-1-55059-691-5 (PDF).—ISBN 978-1-55059-693-9 (EPUB).—ISBN 978-1-55059-692-2 (MOBI)

1. Detector dogs—Training—Handbooks, manuals, etc.   2. Explosives—Detection—Handbooks, manuals, etc.   3. Land mines—Detection—Handbooks, manuals, etc.   I. Haak, Ruud, author   II. Title.

SF428.2.G475 2017   636.7'0886   C2017-901651-2
                                              C2017-901652-0

Contents

Introduction vii
1. Dog and Handler 1
2. Explosives, Weapons, Ammunition, and IEDs 27
3. Training Odors 65
4. Influences on Searching 78
5. Explosive Detection Training 106
6. Search Actions 129
7. Examinations and Performance Assessment 160
8. Mine Detection Dogs 183
9. Stress in Operational Service 217
10. First Aid 243
11. Explosives: Past and Present 267
    Bibliography 295
    Photo Credits 299
    About the Authors 301

Introduction

In the 1970s and 1980s, terrorists operated in solid, organized groups using long-standing techniques. Their goals were generally clearly defined and political, such as the formation of an independent state. Organizations such as the Irish Republican Army (IRA) in Ireland, the Red Brigades in Italy, and *Euskadi Ta Askatasuna* (ETA) in Spain usually focused their efforts on embassies and military targets as a way to get the attention of national governments. Some actions involved civilians (e.g., hijacking aircraft and setting off bombs in London), but the death and injury of civilians was considered a means to an end: putting pressure on states to accept the group's demands.

Since the 1990s, these traditional motives in terrorism have become clouded. Motives have become broader, with religious goals joining and sometimes superseding political ambitions. Members of terrorist groups are more diverse and distributed geographically, making them incredibly difficult to identify. Individuals and small cells may operate independently, with little or no contact with a movement's leadership. Directions for homemade weapons are easily available, and perpetrators even use themselves as weapons (e.g., suicide bombings). In addition, targets are not easy to identify; today anything and anyone can be the target of a terrorist attack. The hijacking of aircraft and ships is no longer just a tactic to exert political pressure, but is now also a way to acquire an offensive weapon for attacks. The best-known example of this, of course, was seen on September 11, 2001.

Dogs have been used to detect mines and other explosives for many years. Even before World War I, dogs were trained to detect the chemical signature of explosives and weapons. Since World War II, dog–handler teams have been used extensively by the military to locate mines. However, the first mine action programs, including those using dogs, were inefficient and unsafe, partly because the demining organizations still had to learn their craft, partly because they had few resources to work with, and also because they did not yet have safe, effective methods of searching for mines with dogs.

Most operational searches for explosives find nothing, which can be viewed as a success: where there is no bomb, none can explode. The work of explosive detection is very serious; mistakes can be catastrophic. This enormous responsibility must always be kept in mind while training explosive or mine detector dogs. Dogs play a critical role in ensuring accuracy. A well-trained explosive or mine detection dog has an investigative accuracy level of 95 percent, which is 40 percent higher than the performance a human has in the search for the same explosive.

As specialists in explosive detection, dogs do a serious job, although the dogs consider their job a game. With the reward of play, a favorite toy, or food each time they successfully find a target scent, dogs can be trained to signal when they smell explosives.

We wish to thank Claudia and André Boomaars of Dog Training Center Oosterhout (www.hondencentrum-claudia.nl) for the photos of our training methods and the information they contributed to this book. We also thank the much-too-early-deceased Sgt. 1. Ed Snoek, commander of the dog section of the Royal Dutch Airforce at Airbase Volkel, the Netherlands, and also Nico Ram, police dog training instructor of the regional police, Rotterdam-Rijnmond, for all the advice and information they gave us during the many years we were in contact, and for their help in training our dogs.

Dr. Resi Gerritsen and Ruud Haak

Disclaimer

While the contents of this book are based on substantial experience and expertise, working with dogs involves inherent risks, especially in dangerous settings and situations. Anyone using approaches described in this book does so entirely at their own risk, and both the authors and publisher disclaim any liability for any injuries or other damage that may be sustained.

1

Dog and Handler

Selecting a Dog for Explosive Detection

Success in the special training for explosive detection begins with making a careful choice of the right dog. Dogs that are nervous or frightened, dogs with too much temperament, or dogs that are too self-confident or stubborn are not good choices. With a lot of perseverance, an experienced handler may achieve something with such a dog, but for the dog itself, the training and work will be a mental torment, which will be expressed sooner or later in serious disorders.

Figure 1.1 Search work is strenuous, both mentally and physically. Only healthy dogs can be used for the heavy training required for explosive detection.

Search work is strenuous, both mentally and physically. Only healthy dogs can be used for the heavy training required for explosive detection. Avoid dog breed lines with hereditary issues such as hip and elbow dysplasia, which prevent normal movement. But other hereditary physical defects, such as epilepsy and eye disorders, also make a dog absolutely unsuitable for work in explosive detection. In addition, many kinds of illnesses and medications affect the nose (see chapter 4, Influences on Searching). Training a dog while its sense of smell is not optimal will cause all kinds of unnecessary stress, which in turn will be detrimental to the training.

RECOMMENDED PHYSICAL QUALITIES
For successful explosive detector dog training, we recommend that the dog

- preferably belong to one of the following breeds or crossbreeds: Malinois, German or Dutch shepherd, Labrador, or spaniel;
- have an excellent nose;
- have an optimal sense of sight and hearing;
- be absolutely healthy, and sound in life and limb;
- have a strong and muscled body;
- walk and move with ease;
- be in optimal condition and have strong stamina;
- have strong legs and feet with strong soles; and
- be adapted to the weather and climate in which it has to work.

Explosive detection is physically demanding, but it also requires intensive mental work: the dog has to learn to recognize several target odors and then detect them in every possible location and in all kinds of stressful situations. Of all traditional search dog activities, explosive detection work may be the most demanding in terms of cognitive abilities. The work requires a stable, adult mentality in the dog.

Preparing a dog for detection work should include good socialization, general obedience training, and a stimulation of its search and bring drives through games. Here, care should be taken that the dog learns to search with its nose and that it does not become too possessive of a training tool, such as a ball.

The mental characteristics we require for the training of explosive detector dogs are only found in mature dogs, although some characteristics will develop during the training and cannot be fully tested beforehand. For example, you can try to test a dog's willingness to work before selecting it for training, but it can be difficult to measure the dog's ability to cope with routine before training begins. The ability to cope with mistakes is another characteristic you cannot really test beforehand, but it is a very important quality in dogs that must undergo strenuous training.

RECOMMENDED MENTAL QUALITIES

For successful explosive detector dog training, we recommend that the dog

- show social behavior with humans and other animals;
- have a placid composure (be self-confident and stable, not nervous or afraid);
- possess a lively and interested temperament;
- show a willingness to work even if there is no immediate reward;
- show intelligence, particularly the ability to quickly learn to respond to a cue;
- have a good search drive, with the natural ability to use the nose to find objects;
- not have a prey drive that is overly strong; if the dog defends its reward too strongly, it will be focused on the reward itself too much, which will prevent it from searching well;
- have a high bring drive: by retrieving the reward to its handler, the dog shares it with him, which is good for the team;
- show stress resistance; and
- have the ability to cope with mistakes: if corrected (a verbal correction should be sufficient), the dog should remain composed, willing to work, and not lose its search and bring drive. Dogs that cannot cope quickly with being corrected are difficult to work with.

Training will be successful only if your starting material is good, so look carefully at the characteristics of the dog you want to train. However, it is equally important to look at the characteristics of the handler who is going to teach the dog and to look at the kind of team the handler and dog make.

Selecting a Handler

The physical strain for a handler training an explosive detector dog is not excessive; however, the work does require frequently bending down, squatting, and kneeling. These activities must not be a problem for the handler.

A handler must also have a stable character and not be easily agitated by his dog's behavior. He must know how to interpret the behavior of different dogs and be able to read their signals quickly and accurately. The handler must have patience and be willing to review his own training critically and, when needed, go back a step in training. He must also be aware of the pitfalls he can come across in this work, especially the Clever Hans effect (see "Handler Cues," page 6). This means he has to accept that it is good if the dog is not always focused on him, which is quite different from normal obedience work. The handler must realize that the dog is the only member of the team that can smell well enough to detect hidden explosives. The handler must never try to force his dog into making an alert and instead must adapt his training to help the dog understand what is expected of it.

In short, the handler must be an intelligent and sensitive trainer who stays one step ahead of his dog all the time. So if you want to train a detector dog, begin by looking at yourself critically. Know that an inadequate handler can ruin a potentially good dog. On the other hand, a good handler can go quite a long way with an average dog, but he will not be able to achieve the high standard necessary for operational work. Both members of the team must be top-notch to achieve success in this line of work.

Figure 1.2 Although the characteristics of the dog are essential to a good explosive detection dog team, the characteristics of the handler who is going to teach the dog are also important.

Teamwork

No matter how careful you are about selecting a dog and pairing it with a good handler, mistakes can happen. Once training begins, if things do not go well, stop. The handler should like the dog he works with, and there should be no tension between the dog and handler, neither during training nor outside of training. It is also important that activities outside of training suit the dog and handler and improve their relationship, not create tension. If there is stress between the handler and his dog, it will show up in the training and play an important, negative role.

HANDLER CUES

Everyone who has ever tried to teach a dog something knows that dogs respond very well to handler cues. Most people also realize dogs pick up cues they were not specifically trained to recognize. For example, if you put on your walking shoes, your dog will stick to you like glue because he hopes to go for a walk. Dogs know the cupboard where their treats are stored and will appear by your side as soon as you open the cupboard door. The question is how subtle the cues can be and if dogs can pick up cues you are completely unconscious of.

These subtle cues are called "Clever Hans" cues, after a horse who lived at the turn of the twentieth century in Germany. The horse was owned by Wilhelm von Osten, who discovered that Hans could count and do sums. Von Osten would ask Hans, "How much is five and two?" and Hans would start tapping his hoof, stopping after seven. This amazing ability led to widespread discussion about the intelligence of animals in general. However, by watching both von Osten and other people giving mathematical problems to Hans, the German comparative biologist and psychologist Oskar Pfungst deduced in 1911 that Hans could not do math. Rather, the horse was responding to the questioner's slight leaning forward as a cue to stop tapping his hoof when he had reached the correct answer.

Another, much less well-known doubter of Hans's abilities was Emilio Rendich, a painter. He had also observed that Hans responded to von Osten's leaning forward and backward. He trained his dog Nora to respond to small physical cues in much the same way that Hans did. Nora would start responding to Rendich's question, and when the correct figure was reached, Rendich would lean forward and Nora would stop.

More recently, Ádám Miklósi and his team at the Eötvös Loránd University of Budapest, Hungary, has studied this subject. Miklósi's team confirmed that dogs are able to use human gestures such as pointing, bowing, nodding, head turning, and glancing as cues for finding hidden food. Dogs were also able to generalize from one person (the owner) to another familiar person (the experimenter) in using the same gestures as cues. Miklósi and his team suggest that the phenomenon of dogs responding to human cues is better analyzed as a case of interspecies communication than in terms of discrimination learning. In other words, the dogs' understanding of nonverbal cues is a form of communication with humans rather than a simple learned response to specific stimulation. The importance of these experiments is that they illustrate how well dogs can learn to "read" us.

During training, we want dogs to learn to respond to the **relevant** cue, such as the odor of an explosive. So when searching for an odor, the only cue must be the odor. Observing handlers with their dogs, we sometimes see handlers providing obvious, even if unintentional cues. We know dogs carefully watch their handler while searching, and a minimal movement, even a glance or small step backward, is enough for a dog to immediately lie down without any indication of an explosive odor.

So how can we prevent ourselves from cueing the dog in some way, if they can pick up and use such minimal signals? The answer is obvious: work "blind" or "operational," as described in chapter 5, Explosive Detection Training. Do not know the position of the matching odor in a lineup, do not know the location of a hidden cache of explosives, and preferably have no one close by who knows since this person may also unconsciously cue your dog.

The Basics of Dog Behavior

To successfully train explosive detector dogs, handlers need to understand several basic elements of dog behavior and learning. This knowledge will help the handler properly assess and select a dog for training and then also train the dog and manage its work in the field. What follows is a summary of some of the basics about dog behavior that every handler should know. Each idea is discussed in more detail in our book *K9 Behavior Basics: A Manual for Proven Success in Operational Service Dog Training* (Brush Education, 2013).

STIMULATION → RESPONSE

Behavior is a sequence of actions performed by an animal (in our case, the dog) after being stimulated to do so. An animal always acts as result of a stimulus, which can be conscious or unconscious. This stimulus can reach the animal from the outside or can originate in its own body. An example of an external stimulus is seeing some kind of danger approaching; with such a stimulus, the animal might react by escaping. Hunger is an example of an internal stimulus; hunger prompts an animal to search for food. Not every animal reacts in the same way to a certain stimulus, which is why there are big differences in behavior between individuals of the same species.

HEREDITARY BEHAVIOR

An important part of behavior is determined by heredity, and in principle hereditary behavior does not differ from hereditary characteristics such as the color of the coat, the shape of the ear, or the place or position of the limbs.

Innate behaviors are acts determined by heredity and that are already partially present at birth. These are, in the beginning, simple acts, such as urinating and defecating when the female licks the puppies and pushing with the front legs against the mother's nipple to get the milk out of the deeper regions of the milk glands. In a later stage of the dog's life, various behaviors the dog was never taught will appear, such as turning around before lying down and scratching away soil after answering nature's call. These are also considered innate behaviors.

Acquired behaviors are also determined by heredity but have to be further developed by learning. These behaviors are learned in the so-called socialization period, which is from about the third to twelfth week after birth. In this period, the dog learns to react to siblings, other dogs, people, odors, sounds, sight, and so on.

Trained behaviors are the strengthening or suppression of innate and acquired behaviors. This training begins with obedience training, but extends to other training, such as that needed for a detector dog. When at least part of the trained behavior is not innate or acquired, or if there is no hereditary tendency for a certain behavior, then learning that behavior makes no sense to the dog. This is a key understanding: trying to train a dog to perform an action that has no basis in the dog's natural behaviors will be frustrating and, most likely, unsuccessful.

Good trainers know how to frame a human goal in a way that works with, not against, a dog's natural biology.

Yet puppies of the same parents can be very different in their behavior patterns. This variation arises because of differences in genetics, differences in the socialization of the puppies, and differences in the way the dogs' owners try to train them. Parents with a good aptitude for training usually have descendants with a good aptitude for training. However, these promising descendants still have to develop their skills through proper socialization, education, and training.

INSTINCT

A dog's response to external stimuli is always functional and significant. Its behavior has the goal of self-preservation and thus, survival of the species. Behavioral responses to external stimuli are called *instinctive acts*. An instinctive act is innate behavior that is typical for the species. An instinctive act is the ability of an animal, in a situation it has been never been in before, to react to certain stimuli in such a way that its survival will not be in danger. The instinct thereby ensures the survival of the species. For example, an animal will attempt to flee a house fire or forest fire even if the animal has no experience with such an event.

Instinctive acts are further developed by experience and exercises. In young dogs, instincts develop by playing together and imitating the behavior of older animals. In the play of puppies, for example, they develop the acts necessary for hunting. In turn, the puppies are hunter or prey, or we see them shake rags or toys in an imitation of shaking prey to death. Through play, the reactions of the young animals sharpen and their skills develop, while they also learn to control their bodies.

DRIVE

Along with understanding the role of instinct in a dog's behavior, handlers should also understand the concept of drive. A drive happens without the animal's will. It is aroused by certain stimuli that push, or drive, it to certain acts. These drives underpin the reactions we call the instinctive acts.

The dog's drives, along with its organs of sense and its temperament, form its "doggy" character. It is difficult to divide instinctive acts according to different drives, because many times an act will fit more than one drive. That's why we like to speak of a drive complex, because we believe the drives are interwoven, creating the characteristics of the dog. Dogs have drive complexes for food acquisition, reproduction, flight, and aggression. These drive complexes can activate various drives in the dog, which then result in certain instinctive acts.

For example, the hunting, prey, tracking, search, pack, and bring drives form a chain, which take care of acquiring the food necessary for canids living in the wild. For our modern dog, for whom the problem of food acquisition no longer exists, these drives can show up independently of each other. Then we see, for example, that the hunting drive can be present without the prey drive, or that the bring drive has nothing to do with food. For our dogs, the hunting drive, as well as the prey and bring drives, can be worked off by replacing prey with a toy, a stick, a ball, or, for greyhounds, a piece of rabbit skin.

Dog training is most effective if it is based on the natural ability and drive complexes of the dog and, when instinctive acts are triggered, the dog can work them out until the end. Every interruption of an instinctive act creates frustration for the dog because it is driven to perform the act. The interruption makes the dog unhappy about the work we want it to perform because stopping the act goes against its nature.

DRIVES IMPORTANT FOR EXPLOSIVE DETECTOR DOGS
Here we will discuss the drives that are particularly important for explosive detector dogs.

HUNTING DRIVE
By *hunting drive,* we mean the characteristic drive of dogs to scent for game or to search for and chase game on sight. This drive goes back to the forefathers of the dog, wolves, and finds its origins

in the pressure to find food. The hunting drive is still present in our modern dogs in a more or less emphatic form, although it has nothing to do with feeling hungry or with the pressure for food acquisition. The hunting drive is therefore not only present in hunting dogs, but also in just about every dog, with the exception of some house pets.

PREY DRIVE

The *prey drive* is very similar to the hunting drive. Originally the prey drive grew out of the attempt to hunt, catch, and kill game to satisfy the animal's hunger and that of their young. This drive is also present in many modern dogs; however, it is now often focused on chasing toys. Chasing game is no longer taught to young dogs (except, of course, in training hunting dogs), and the prey drive is now expressed in chasing, catching, and shaking articles to "death."

TRACKING DRIVE

The *tracking drive* is expressed in the willingness of the dog to follow a game track or pick up a human track (smelling with the nose near the soil) and in striving to follow that track with enthusiasm and perseverance.

SEARCH DRIVE

By *search drive* we mean the dog's interest in catching game (or hidden objects, people, or odors), not only by using its nose, but also with the support of the eyes and ears, and in following the found odor by air scenting, with a high nose, enthusiastically and in a determined way.

PACK DRIVE

The *pack drive* is demonstrated by dogs striving for temporary or long-term group relationships. For most dogs, humans and human society have become their pack (group). The human family replaces the pack and becomes the dog's familiar social and family circle. In this pack, the dog will then orient all its drives and instincts (in a somewhat changed form) toward living communally.

BRING DRIVE

The *bring drive* is expressed by wild canids (under the influence of the pack drive) when they bring prey or parts of it to the lair, where the mother and young dogs are waiting. Given their prey and bring drives and some focused exercises, the dog can be trained to pick up and bring replacement prey to the handler, which is usually called retrieving.

PLAY DRIVE

The *play drive* is especially present in young dogs, but usually is effective until the dog is quite old. This drive has a strong relationship with the motion and occupation drives. By play-skirmishing with packmates or by playing with objects, the young dog learns to use and control its skills and power, both physical and mental. Play helps it prepare for the more serious tasks of life, such as hunting, reproduction, and defence.

MOTION AND OCCUPATION DRIVES

The *motion* and *occupation drives* originate in the constitutional circumstances of the animal, its temperament and muscular strength, as well as its circumstances, health, feeding level, and training. In canids living in the wild, the motion and occupation drives are satisfied by the struggle of daily existence: food acquisition, skirmishes with packmates, and avoiding enemies. Because our modern dog doesn't have to struggle for existence anymore, it feels, depending on its age, temperament, and physical circumstances, a more or less intense pressure to release stored bodily and mental energy in movement, or in some sort of work. This need to do something is more intense in young dogs and certain working dog breeds.

INTELLIGENCE

Along with a dog's drive complexes, a dog's intelligence will greatly affect its success as an explosive detector dog. We distinguish between three forms of intelligence: the instinctive, the practical, and the adaptive.

By *instinctive intelligence* we mean all hereditary skills and behavior. For instance, the hunting drive is instinctive: every puppy runs after a moving object.

By *practical intelligence* we mean the speed with which, and the degree to which, the dog conforms to the desires of the handler. Roughly said, practical intelligence is how quickly and correctly the dog learns the different exercises in training.

Adaptive intelligence can be divided into two abilities. One is the dog's learning proficiency, which means how quickly it develops adequate behavior in a new situation. The second is the dog's problem-solving ability, which is the dog's skill in choosing the correct behavior to solve problems.

TEMPERAMENT

Temperament is expressed in the psychological skills and degree of reaction to different "prickles" (stimulations) from the environment. The more lively a dog is and the more intensive its response to its surroundings, the more full of temperament it is. The slower and less the dog reacts to its environment, the less temperament the dog has. For example, a dog with a strong guard drive that is full of temperament will focus intently when a small prickle from its surroundings occurs (e.g., a person approaching from far away). Dogs with such a temperament are happy and attentive, and always stay active.

It is important to recognize the difference between a dog full of temperament and a nervous dog. Some handlers want dogs that, when something happens, are immediately itching to react. They say the dog has temperament, but that is not true: it is three-quarters nervousness, often combined with a big part of sharpness (a hostile response to the unknown). Whereas the dog full of temperament will attentively but calmly watch an unknown person approaching from the distance, a nervous dog will excitedly jump back and forth, bark, squeak, and possibly run in agitated circles.

Figure 1.3 A dog's training should include its future working places such as airplanes and luggage handling bays. It needs to get used to the sounds, sights, and smells of locations where it will have to concentrate on its work.

SELF-CONFIDENCE AND COMPOSURE

A dog is self-confident when its attitude is free of nervousness, fear, or jumpiness. Sudden and unexpected prickles, such as gunshots, traffic noise, or waving flags, do not bring it out of balance.

Composure is an important factor for an explosive detector dog. An adult dog must stay absolutely calm and show self-confidence, even when placed in completely unfamiliar or challenging circumstances such as crowds or urban traffic.

The dog must also be reliable, so its performance is without surprises. Dogs that are too independent and that "resist" are disturbing in daily contact and not recommended for explosive detector dog training.

WILLINGNESS TO WORK

A dog you have to wake up before going to work won't likely become a good explosive detector dog. A dog that likes to work shows interest when it sees its handler is getting ready to go. What is also, maybe even more, important is that the dog has to show both before and during work an almost tireless willingness to work.

Figure 1.4 It is important that the handler and dog like each other and have no tensions between them, neither during training nor outside of training.

Figure 1.5 Here a dog handler with the US marines plays with Cookie, an improvised explosive device (IED) detection dog in Afghanistan in 2012.

To be able to do this, the dog must be in very good health and have stamina. In short, you want a dog in which you see a definite willingness to work and which needs no encouragement to continue and concentrate on its work.

TOUGHNESS AND SOFTNESS

By toughness we mean the ability to suffer unpleasant prickles or events, such as pain or punishment, without being put off (even temporarily), and to forget pain or punishment just as quickly (low sensitivity). A tough dog will not be prevented from carrying out the handler's commands even if it is hurt or in pain. Softness is the opposite. A soft dog will be strongly affected by unpleasant events or frightening circumstances and will avoid such situations or prickles in the future (high sensitivity). However, softness must not be confused with fear of pain. Some dogs are very sensitive and squeal at the slightest pain, such as an injection. But they will not lose their confidence in the person who causes the pain.

INTERACTING CONDITIONS

Three interacting conditions influence the achievements of a dog: the physical, the mental, and the working conditions.

Physical condition: The dog should have well-trained muscles and be fed correctly. When physical condition is lacking, the dog will be exhausted after only a brief exertion. With poor or insufficient feeding, the dog will be dominated by hunger, leaving it with a lack of concentration, insufficient energy to perform, and intense nervousness.

Mental condition: The dog should have the ability to independently and enthusiastically work out exercises without pressure or compulsion from the handler. When a dog's mental condition is lacking, we see apathy, stress, or physical tiredness.

Working condition: A dog with good working condition shows the ability to concentrate long enough to complete a task. When working condition is lacking, we see dogs that need a break after a short time because of concentration problems.

PHYSICAL CONDITION

To perform well, a dog needs optimal physical fitness. This can be achieved through endurance training. For dogs, this training can be swimming or trotting beside a bicycle or on a treadmill.

Endurance training asks special requirements from the dog's internal organs, such as the heart and lungs, but also from the muscles, foot pads, and skeleton due to the demands of locomotion. Therefore, the dog should first have a veterinary check-up before beginning endurance training. Plan this training carefully and your dog can acquire a good muscular mass and easy, effective movement. The training must gradually and properly stimulate the muscles and the skeleton, while avoiding sudden movements and risks to the joints.

TIPS FOR ENDURANCE TRAINING

- The trotting tempo of the dog should be from 7–9 miles per hour (12–15 km/h).
- Do not allow your dog to pull on the leash too hard, and do not fasten the leash to the bicycle or around your hand: if the dog suddenly runs to the side, it will pull you down.
- The dog should preferably be at least one year of age before starting endurance training.
- The temperature should be less than 20–25°C.
- Take good care of your dog's foot pads and examine them carefully for injuries. To examine your dog's pads, pull the legs carefully backward—never to the side. Superficial injuries can be treated by application of products such as Friar's Balsam, Espree Paw Balm, or another natural paw wax and giving the dog rest. Puncture wounds must be treated by a vet.
- Always monitor your dog's condition carefully during training. Dogs usually warn us too late that the training is too much for them. On a cycle, keep in mind that you still have to cycle back home, so you don't want to injure or exhaust your dog.
- Don't feed your dog or allow it to drink too much water before an endurance training session.
- Before you begin, do a good warm-up, as described on page 224.

SAMPLE ENDURANCE TRAINING SCHEDULE

This endurance training schedule is to prepare for a 12 mile (20 km) endurance test in which dogs must first trot about 5 miles (8 km) beside their handler's bicycle, then they have a break for 15 minutes. They continue with another trot for about 4 miles (7 km), followed by a second break of 20 minutes, and then a final trot for the remaining 3 miles (5 km). At the end of the test, the dog must be able to do a few simple obedience exercises, such as heeling and jumping. Start training about six weeks before the day of the test.

The schedule that follows can be adjusted to specific training needs, and it can also function as regular stamina training.

- *Week 1*: Four times (every other day), cycle about 3 miles (5 km). On alternate days, cycle 2 miles (3 km). On your first day, start with a 2 mile ride. Observe your dog carefully, and if he shows symptoms of tiredness, stop and rest, walk back home, and revise the overall training schedule to begin with shorter distances.
- *Week 2*: Four times (every other day), cycle about 4 miles (7 km); on alternate days, cycle 2.5–3 miles (4–5 km).
- *Week 3*: Three times (about every other day), cycle 6 miles (10 km), with a break after 3 miles (5 km). On alternate days, cycle about 3.5 miles (6 km).
- *Week 4*: Two days cycle 9 miles (15 km) with a break after 5 miles (8 km); on alternate days, cycle about 3.5 miles (6 km).
- *Week 5*: One day at the beginning of the week and one day at the end of the week, cycle 12 miles (20 km), with a break after 5 miles (8 km) and after 9 miles (15 km); the other days, cycle about 3–5 miles (5–8 km) to keep muscular strength.

The breaks in this schedule have to be at least 10–15 minutes. During this time, check your dog's pads and give him some water. Once the dog is running longer distances, you might add glucose polymers (about 1.5 g carbohydrate/kg body weight) to its water.

On paved streets, don't let your dog trot too close to the side of the road. Traffic shoves small stones, pieces of glass, and other sharp objects to the sides of the road, increasing the chance of wounding your dog's pads. Wet asphalt and concrete also pose a higher risk for injuries to the pads. Under such circumstances, take another route or shorten the training.

MENTAL CONDITION

The Webster's general definition for stress is "any stimulus, such as fear or pain, that disturbs or interferes with the normal physiological equilibrium of an organism." It may also be defined as physical, mental, or emotional strain or tension. Both definitions are applicable to the effect of stress on a dog's performance because both physical and emotional stress may result in physiologic changes that reduce a dog's working potential.

Yet stress is an absolutely natural reaction of an organism toward certain stimuli, challenges, and loads, the so-called *stress factors* or *stressors*. For normal physical and mental development, every animal needs appropriate loads (stressors) that lead to clashes with its environment. These stressors help the animal learn to quickly respond and adapt to its biosphere. The body does not differentiate between positive stress (eustress) and negative stress (distress). Every strong stimulus produces the same physical pattern of reactions.

In a positive way, stress results in an increased supply of energy from the body, which allows quick reactions and increased physical capabilities, leading to an animal's optimal preparedness for the challenges of the environment. For example, an animal experiencing the stress of a predator's sudden appearance will have the rush of energy needed to allow it to escape the danger.

Stress becomes negative when it is continuous (chronic) or extremely strong. Negative stress can result in diseases of the immune system or kidneys, and gastrointestinal or cardiovascular problems. In dogs, chronic negative stress can also be seen as a high aggressive impulse.

Whether a stressor is positive or negative depends on its effects on the body, which can differ from individual to individual in a species. The threshold for physical or mental damage from stress depends on many factors, such as the animal's heredity, health, experiences, and so on.

STRESSORS

The experience of stress, and the means by which an organism develops a way to cope with stress, can differ in humans, as in dogs. A situation that one dog faces calmly can be a heavy burden for another dog. There are five main categories of stressors that affect dogs (and humans, for that matter).

- *External stressors*: inundation with stimuli of the sense organs (e.g., light, noise, odor, heat, cold) or withdrawal of stimuli (deprivation), pain stimuli, and real or simulated dangerous situations.
- *Stressors that prevent the satisfaction of primary needs*: sleep deprivation, withdrawal of food or water, no or less bodily contact, prevention of movement (chaining up or kenneling).
- *Performance stressors*: physical overexertion, over- or undertraining, improper training methods, excessive demands in training or operational service, too much responsibility, inappropriate activity for the breed of dog, forthcoming tests, failures, reprimands, or punishment.
- *Social stressors*: isolation, less or no contact with other dogs, incorporation into a new dog group, removal from a dog group, change of human partner.
- *Mental stressors*: conflicts, uncontrollable situations, anxiety, uncertain expectations, unpredictable and inconsistent human behavior, noisy surroundings, irregular days, constantly changing environment.

WORKING CONDITION

By working condition, we mean the dog's ability to be engaged in a task. For working dogs, this is the work they are trained for, such as explosive detection. A dog with a good working condition is well able to perform its assigned duty for a reasonable time without a decrease in performance level. This working condition has to be built up gradually.

The two most important factors that determine a dog's working condition are motivation and concentration. If a dog has no predisposition for motivation and concentration, it cannot be brought to a high performance level.

MOTIVATION

Abraham Maslow describes motivation as "an energy and tension oriented toward a certain goal." Motivation produces a selective attention for certain stimuli, without being distracted by other stimuli.

An example is the way a tracking dog follows a human track. From the start, the dog focuses on the human footprints on the ground, and as long as it is able to find these footprints, it will stay with its nose on the track. The dog will not be diverted by flowers, objects, changes in the terrain, or other distractions. Only if it is not able to perceive the odor of the track anymore will it try to find another way to come to the end of the track by perceiving stimuli that were previously ignored, such as visual cues.

Motivation can be seen as the mainspring or origin for a certain behavior. It directs the behavior—a driving force, like coals heat the fire. Through conditioning, an animal can be motivated to increase or decrease this behavior. Motivation can be sparked by the interaction between a certain physiologic state of the organism and certain environmental stimuli. So if a dog is hungry and it smells food, it will be motivated to scent the air or ground to locate the food. In this example, the smell of food is the start-stimuli. Such start-stimuli can arouse certain reactions (drooling, sniffing the air or ground) and at the same time serve as signal-stimuli that steer the behavior in a certain direction. So a dog conditioned to detect explosives might see the handler's command or hand signal as a start-signal and will be motivated to find explosives to receive its reward.

To attain optimal performance, a dog needs a certain amount of tension. If tension is too low, the stimuli does not prompt a response; if tension is too high, the dog may respond to its own stress rather than the correct stimuli. So in a searching situation, a handler who doesn't appear interested or excited about the search would create a low-tension environment, and the dog might not search well. But if the handler is over-tense, perhaps shouting or seeming agitated and angry, the dog might experience the situation as too tense, making it want to hide or retreat instead of search.

Figure 1.6 This is what we want as a good response: a sitting alert without touching the object. The dog shows good concentration.

Figure 1.7 In this alert, the dog shows too much interest in the object and touches it. He may be hypermotivated.

Hypermotivation in dogs leads to poor performance of their duty. Hypermotivated dogs are active and agile, but they are not purposeful in their work and they may persist in inappropriate, ineffective behaviors. Their level of tension is too high.

CONCENTRATION

Many people misunderstand the concept of concentration. Most of the time it is only used if talking about the ability to focus attention on an unpleasant task. A much better understanding is that

Figure 1.8 An explosive detector dog should be used to seeing and working near an explosive ordnance disposal robot.

concentration is the ability to isolate a part from a complex and to stay occupied with it. When a duty is experienced as pleasant, concentration goes more or less smoothly. But if the task that has to be performed is experienced as unpleasant or negative, concentration is often less intense and short-lived.

A task or command initially experienced as negative can become positive if the dog clearly understands exactly what is expected. This shift often happens in training courses. A task might be experienced as unpleasant when a dog is first learning it because it doesn't know what the handler wants. However, once the dog knows what it has to do, the dog performs the order with pleasure. It will concentrate without problems on its duty. But if the order or task remains unpleasant, and the dog has to be forced again and again to repeat it, the activity will take a lot of its energy, and it will not persist for long. To avoid giving your dog negative experiences, be clear with instructions and watch it all the time to be sure it understands what it needs to do. If your dog shows uncertainty, find another method of communicating what you want it to do.

Figure 1.9 Get your dog used to seeing people in bomb suits during early training.

BUILDING UP A DOG'S WORKING CONDITION

Even if a dog's motivation and concentration are excellent, working condition cannot be improved without the foundation of good physical and mental conditions. With poor physical condition, or with a lack of energy caused by hunger, neither dogs nor humans are able to stay motivated to work out a task over a long period. They get tired quickly, and with that, concentration becomes impossible. Without concentration, an overdose of stimuli works at the brain, and motivation will not be purposeful. The same counts for mental condition: a stressed human is often unable to accomplish his task, suffering from overstrain or burnout. That goes for dogs, too.

Figure 1.10 A US marine interacts with an IED detection dog after searching a compound in Afghanistan in 2013.

Figure 1.11 A dog handler gives a command to Sassy, his tactical explosive detection dog, while checking a vehicle in Afghanistan in 2012.

So to develop optimal working condition, a dog first has to have optimum physical and mental condition. With those conditions as a foundation, working condition can be built up gradually in the following aspects of the job:

- *Length of working time*: increase gradually.
- *Number of distractions*: sounds, people, objects, other dogs, and so on.

- *Conditions*: at night; in crowds and noise; in all weather conditions; in or near houses, barns, cowsheds, warehouses; in cars, aircraft, and ships; directly starting out of the car or kennel; postponement of rewards; and so on.
- *Surroundings*: towns, cities, harbors, passenger terminals, woods, mountains, sand plains, water, concrete slabs, and so on.
- *Level of difficulty*: building in more and more obstacles and hindrances (literally and figuratively) to the task.

Not all of these components will be equally important for every explosive detector dog. Each handler has to decide which components are important for his dog and train those. Never forget to build working condition gradually and add components one at a time. By changing more than one component at a time, there is a chance that the dog will react negatively and be unable to perform its duty. This type of stress only breaks down the dog's confidence, which you want to avoid. Your job as trainer is to help build your dog and its confidence up.

It is of great importance in training that dogs are challenged to solve problems by themselves. For example, dogs might be challenged to surpass an obstacle to investigate an explosive odor. But they must have a real chance to solve the problem so they can experience success. This success increases the dog's motivation and concentration for the next task and builds up its working condition.

2

Explosives, Weapons, Ammunition, and IEDs

Explosive substances are mainly used for military purposes. However, we also see applications in the civilian sector in demolition, fireworks, explosive welding, mining, seismic soil testing, aerospace, and avalanche control.

Figure 2.1 US explosive ordnance disposal (EOD) specialists move unexploded ordnance during training.

Describing Explosives

An explosion is a sudden increase in the volume of a quantity of materials and the release of energy in a violent manner, usually accompanied by high temperatures and the release of gases. An explosion causes shock waves in the medium in which it occurs. Explosions can occur in the air, water, or ground, causing different effects in each medium. Explosions are categorized as either *deflagrations* (if the shock waves are subsonic, moving slower than the speed of sound in the same medium) or as *detonations* (if the shock waves are supersonic, moving at faster than the speed of sound in the same medium).

Many explosives have a *phlegmatizing agent*. A phlegmatizing agent helps to stabilize or desensitize the explosive. It is used to improve the handling properties of an explosive (e.g., when munitions are filled in factories) or to reduce the explosive's sensitivity, brisance, or detonation velocity, each of which is discussed below.

SENSITIVITY

The *sensitivity* is the ease with which an explosive substance comes to reaction. The transition to an explosion can be caused by an impact, friction, heat, or spark (including static discharge). The sensitivity of an explosive substance depends on factors such as the density of the explosive or explosive composition; the pressure the material is under; if granular, the grain size; and any additions. Manufacturers try to produce explosive substances with low sensitivity and reliable operation. In particular, military explosives are fairly insensitive to ensure that military personnel can handle them as safely as possible. Personnel must be able to use explosives without fear that they will explode as they work with them, especially under stressful situations such as enemy fire.

BRISANCE

The term *brisance* refers to the power of a material's explosive force. Brisance is determined by the speed of the shock wave following a detonation. So the greater the *detonation velocity*,

Figure 2.2 Explosions are categorized as either deflagrations (if the shock waves are subsonic) or as detonations (if the shock waves are supersonic). This photo was taken at the test center for weapons and ammunution of the Department of Defense of the Netherlands.

the greater the brisance of an explosive. At least three factors are known to influence the detonation velocity of an explosive substance: the method by which a blast is initiated, the size and physical composition of the explosive, and physical conditions such as density and temperature. This means that, depending on these factors, the same explosive can have more or less brisance in its effects.

Explosives that deflagrate have a low brisance power and are classified as "low explosives." Explosives or compositions that detonate have a higher brisance and are classified as "high explosives."

LOW EXPLOSIVES

Low explosives (LEs) deflagrate and produce a mild shock wave and gas, light, smoke, or fire. Their reaction is not as violent as high explosives and there is not always a "bang." Examples include black powder (gunpowder) and smokeless powders that are used as propellants. Pyrotechnics (fireworks) are also low explosives. Ignition of low explosives usually happens through the heat of a flame. The item that produces this flame is called the *percussion cap* or *igniter*.

HIGH EXPLOSIVES

High explosives (HEs) have the ability to destroy material through shock waves and extreme pressure. Their reaction is very fast (up to 6 miles per second or 10,000 m/s) and violent. When an object such as a bullet is moving at supersonic velocity through a medium, it generates shock waves, a front of compressed medium. The passing of such a front is discernible: we hear a thunderclap or resounding "bang"—the "sonic boom" that occurs when a front breaks the sound barrier (travels faster than the speed of sound). TNT is a well-known HE used for both military and civilian purposes.

The only way HEs can be initiated is through a shock wave produced by a *blasting cap* or *detonator*. A detonator is a tool to prompt a stable explosive to explode. The detonator is usually connected to a wick or electrical connection and placed in or directly on the explosive. The detonator consists of a small amount of very sensitive explosive material, such as lead azide or mercury fulminate, which readily explodes from a small shock or contact with heat. This sensitive material gives the blast enough force to ignite the main charge.

High explosives are conventionally subdivided into two classes and differentiated by sensitivity:

- *Primary high explosives* are extremely sensitive to shock, friction, and heat and are mostly used in detonators or blasting caps and in igniters.

- *Secondary high explosives* are relatively insensitive to shock, friction, and heat and are used as the main charge in many projectiles. They are ignited by detonators that have a small amount of primary high explosive in them.

EXPLOSIVES, WEAPONS, AMMUNITION, AND IEDS 31

Figure 2.3 A checkpoint where officials search for suspects, weapons, and ammunition. If there is any suspicion of an explosive, the detector dog will be called in.

Figure 2.4 Sharpshooters, along with military dogs, often monitor the loading of military equipment in risk areas to prevent attacks.

COMMON MILITARY AND COMMERCIAL EXPLOSIVES*

EXPLOSIVE	COMPONENTS
Amatol	Ammonium nitrate + TNT
Ammonal	Ammonium nitrate + TNT + aluminum (Al)
ANFO (Amex or Amite)	Ammonium nitrate + fuel oil (diesel)
Black powder	Potassium nitrate + C + S
Composition A-3	RDX + wax
Composition B	RDX + TNT
Composition C-2	RDX + TNT + DNT + NC + MNT
Composition C-3	RDX + TNT + DNT + tetryl + NC
Composition C-4	RDX + plasticizers
Composition D	Ammonium picrate
Cyclotol	RDX + TNT
Detasheet (Flex-X)	RDX + plasticizers
DBX	TNT + RDX + ammonium nitrate + Al
Demex 200	RDX
Detonation cord (commercial)	PETN
Detonation cord (military)	RDX or HMX
Dynamite (ammonia)	NG + NC + sodium nitrate
Dynamite (gelatin)	NG + NC + ammonium nitrate
Dynamite (military)	TNT
HBX-1	RDX + TNT + Al
Helhoffnite	NB + nitric acid
HTA	HMX + TNT + Al
Nitropel	TNT
Non-el cord	HMX
PE-4	RDX + plasticizer
Pentolite	PETN + TNT
Picratol	TNT + ammonium picrate
Primasheet 1000	PETN + plasticizers
Primasheet 2000	RDX + plasticizers
PTX-1	RDX + TNT + tetryl
PTX-2	RDX + TNT + PETN

Red diamond	NG + EGDN + sodium nitrate + ammonium nitrate
Semtex A	PETN + plasticizers
Semtex H	RDX + PETN + plasticizers
Smokeless powder (single based)	NC
Smokeless powder (double based)	NC + NG
Smokeless powder (triple based)	NC + NG + nitroguanidine
Tetrytol	TNT + tetryl
Time fuse	Potassium nitrate + C + S
Torpex	TNT + RDX + Al
Tritonal	TNT + Al
Water gel/slurry (Aquaspex)	NG
Water gel/slurry (Hydromex)	Ammonium nitrate + TNT
Water gel/slurry (Powermex)	Ammonium nitrate + sodium nitrate + EGMN
Water gel/slurry (Tovex)	Ammonium nitrate + sodium nitrate + MMAN

*Adapted from Mistafa, R. (1998), Yinon, J. (1993, 1999)

ABBREVIATIONS:

Al (aluminum)
C (carbon)
DNT (dinitrotoluene)
EGDN (ethylene glycol dinitrate)
EGMN (ethylene glycol mononitrate)
HMX (octogen)
MMAN (monomethylamine nitrate)
MNT (mononitrotoluene)
NB (nitrobenzene)
NC (nitrocellulose)
NG (nitroglycerin)
PETN (penthrite)
RDX (hexogen)
S (sulfur)
TNT (trinitrotoluene)

Figure 2.5 A Dutch EOD technician wearing a bomb suit on his way to an object after the alert of an explosive detector dog.

Figure 2.6 A US soldier searches a field for unexploded ordnance during a certification exercise designed to mimic real-world scenarios and test EOD personnel on their capabilities.

APPEARANCE

Explosives can be many different colors, including white, pink, green, brown, blue, gray, and yellow. Various forms of explosives are used and packaged in different ways.

- *Plastic explosives* are soft and malleable; they can be molded by the user in any desired shape and are therefore especially suitable for improvised, shaped charges (an explosive charge with a cavity that focuses the blast into a small area).
- *Liquid explosives* are not used a lot; most of the time liquids are used in water-gel explosives (slurries).
- *Slurry explosives* are composed of plastic and liquid explosives; they are often packaged as "sausages." Slurry explosive compositions are widely used in commercial blasting operations such as mining because they are safe and relatively inexpensive, they propagate at high density, and they can be used in wet conditions.
- *Putty-like explosives* can be applied with a caulking gun; they are often used for demolition operations.
- *Foam explosives* are sometimes packaged in aerosol containers for easy application; they are often used in demolitions.
- *Sheet explosives*, also known as rubberized explosives, are thin, flexible sheets with a rubbery texture. They are often used as a flexible, self-adhesive explosive tape for cutting out windows or other openings. These explosives are also used for letter bombs.
- *Solid explosives* can be manufactured in any desired shape. After heating, these explosives are molded into the desired shape and then cooled.

Pyrotechnic Compositions

Fireworks are powders, salts, or other compounds that deflagrate and generate a special effect, such as a flash, flame, or light (white or colored); a pop, whistle, or other sound; smoke (colored or uncolored); and/or a shock wave. Fireworks have fascinated humans for hundreds of years because of the special effects they create. In the beginning, fireworks had ornamental use in particular festivities; later fireworks were used as a warning, distress signal, or torch. Some people spend hundreds of dollars on fireworks during New Year or other celebrations. Furthermore, some daredevils risk their lives trying to make their own fireworks using jam jars or iron pipes. Information on how to make fireworks is often obtained over the Internet, but the directions there are generally highly unreliable and often dangerous.

MILITARY FIREWORKS

The military makes extensive use of fireworks for various purposes, such as creating a bright flash of light at night to take pictures from the air. Military fireworks are also used to create smoke for signals, to mark landing zones, or to set up smoke screens. Such smoke is often created using pots, tins, or canisters containing an explosive mixture (often hexachloroethane and zinc powder) that, through the chemical reaction started after ignition, forms very small solid particles, which propagate in the air as a smoke. Sometimes a dye is added to color the smoke.

Smoke grenades are also used. Once thrown, they produce a thick screen of smoke, sometimes called HC or HCE (hexachloroethane) smoke, which is a mixture containing roughly equal parts of hexachloroethane and zinc oxide and approximately 6 percent granular aluminum. Smoke grenades generally emit far more smoke than smoke pots and are used as a signaling device, to mark landing zones, or to create a hiding screen for people during operations. They are normally not used as a weapon and hits are usually not fatal, but they can cause injury. In addition, the smoke can be toxic because of the production of zinc chloride as a byproduct.

In military exercises or demonstrations, pyrotechnics are also used to simulate the effects of fire, weapons, and ammunition. Such pyrotechnics can create many desired effects (and thus occur in many different compositions). Some mimic explosions and flames, others the firing of a bang rocket or grenade explosion, and some sound like machine gun fire.

Weapons

Most military weapons harness the power of explosives to fire projectiles at high velocity. *Ammunition*, or *munitions*, is the collective name for projectiles and their driving charge. The purpose of ammunition is to project force against a selected target.

A *bullet* is a projectile made of solid metal. A hollow projectile that carries explosives or another payload is called a *shell*. The *caliber* is the measurement of a tube-launched projectile at its thickest part. Bullets are mostly fired from small-arms weapons (caliber up to .78 inches, 20 mm) and shells are mostly used in artillery (caliber larger than .78 inches, 20 mm). This is not a firm rule, however; some small arms fire shells and some artillery fire solid metal projectiles.

BULLETS

The first firearms were used in the fourteenth century after the invention of gunpowder. These early firearms had a smooth-bore barrel and fired round bullets. With the introduction of rifling, which are spiral grooves running down the barrel of firearms, the shape of the bullet changed to a more cylindrical shape, pointed at the front end and sloping back to the rear. A cylindrical bullet can handle much more gas pressure, so bullet speed and firing distance increase significantly. The rifling of the gun barrel provides the bullet a more stable flight, which gives greater accuracy over longer distances. Some types of bullets have a hollow cavity at the back, filled with a flare mixture that ignites when the bullet is fired, producing a bright red light during flight. These "tracer" bullets are used in machine guns and submachine guns, enabling the gunner to bring his line of fire on the target. Tracers can also set a target on fire.

Bullets are traditionally molded from a mixture of lead and tin. Because lead and tin are very soft metals, some bullets are jacketed with copper or steel to make them harder. Steel jacketed bullets are then dipped in copper to prevent the steel from damaging the gun's rifling. Most of the bullets used today are molded from bismuth alloys to prevent the release of toxic lead into the environment. Non-lethal rubber bullets are used for some police purposes, such as riot control.

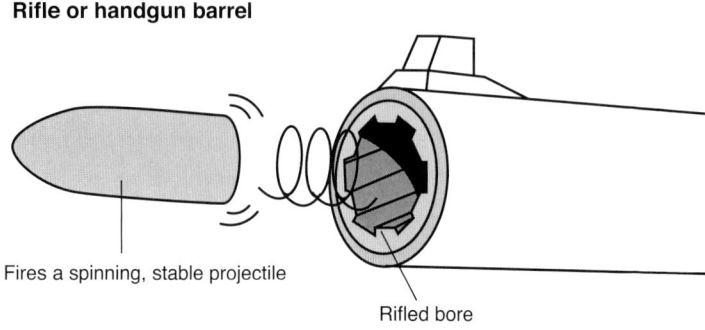

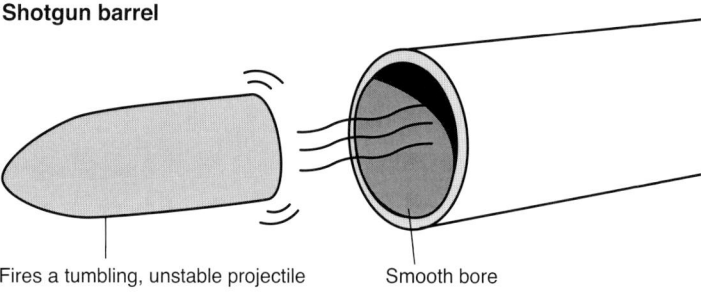

Figure 2.7 A smooth-bore versus rifled-bore barrel.

SHELLS

Shells are basically big, hollow bullets that carry some sort of payload toward the target. This payload can range from an HE, a smoke mixture, a chemical (gas) mixture, and sub-munitions (i.e., ammunition within ammunition, by which many smaller bomblets are released after the main detonation) to pamphlets or illuminating flares. While bullets affect the target through kinetic energy (they move so fast that they penetrate the target), shells affect their target through a second effect, such as the detonation of an explosive payload, the creation of a smoke curtain, the dispersion of a gas cloud, the expulsion of sub-munitions or pamphlets, and so on. Shells are not economic in small sizes and are therefore used in bigger calibers from around 0.78 inches (20 mm) upwards and are fired by artillery, tanks, battleships, and aircraft cannons. The caliber of a shell is measured in millimeters, centimeters, or inches, depending on the country of origin.

Figure 2.8 A rusty bomb shell case from World War II.

Almost all ammunition is painted and stenciled in specific colors for protection from weather, camouflage, and identification.

Types of Ammunition

Bombs, grenades, mines, and torpedoes count as ammunition, but most commonly, the term means ammunition cartridges for firearms. A *cartridge* is a complete round of small-arms ammunition—everything needed to fire a gun one time.

Types of ammunition (commonly shortened to ammo) include the following:

- Small-caliber ammunition
- Hand grenades
- Rifle grenades
- Artillery ammunition
- Mortar ammunition
- Landmines

- Rockets
- Aircraft bombs
- Underwater mines (sea mines, torpedoes)

Figure 2.9 This army box of ammunition contains an ammo belt and hand grenades.

Figure 2.10 The FN MAG is an automatic, air-cooled, light machine gun. Its ammunition is fed through a cartridge band, reaching a rate of fire from about 700 to 750 shots per minute. After firing the bullets, the spent cartridge casings are removed through an ejection port.

SMALL-CALIBER AMMUNITION

Small-caliber ammunition is used for pistols, revolvers, rifles, and machine guns. All have a caliber less than .78 inches (20 mm) and consist of the following components:

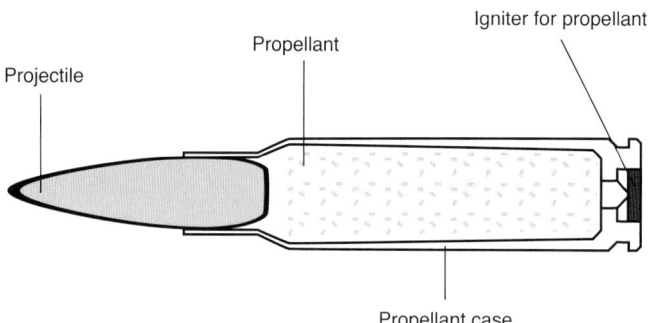

Figure 2.11 The main components of small-calibre ammunition.

- The *projectile*, also called *bullet*, will eventually create the damage at the target. The projectile is usually cylindrical and made of a heavy metal so it will deliver a maximum force on the target. The nose may be round, as in the .45 caliber bullet, or it can be ogival (a curved surface that comes to a point), as for most service rifles and machine guns. The base may be square or boat tailed.
- The *propellant*, also called the *propellant charge*, which consists of a quantity of smokeless powder that provides enough gas pressure to move the bullet forward through the barrel toward the target, but not so much that it will blow the barrel of the weapon.
- The *propellant case*, also called the *case* or *cartridge case*, holds the propellant, keeps it dry, and acts as a housing for the primer. It is often made of brass.
- The *primer*, which is also called the *igniter for the propellant* or *percussion cap*, turns the mechanical impact of the firing pin into a flame that ignites the propellant.

Operation: The complete round (cartridge) is put in the chamber of a pistol or rifle. When the trigger is pulled, the firing pin hits the primer, which is a small, disposable copper or brass cup, 1 to 2 millimeters in diameter. In the cup is a precise amount of stable, but shock-sensitive explosive, such as lead azide. When the firing pin hits the outside of the cup, it bends and the explosive is crushed. This causes the chemical compound to explode, sending a flame to the propellant through two flash holes in the percussion cap. The propellant then sets fire and produces a high gas pressure that pushes the projectile (bullet) loose from the propellant case, forcing it through the barrel of the gun toward the target. The speed of the bullet when leaving the barrel can be up to 0.62 miles per second (1,000 m/s). This whole sequence of events takes no more than 0.01 seconds. The high speed of the bullet, together with its weight, cause great damage to the target.

Special attention: Never put small-caliber ammunition on top of each other; the bullet of one can set off the percussion cap of another.

HAND GRENADES

Hand grenades are short-range projectiles intended to be thrown with the hand, whether or not they are provided with an explosive and igniter. For military forces, hand grenades are thrown by a soldier (grenadier) from his own position to the position of the target. Some are also designed for use by police in riots.

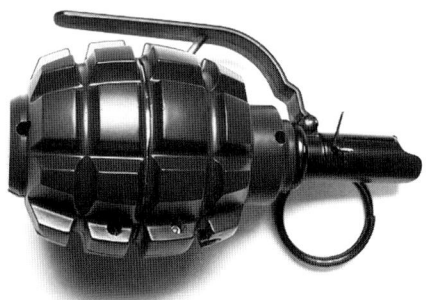

Figure 2.12 Most types of hand grenades consist of a fist-sized body, a bracket, and a safety pin.

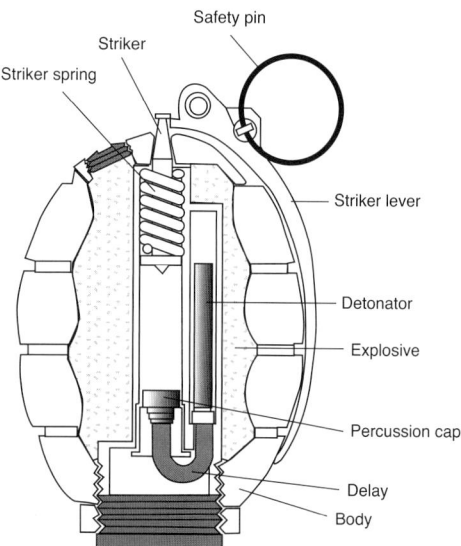

Figure 2.13 The main components of a hand grenade and steps in its operation:
1. Once the safety pin is removed, the striker lever must be held in place.
2. Once the grenade is thrown, the striker lever releases the striker, which releases the high pressure spring that hits the percussion cap.
3. The chemical or powder delay is ignited, providing about a 4 second delay until the flame reaches the detonator.
4. The detonator ignites, which then detonates the main explosive.

EXPLOSIVES, WEAPONS, AMMUNITION, AND IEDS 43

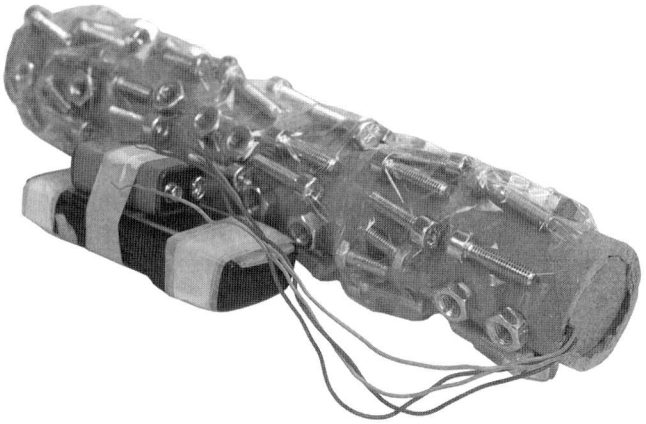

Figure 2.14 A pipe bomb with fragmentation.

A hand grenade can be filled with an explosive, a chemical, a pyrotechnic, or a powder charge. The main types of hand grenades include the following:

- *Fragmentation (frag) grenades*: made of metal or any other material that produces fragments. The fragments are projected in all directions at high velocity when the HE filler detonates. Frag grenades can be ball shaped, oval, or cylindrical and can be pre-fragmented.
- *Offensive grenades*: designed to produce a loud explosion with a minimum of fragments, so they are friendly for a force's own personnel in close-combat situations. The body is smooth and made of thin metal, plastic, or impregnated cardboard.
- *Anti-tank grenades*: designed for use against armored vehicles. They have a shaped charge and the fuse detonates upon impact. The body of the grenade is made of plastic or thin metal.
- *Smoke emitting grenades:* burn and produce smoke when ignited. The smoke comes out of emission holes in the body of the grenade, which is made of thin metal.
- *Burst smoke grenades*: filled with white phosphorus and have a small charge that will burst open the body of the grenade and spread burning white phosphorus up to 82 feet (25 m). The body of the grenade is made of thin metal or plastic.

- *Riot control grenades*: basically the same as smoke emitting grenades, but instead of a smoke composition, these grenades are filled with a riot control agent such as a tear gas—o-chlorobenzylidene malononitrile (CS), chloroacetophenone (CN), or diphenylaminearsine (DM, or Adamsite)—or pepper spray—oleoresin capsicum (OC) or pelargonic acid vanillylamide (PAVA).
- *Incendiary grenades:* have a burn-sustaining charge used to set something on fire.

Operation: The grenade starts to function the moment the safety pin is removed and the grenade leaves the hand of the person who throws it. Then a mousetrap-type mechanism forces away the safety lever and the firing pin hits a percussion cap. After a 3 to 5 second delay, the grenade detonates.

Special attention: Duds of hand grenades are extremely dangerous. They often have a spring-loaded firing mechanism that can be set off with just a slight movement.

RIFLE GRENADES

Rifle grenades are not thrown, but instead are projected up to 1,150 feet (350 m) with a standard service rifle. These grenades are developed to fill the gap between the distance that a hand grenade can be thrown and the minimum firing distance of mortars.

The main types of rifle grenades include the following:

- *Anti-personnel grenades:* fragmentation grenades, sometimes with the same body as a hand grenade, but adapted with a stabilizer and time-delay or an impact-type fuse, sometimes called a direct-action fuse. A direct action fuse causes detontation upon impact with a hard surface.
- *Anti-tank grenades:* shaped-charge grenades for use against light-armored vehicles. They use an impact fuse.
- *Smoke emitting grenades*: basically the same as smoke emitting hand grenades, but adapted with a stabilizer and time delay or an impact fuse.

EXPLOSIVES, WEAPONS, AMMUNITION, AND IEDS

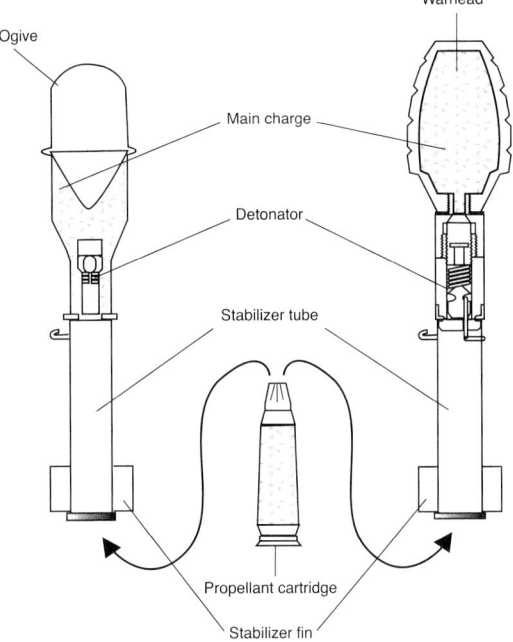

Figure 2.15 Example of a rifle grenade cartridge.

- *Burst smoke grenades*: have an impact fuse and a small HE bursting charge that breaks the warhead open and spreads burning white phosphorus.

Special attention: It is often difficult to establish whether a rifle grenade has been fired. When in doubt, assume it is a dud-fired projectile and treat it with appropriate precaution.

ARTILLERY AMMUNITION

Artillery is a general term covering several varieties of large-caliber weapons (greater than .78 inches, 20 mm) that are capable of firing explosive shells and are of such size and weight that they require a special mount for firing and transport. Weapons covered by this term include traditional tube artillery such as howitzers, cannons, and mortars, as well as modern rocket artillery.

Howitzers are used to fire explosive shells at ground targets up to about 15–19 miles (25–30 km) away. Howitzers are distinguished

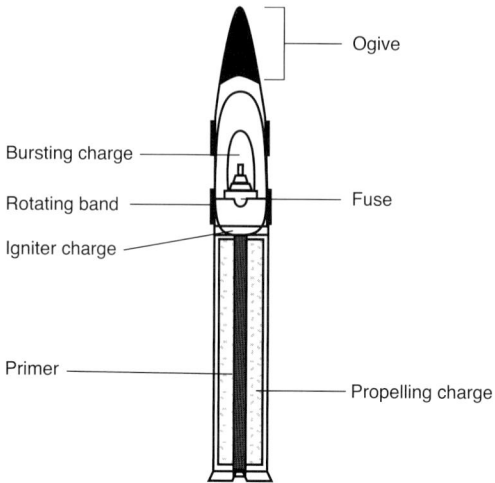

Figure 2.16 An example of artillery ammunition.

from other types of tube artillery because they can shoot at both high- and low-angles. Modern howitzers are commonly either self-propelled or towable. During World War II, a 2.95 inch (75 mm) howitzer was common. This howitzer could be disassembled into components and carried by mule through difficult terrain. Howitzers of such small caliber have generally been abandoned in favor of larger calibers with greater capabilities. Modern howitzers fire 4.13–6.10 inch (105–155 mm) diameter shells at a maximum rate of approximately 10 per minute. Small howitzers can be towed by a five-ton truck or airlifted by helicopter.

Cannons are artillery weapons that fire projectiles from a long, rifled barrel at high velocity in a low, flat trajectory. The projectile usually carries a charge that explodes when it hits its target. Some cannons use ammunition that can pierce armor. Cannons are widely used on warships, armored combat vehicles, and tanks. The first artillery cannons were loaded from the front (muzzle) of the barrel and fired simple projectiles that did not explode. Later cannons fired ammunition that released shards of metal, called *shrapnel*, in the air. Modern cannons are loaded from the back, which increases the speed and ease by which they may be fired.

Artillery ammunition includes ammunition for cannons, recoilless guns, and large-caliber grenade launchers. The ammunition can be placed in the gun in three different ways:
- fixed (the propellant case, the projectile, and the igniter for the propellant are built together in a cartridge and loaded in the gun as one item);
- semi fixed (the propellant case and the projectile are not built together); or
- separated (the propellant comes in a cloth bag and the projectile and igniter for the propellant are also separate). All three items are loaded separately.

Operation: All ammunition needed to fire the gun is put in the chamber of the gun. When the gun is fired, the firing pin hits the percussion cap and, because of friction, the igniting powder flames up, or ignition of the propellant can take place electrically, with a heat-sensitive igniting powder. The flame is then passed on to the propellant through flash holes in the percussion cap. The propellant sets fire and produces a high amount of gas pressure. This gas pressure pushes the projectile through the barrel of the gun toward the target. Muzzle speed can be up to 1,000 meters per second.

A rotating band is a soft copper band on the projectile. When the weapon is fired, the soft metal fits tightly into the rifling in the barrel, keeping all the gas pressure behind the projectile to force it from the muzzle. The rifling also makes the projectile rotate along its center line, giving it a stable flight. Rotation can be up to 10,000 revolutions per minute. Sometimes there will be two rotating bands instead of one.

Another component can be a tracer, which allows anti-tank (AT) and anti-aircraft (AA) gunners to follow the projectiles and bring the line of fire at the target.

Special attention: To know if a projectile is relatively safe or not, it is important to know whether the projectile has been fired. This can be seen on the rotating band: when grooved, assume that the projectile has been fired and therefore is in an extremely dangerous condition.

MORTAR AMMUNITION

Mortar ammunition are projectiles for muzzle loaded, high-angle firing weapons used in areas where direct fire cannot reach the target, such as built-up areas and mountains. Like cannons, the first mortars fired shells that did not explode. Later mortars fired shells filled with gunpowder. These shells had fuses and could be set to explode on impact, or just before they hit the ground. Modern mortars fire shells with different payloads, such as HE, smoke, and illuminating flares.

Because mortar ammunition is muzzle loaded, many, if not most, projectiles are fin stabilized instead of spin stabilized by means of a rotating band. The stabilization fins are attached to a tail pipe that is screwed on to the projectile. The tail pipe also holds the propelling charge.

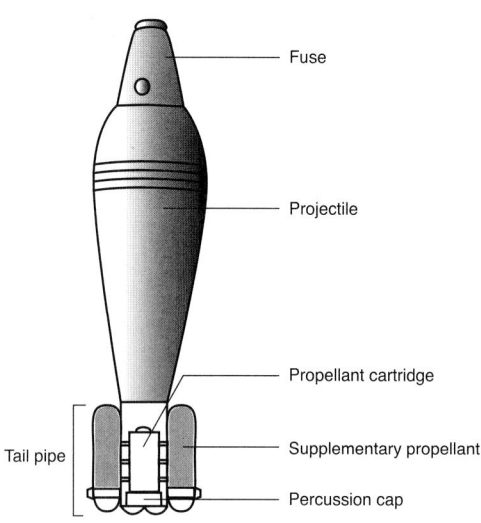

Figure 2.17 The main components of mortar ammunition.

Operation: The projectile is loaded through the front end of the muzzle and slides down the tube until it hits the firing pin at the bottom. The percussion cap then ignites the propellant and the projectile is fired out of the muzzle toward the target. The rest of the functioning is the same as artillery ammunition.

Special attention: Dud-fired mortar projectiles are more dangerous than other artillery projectiles because they can be more difficult to identify because most mortar projectiles don't have rotating bands. Instead, look for burn marks around the holes in the tail pipe and a dent in the percussion cap.

LANDMINES

Landmines are ammunition specially designed to deny access to a certain area; they are activated by the target itself.

There are two main types of landmines:

- *Anti-tank mines*: used to destroy vehicles and therefore will not normally detonate when a person steps on them. Modern, sophisticated mines have self-destruct mechanisms or a mechanism that makes them safe after a certain period. There are three sub-types of anti-tank mines:
    - *Blast mines* have 11–22 pounds (5–10 kg) of HE and are set off by a pressure of more than 275 pounds (125 kg).
    - *Off-route mines* are heat-seeking rocket launchers. They are placed 32–82 feet (10–25 m) from a road or other vehicle route and will fire a heat rocket when a vehicle passes and activates the mine.
    - *Plate mines* have 4–11 pounds (2–5 kg) of HE. When the mine is set off, it releases a high velocity, convex-shaped projectile that penetrates the belly of the tank.
- *Anti-personnel mines*: designed to wound, not kill, soldiers who step on the mine or set the mine off by tripwire. Modern, sophisticated mines have a self-destruct mechanism or a mechanism that makes the mine safe

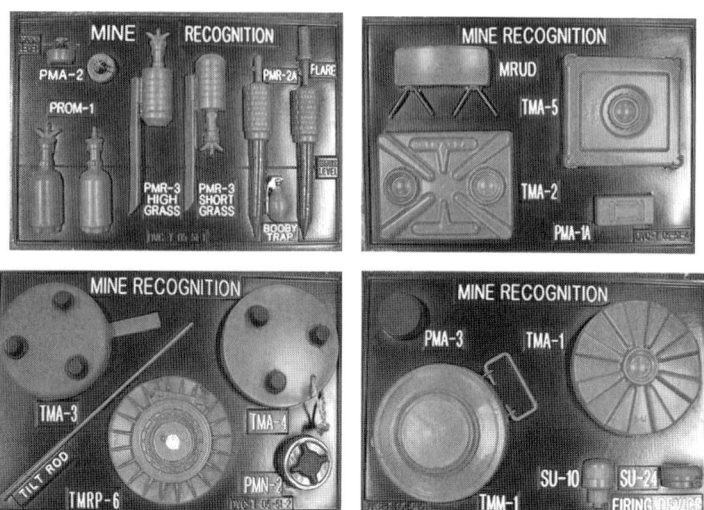

Figure 2.18 A Bosnia mine recognition set. This device is used as a graphic aid to teach soldiers how to recognize mine hazards. The four boards show the actual dimensions of the mines personnel are most likely to encounter.

after a certain period. There are four sub-types of anti-personnel mines:

- *Blast mines* will wound people who step on them with a blast of detonating HE. Blast mines have a thin housing with 0.9–8 ounces (25–225 g) of HE inside. The mines are placed on the surface or buried just below the surface. As little as 7 ounces (200 g) of pressure can activate the mine.

- *Fragmentation mines* will wound people with fragments after they detonate. Fragmentation mines have a thick casing that can be pre-fragmented. They are placed above the surface and usually operated by tripwires. Their effective radius is about 65–80 feet (20–25 m).

- *Bounding fragmentation mines* wound people by fragments after they detonate. Bounding fragmentation mines are buried below the surface and are launched about 1 yard (1 m high) before they detonate.

- *Directional fragmentation mines* produce fragments only in a certain direction. They are placed above the surface and are operated by tripwire or electrical contact.

Special attention: Because landmines are static munitions, they stay effective for a long time, sometimes decades after a war has ended. When dealing with landmines, watch for booby-traps, anti-handling devices, and anti-lifting devices.

ROCKETS

Rockets are projectiles propelled by gas pressure produced at launch and during flight by an LE in the rocket motor. The main types of rockets are anti-tank rockets, anti-personnel rockets, and smoke rockets.

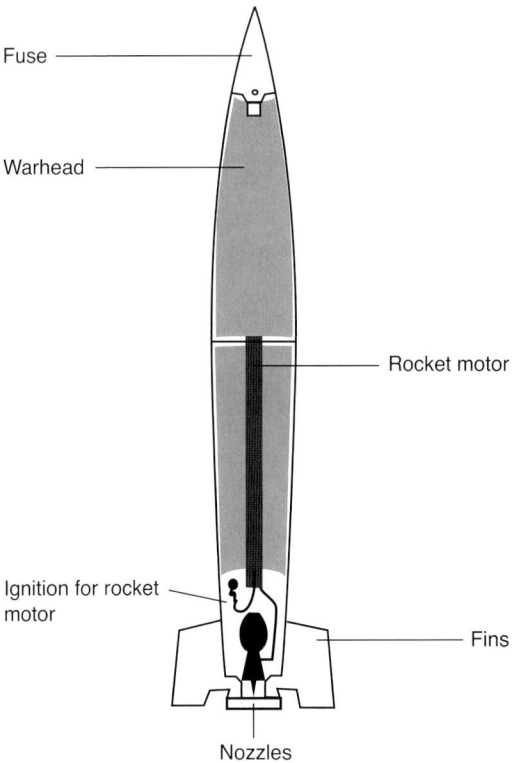

Figure 2.19 Rocket components and structure can vary. This drawing shows the main parts of a BM-21 rocket with an impact fuse. The BM-21 is a vehicle mounted, multiple barrel rocket launcher first designed in the Soviety Union after World War II, but now copied and used throughout the world.

Operation: Rockets are propelled by the gas pressure produced in a chemical reaction in the rocket motor. The high-pressure gas escapes through nozzles, producing a propelling force that continues during flight.

Rocket sizes can range from those small enough to be shoulder launched to those 82 or more feet (25+ m) long that can carry people into space. Rockets that can be guided during flight are called missiles.

Special attention: Smaller rockets with solid propellants that are shoulder fired or fired from the back of trucks often have electric igniters and electric fuses. This makes them sensitive to static electricity. Ground yourself before touching a rocket to avoid a flow of electricity from your body to the device.

AIRCRAFT BOMBS

Aircraft bombs are munitions that are carried inside the fuselage (bombers) or outside the fuselage (fighter-bombers) of an aircraft. Air-dropped from a certain height and at a certain speed, they function at a preset time or position. Originally, aircraft bombs were all of the "free fall" type, but during the 1960s, guidance systems for bombs were developed to make them "smart." Free fall ("dumb") bombs are used for carpet bombing; specific targets are attacked with smart bombs.

UNDERWATER WEAPONS

Sea mines and *river mines* are specially designed to destroy ships in open water. They are static weapons, which means the target (ship) comes to the weapon. Sea mines are placed by another ship or by airplanes. Sea mines can lie on the bottom, they can be anchored at the bottom and drift somewhere between the bottom and the surface, or they can float on the surface. Sea mines can be activated by a contact fuse or an influence fuse, which is designed to detonate an explosive at a certain distance from a target. The main charge of a sea mine consists of 440–2,200 pounds (200–1,000 kg) of TNT or another equivalent HE.

Torpedoes are also specially designed to destroy ships in open water. Unlike a sea mine, a torpedo is dynamic, which means it moves to the target. Torpedoes are fired from ships, submarines, airplanes, or helicopters and are propelled by an underwater motor. They explode when they make contact with the target or when they are close to the target.

UXOs

A "blind," or UXO (**u**n**e**xploded **o**rdnance), is an explosive or weapon that did not fire at the intended time. It includes any kind of military or civilian explosive: fireworks, shells, aerial bombs, poison gas grenades, and even nuclear weapons. Most UXOs are fireworks or unexploded military ordnance. UXOs are extremely dangerous because, although they refused to explode when ejected, hitting the target, or dumped, they may still explode by touch, shock, vibration, or even a slight bump.

Figure 2.20 A US army EOD technician lays out old Soviet land mines recovered from Bagram Air Field, Afghanistan, during a controlled detonation operation near the base. The three-person EOD team destroyed more than 600 pounds of old, recovered, and captured munitions during the operation.

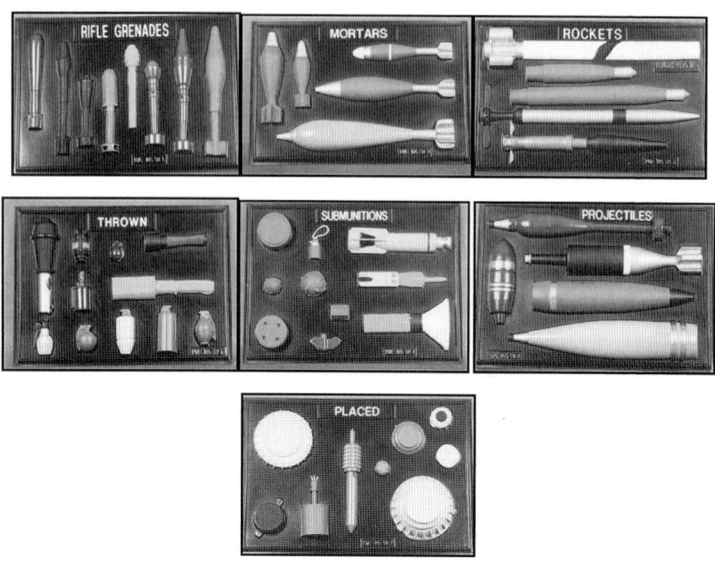

Figure 2.21 Unexploded ordnance recognition 7-board set. This device is used for instruction on UXOs. The boards show the actual dimensions of mortars, rockets, sub-munitions, projectiles, and other types of ordnance.

For example, in a shell, the fuse (igniter) keeps the shell safe from accidental detonation during storage, handling, and a launch through the barrel, whereafter the fuse detonates the shell at the correct moment. To achieve this, the fuse has several safety mechanisms that are successively withdrawn during the sequence of firing. In some instances, one of these safety mechanisms is not disabled after firing, so the shell fails to work when it reaches the target. The shell becomes a UXO with an only fragile hold on stability. UXO hand grenades are a special danger due to rusted or otherwise compromised safety pin springs. In chemical grenades that have been left to rust, phosphorus may spontaneously ignite, which will then ignite the detonator.

> Some UXOs, such as landmines, were placed as traps during war. These traps may have become unstable due to age and weathering.

Improvised Explosive Devices

An *improvised explosive device* (IED) is an explosive manufactured by non-professionals. The term was first used by the British Army in the 1970s to describe bombs and booby-traps made from agricultural fertilizer and Semtex (a type of plastic explosive) created by the Provisional Irish Republican Army (IRA).

The reasons for making IEDs can vary. Explosives are sometimes created as a hobby and are detonated in places where they can do little harm. Occasionally, buffoonery with explosives occur: for example, someone detonates a firework bomb in someone else's garden.

Terrorism is nowadays a main reason to make an IED. Terrorists often buy or steal professional explosives, although some, such as Timothy McVeigh in the Oklahoma City bombing in 1995, produce their own explosives. Today we are confronted almost daily with terror attacks both at home and abroad. Such attacks often create many civilian victims and do great material damage. Along with explosive substances, an IED can also contain incendiary or noxious chemicals.

A vehicle-borne IED, or VBIED, is a military term for a car bomb or truck bomb, but a VBIED can employ any type of transportation, including bicycles, motorcycles, donkeys, and so on. VBIEDs can carry a relatively large payload and can be employed by insurgents or detonated from a remote location. VBIEDs create additional shrapnel through the destruction of the vehicle itself, and they may use vehicle fuel as an incendiary weapon. A suicide by VBIED is known as an SVBIED. Of increasing popularity among insurgent forces in Iraq is the house-borne IED, or HBIED, which takes advantage of the common military practice of clearing houses. In an HBIED, insurgents rig an entire house to detonate and collapse shortly after a clearing squad has entered.

Figure 2.22 A time bomb placed in a car.

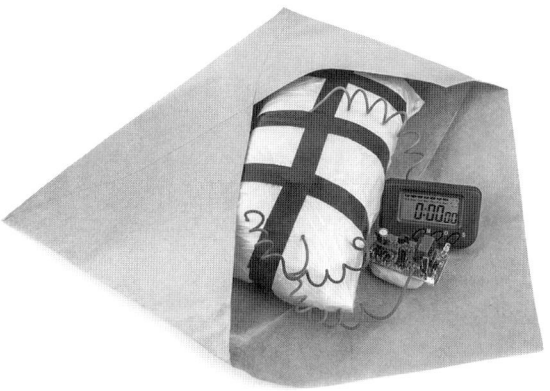

Figure 2.23 Handmade explosives in a letter bomb.

VISIBLE OR HIDDEN

A bomber may try to cause disruption by placing an easily recognizable IED in a public location. If authorities suspect that an object is or contains a bomb, they will take comprehensive measures, such as evacuating a building, to rule out any risks. Suspicious objects can turn out to be completely innocent, but they can also be left as a joke or malicious act, whether or not combined with a bomb threat. Fake bombs can also be used to test security.

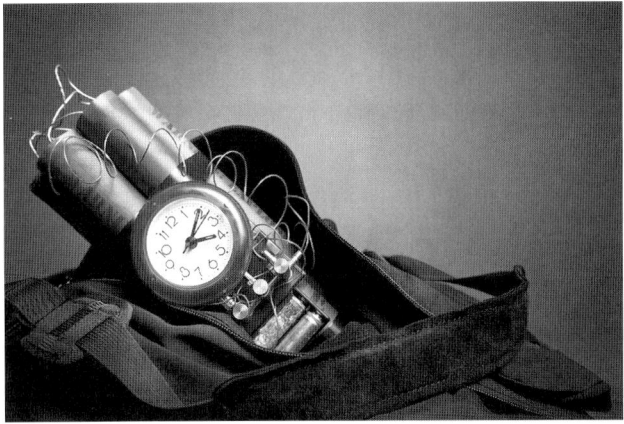

Figure 2.24 Many public buildings are on alert for unattended parcels and luggage in case they contain explosive devices such as this time bomb.

Usually an IED will be placed in a nondescript package such as a cardboard box, briefcase, purse, or letter. Sometimes IEDs are built into personal consumer goods, such as a car, bag, laptop, or mobile phone. In such situations, evidence of damage on the object or a person's temporary loss of personal belongings can signal the possible presence of an IED.

IED DESIGN

IEDs are diverse in design and may contain many types of initiators, detonators, and explosive loads. In addition to an explosive (main) charge, IEDs can include a variety of other hazardous substances, such as suffocating, aggressive, biological, chemical, or even radioactive materials. IEDs can be composed of military or civilian explosives, homemade explosives, or a combination. Military explosives or explosive components can be obtained relatively easily in areas where tension or war prevails. Military explosives are tested, reliable, and ready to use, so for bomb makers these products are easy to employ. The same applies to explosives stolen from civilian operations, such as demolition, mining, seismic, and soil survey businesses. It is also quite possible to use

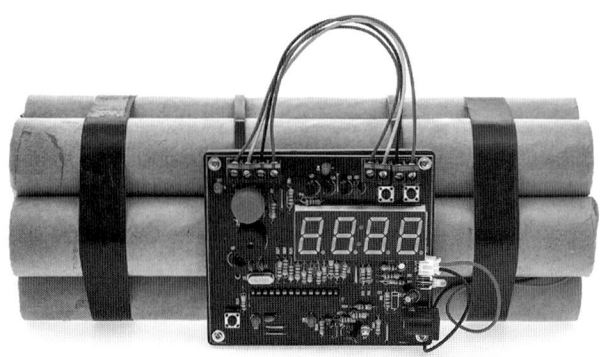

Figure 2.25 A TNT time bomb.

easy-to-purchase products from drugstores, pharmacies, hardware stores, and supermarkets for making explosives. Details on the exact composition and mixing ratios of the various ingredients are readily available at libraries or on the Internet, but this information is not always complete and accurate, so homemade explosives cannot be created safely and reliably.

The most frequently encountered substances used to make IEDs are discussed below to help you understand which substances you may be searching for. However, so that this information will not be used inappropriately, we will not say which substances might be mixed, will provide no mixing ratios, and will not discuss production procedures.

ACETONE PEROXIDE

Acetone peroxide requires only acid, hydrogen peroxide, and acetone, ingredients that can be purchased easily. Acetone peroxide has a high brisance and detonates at a velocity of 3.3 miles per second (5,300 m/s). Even a few grams can cause a considerable explosion. It is often used as a detonator and has been employed many times by suicide bombers. The disadvantage is the extreme sensitivity of the material, which has cost many people a few fingers, eyes, or even their life.

ALUMINUM POWDER

Aluminum powder is a highly flammable gray powder created as a byproduct from the machining of aluminum. It is used in an explosive mixture to make the resulting explosion burn with a high temperature, thereby making a more deadly and harmful weapon.

AMMONIUM NITRATE

Some fertilizer is composed of ammonium nitrate mixed with other substances. However, it is not difficult to separate the ammonium nitrate from the other substances. In particular, the fertilizer mixture calcium ammonium nitrate contains only calcium carbonate (lime) and ammonium nitrate, which can easily be separated from each other because ammonium nitrate is highly water soluble, and calcium carbonate is not. Even though ammonium nitrate in pure form is an explosive (with a detonation velocity of about 1.55 miles per second, or 2,500 m/s), causing it to detonate it is extremely difficult.

Ammonium nitrate can be made more sensitive to detonation by mixing it with other substances; the best known and most widely used combination is ammonium nitrate and diesel, a combination known as ANFO (**a**mmonium **n**itrate **f**uel **o**il). Mixing ammonium nitrate with nitromethane is even more sensitive as well as more powerful (with a detonation velocity of about 3.9 miles per second, or 6,300 m/s); this combination is called ANNM (**a**mmonium **n**itrate **n**itro**m**ethane). Both ANNM and ANFO are widely used in the mining industry because they are inexpensive, stable, and they have a relatively low detonation velocity in comparison to many other explosives. This ensures mining detonation can be controlled and limited to only intended areas—high detonations underground are far too dangerous.

MAGNESIUM

Magnesium is often used as a main load in IEDs. Magnesium is a flammable metal that burns with very high temperatures in a violent reaction. It is easily available at drugstores and pharmacies.

NITROGEN TRIIODIDE

Nitrogen triiodide is an extremely sensitive contact explosive: small quantities explode with a loud, sharp snap when touched even lightly, releasing a purple cloud of iodine vapor. Nitrogen triiodide can be prepared from iodine and ammonia and is highly unstable. It detonates at the slightest provocation, such as static electricity, an insect landing, or a slight bump.

POTASSIUM CHLORATE

Potassium chlorate is a white crystalline powder containing potassium, chlorine, and oxygen atoms. It is often used in deflagrating mixtures, such as on the head of safety matches and in chemistry labs in schools. Potassium perchlorate has similar properties to potassium chlorate, but potassium perchlorate is used more often than potassium chlorate in pyrotechnics because it is cheaper and much less sensitive to shock or friction.

POTASSIUM NITRATE

Potassium nitrate is not dangerous by itself, but it can be used to create an explosive mixture in combination with fuels such as charcoal, aluminum, or sugar. Gunpowder is a mixture of potassium nitrate, sulfur, and carbon.

SULFUR

Sulfur can be used as an ignition charge or as a main load. Like potassium chlorate, sulfur is often used in the pyrotechnic composition of safety matches. It is highly flammable and burns with a violent reaction.

Detonators

A detonator or igniter is a tool used to cause a stable explosive to explode. The detonator is placed in or directly on the explosive. The detonator consists of a small amount of very sensitive explosive material, such as lead azide or mercury fulminate, which will explode in response to a small shock (from an electrical or mechanical source) or contact with heat (from a wick).

Because it's the easiest to employ, approximately 90 percent of IEDs use an electrical ignition mechanism. To ensure the blast force is sufficient to ignite the main charge, sometimes a second explosive that is not quite as sensitive as the very sensitive material is incorporated into the detonator. Having a progression of explosives gives more time between detonation and the explosion itself.

It is important to know the difference between arming and firing. Providing an IED with an *armament switch* bridges the time between the production of the bomb and the placement of the bomb for its intended use. When the bomb is placed, the arming switch is usually activated and then the bomb is ready to go. For example, an IED might be equipped with a cooking timer that closes an electrical circuit and thereby arms the device. After the IED is installed, the timer might be set to 15 minutes, giving the bomber ample time to leave the building safely. After that quarter of an hour, the bomb is activated and ready to be fired. Subsequently, the bomb is triggered by an ignition, which could occur after a specific delay in time, after disturbance of the IED, or through a controlled command. The *firing device* prevents detonation between activation and the triggering of the explosive.

Detonators may be from the military or civil sector, or they can be homemade in whole or part. Let's take a closer look the latter. A simple electric circuit is often used to activate an IED, but electrical circuits can also be combined with a mechanical or other type of ignition. The main components of electrically activated IEDs are a voltage source such as a battery, an armament switch, a firing device, sometimes a lead-in charge as an explosive to start the main charge, and a main charge.

A firing or arming device can be made from a cooking/kitchen timer, a countdown timer, a cellphone timer, a sleep clock, etcetera. Such a device can also be a pressure switch made of two

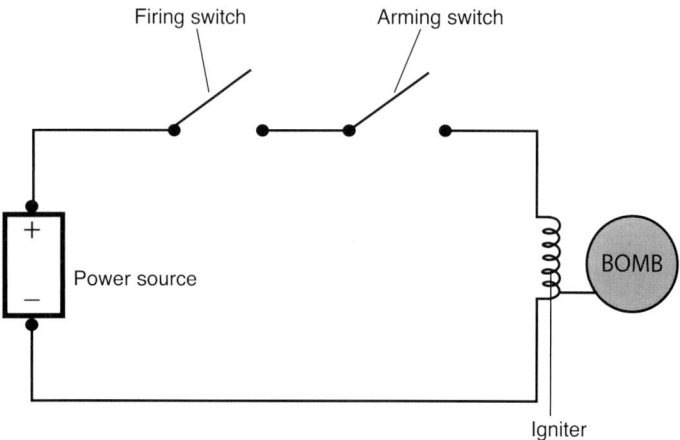

Figure 2.26 The electric circuit of an ignition device.

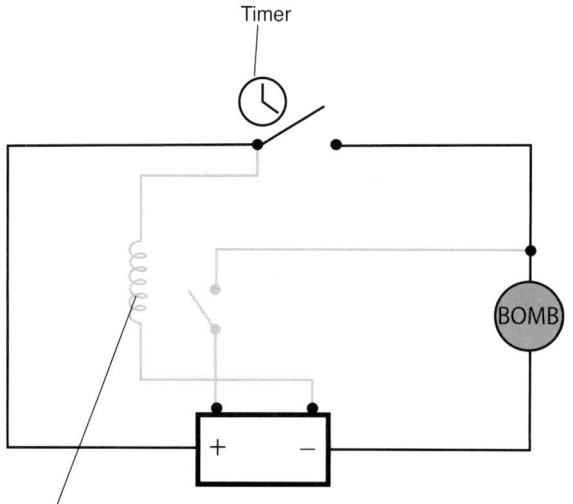

Electromagnet keeps switch off while it's powered

Figure 2.27 Another electric circuit ignition device using a magnet and timer.

sheets of metal foil separated by a soft, perforated, non-conductive substance. The metal sheets are incorporated into an electrical circuit with wires. This device can be placed under a doormat, and when someone steps on the mat, the device is compressed

EXPLOSIVES, WEAPONS, AMMUNITION, AND IEDS 63

Figure 2.28 A steel pipe IED that can be ignited by cell phone.

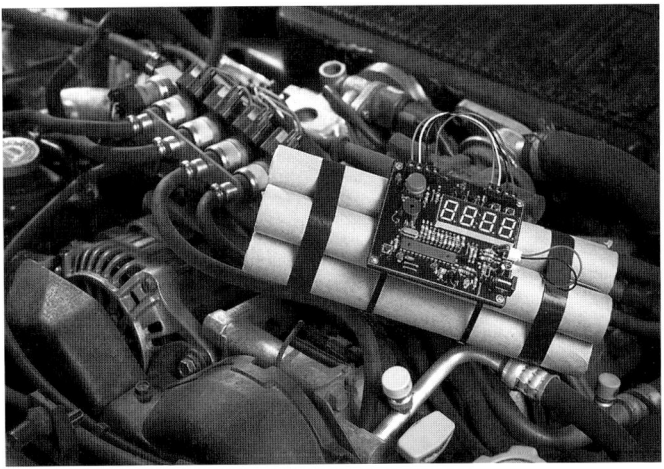

Figure 2.29 A time bomb explosive with a digital countdown timer deployed on a car engine.

and a circuit is completed by foil contact through the perforation holes.

Another firing device can be an anti-cut switch, which is a relay switch put under constant voltage, by which the switch remains open. When the wire is cut, the tension is over and the relay switch closes a circuit. This method can also be used as a time delay: when the battery voltage drops, the relay closes. There are also infrared switches that create a contact as soon as thermal images, such as a human entering a room, are recorded, or acoustic switches that work on sound. A light-sensitive cell switches a contact on or off as soon as sufficient light falls on it. They are very small and easy to build into the inside of an IED.

In some cases, the perpetrator may want to activate a bomb at a precise moment, in which case the ignition device is activated remotely. Command controlled activation can be by radio, by infrared remote control, by a so-called slave-switch that responds to a bright flash of light (e.g., a camera flash) or a certain sound, and, of course, by the use of a cell phone.

> **During all explosive detection deployment, do not use mobile communication devices such as cellphones, radios, and the like: this equipment may activate an IED.**

3

Training Odors

Improvised explosive devices (IEDs), landmines, and other explosive devices emanate a variety of odors from the main charge explosive as well as from the casing (paint, plastic, rubber, cardboard, wood, or metal). A dog can be trained to detect all these odors. If there is no available odor from the main charge, but there are some odor traces from the casing, a dog will detect these traces if it has been trained to do so.

Figure 3.1 The explosive detector dog must be able to detect dozens of individual explosive chemicals.

There are six principle chemical categories of explosives:
- Acid salts (NH_4^+, NO_3^-)
- Aliphatic nitrates ($C-NO_2$)
- Aromatic nitrates ($Ar-C-NO_2$)
- Nitrate esters ($C-O-NO^2$)
- Nitramines ($C-N-NO_2$)
- Peroxides ($C-O-O-C$)

Along with these are dozens of individual explosive chemicals, such as primary explosives, that the explosive detector dog should be able to detect. Common explosives and their properties are shown in Table 3.1.

Table 3.1 Common Explosives and Explosive Compositions

Explosive or Composition	Common Form or Use
Acid salts:	
Ammonium nitrate	ANFO (combined with fuel oil)
	Nitro-carbo-nitrate (NCN)
Ammonium perchlorate	
Potassium nitrate	Black powder/gunpowder (combined with charcoal and sulfur)
Aliphatic nitrates:	
Nitromethane	
2,3-dimethyl-dinitrobutane (DMDNB, DMNB)	
Hydrazine	Rocket fuel
	The liquid component of two-part explosives
Aromatic nitrates:	
Nitrobenzene (NB)	
Nitrotoluene (NT)	
Dinitrobenzene (DNB)	
Amino-dinitrotoluene (A-DNT)	
Trinitrobenzene (TNB)	
ortho-nitrotoluene (*o*-MNT)	
para-nitrotoluene (*p*-MNT)	
2,4-dinitrotoluene (DNT)	
2,4,6-trinitrotoluene (TNT)	Composition B (when combined with an equal part RDX)

Explosive or Composition	Common Form or Use
	Pentolite (when combined with an equal part PETN)
	Note: an inexpensive compound, TNT is a component of 15 explosive compositions.
2,4,6-trinitrophenol (picric acid)	
Nitrate esters:	
Methyl nitrate	
Nitroglycerin (NG)	Some types of dynamite
	Heart medications
Ethylene glycol dinitrate (EGDN)	Some types of dynamite
Diethylene glycol dinitrate (DEGDN)	Detonating cord
	Detasheet (military name Flex-X)
	Semtex (combined with RDX)
Pentaerythritol tetranitrate (PETN)	Penthrite
Nitrocellulose (NC)	Guncotton
	Main component of single-based smokeless powder
NC and NG	Double-based smokeless powder
NC, NG, and nitroguanidine	Triple-based smokeless powder
Nitramines:	
Methylamine nitrate	
Tetranitro-*N*-methylamine (tetryl)	Tetrytol (Tetryl combined with TNT)
Trinitro-triazacyclohexane (RDX)	C-4
Tetranitro-tetrazacyclooctane (HMX)	Her Majesty's Explosive
Hexanitro-hexaazaisowurzitane (CL20)	
Peroxides:	
Triacetone triperoxide (TATP)	
Hexamethylene triperoxide diamine (HMTD)	
Primary explosives:	Note: mixtures of primary explosives are common
Tetramino nitrate	
Mercury fulminate	
Lead styphnate	Blasting caps
Lead azide	

Adapted from Harper et al. (2005) and Furton and Myers 2001.

COMMON EXPLOSIVE DEVICES
Dynamite: usually contains EGDN and/or NG
Landmines: usually contain TNT
Plastic explosives, such as C-4: contain RDX and/or PETN

Choosing Start Odors for Training

Training your dog will require at least one start odor from each of the six explosive chemical classes, plus a low explosive. A starting list therefore includes

- an acid salt such as ammonium nitrate;
- an aliphatic nitrate such as DMNB;
- an aromatic nitrate such as TNT;
- a nitrate ester such as PETN;
- a nitramine such as RDX;
- a peroxide such as TATP; and
- a black powder and a smokeless powder.

Taggants

Along with your start odors, you might want to train your dog on taggants (markers), which are chemical or physical substances

Figure 3.2 One of our old training cases with explosive odors. You may need to change your training odors over time as the substances age and become less detectable to the dogs.

added to explosive materials. Taggant technology was first encouraged by the Institute of Makers of Explosives (IME), which was founded in 1913 to enhance the safety and security organization of the commercial explosives industry. The IME strongly supported the international effort to enhance the detection of explosives by requiring them to contain a detection taggant.

Identification (or post-detonation) taggants have focused on microtaggant technology, which use microchips made of multiple layers of plastic and metal. The idea is that these chips could be placed in explosive products with the hope that investigators could find them after an explosion and trace them, through the manufacturer, to the bomber.

However, although taggant evidence was crucial in the 1980 conviction of James L. McFillin in Maryland for the truck bombing murder of Nathan A. Allen, Sr., taggants haven't proven to be as useful as hoped. First, contamination of bomb sites is often a problem, since microscopic particles of the taggant material might be present at a crime scene from a source other than the explosive material. Second, criminals seldom legally purchase explosives.

Figure 3.3 It is worthwhile training explosive detector dogs to recognize taggants, which are chemical or physical markers added to explosive materials.

Sometimes they steal commercial products, but it is far more likely that the bomb makers will make their own, thus completely avoiding the taggant.

> **Few criminals legally purchase explosives, so taggants are not always useful in tracing bomb makers.**

Moreover, it has been proven that it is unsafe to add microtaggants to certain types of explosives. In 1994, during a manufacturer's test project, the addition of taggants to a molten high explosive (HE) material, which included TNT, destabilized the HE mix, causing the emergency shutdown of the operation. An independent laboratory analysis of the incident conducted by the New Mexico Institute of Mining and Technology confirmed that the microtaggant did indeed destabilize TNT. In fact, the 1979 explosion at an explosive manufacturing plant in Arkansas was likely caused by the introduction of taggants to a molten explosive material. Of course, the danger of destabilizing an explosive greatly detracts from the usefulness of microtaggants.

Despite these problems, after acts of terrorism there are often calls to require taggants in commercial explosives, even though IEDs, which are the main choice of criminals and terrorists, are not generally made with commercial HEs.

Detection taggants are volatile chemicals that slowly evaporate from the explosive and can be detected in the atmosphere by either detection dogs or specialized machines. They are intended to allow for detection of explosives during, for example, airport luggage screening.

Although various technologies can detect even untagged explosives, detection taggants help increase the reliability of these technologies. The inclusion of detection taggants in explosives is mandatory in some countries. Following the bombing of PanAm 103 over Lockerbie, Scotland, in December 1988, the International

Civil Aviation Organization was instrumental in effecting a worldwide requirement for placing a detection taggant in plastic explosives: the 1991 Convention on the Marking of Plastic Explosives for the Purpose of Detection. Incorporation of an approved detection agent in plastic explosives is compulsory for ordnance factories all over world.

Under this convention, manufacturers have a choice between four detection taggant chemicals. In the United States, the marker used is called DMDNB or DMNB (2,3-dimethyl-2,3-dinitrobutane). Other taggants in use in other parts of the world are ortho-mononitrotoluene (*o*-MNT), para-mononitrotoluene (*p*-MNT), and ethylene glycol dinitrate (EGDN).

DMDNB

DMDNB, or DMNB, chemically 2,3-dimethyl-2,3-dinitrobutane, is a volatile organic compound used as a detection taggant for plastic explosives. Plastic explosives can be easily and safely carried by terrorists, so DMDNB is incorporated at a 0.5 to 1.0 percent level in plastic explosives to help authorities detect the substance.

Dogs are very sensitive to DMDNB and can detect as little as 0.5 parts per billion in the air, as can specialized ion mobility spectrometers. Ion mobility spectrometry is a rugged, sensitive, field-portable technique for the detection of organic compounds. It is widely employed at ports of entry and by the military as a particle detector for explosives and drugs.

MNTS

Mononitrotoluenes (MNTs) are a group of organic compounds that are either a nitro derivative of toluene or a methyl derivative of nitrobenzene. Mononitrotoluene comes in three isomers, but only the following two are used as taggants:

- Ortho-mononitrotoluene (*o*-MNT), or 2-nitrotoluene, is a pale yellow liquid with a subtle, characteristic smell reminiscent of bitter almonds. It is non-hygroscopic (won't absorb moisture from the air) and non-corrosive.

- Para-mononitrotoluene (*p*-MNT), or 4-nitrotoluene, consists of pale yellow crystals with the smell of bitter almonds. It is almost insoluble in water.

EGDN

Glycoldinitrate, also known as ethylene glycol dinitrate (EGDN), is an oily yellow liquid explosive obtained by combining glycol with nitrating acid. Glycoldinitrate is, both in regard to preparation and general properties, similar to nitroglycerin. However, EGDN is more volatile and less viscous than nitroglycerin. Glycoldinitrate was first used in the manufacture of explosives: it has a lower melting point than nitrogycerin, so adding it to dynamite produces an explosive that can be used in colder weather conditions.

Thanks to its high volatility, and therefore good detectability, glycoldinitrate was once used as a compulsory addition to Semtex, an odorless all-purpose plastic explosive. After 1995, glycoldinitrate was replaced by 2,3-dimethyl-2,3-dinitrobutane (DMDNB) because it is considerably more stable.

Odor Print

The odor print is not simply the combination of chemicals found in the explosive. The odor print is also determined by an interaction

Figure 3.4 US soldiers search a field for unexploded ordnance during a certification exercise for explosive ordance disposal (EOD) personnel. EOD teams normally employ dog–handler teams and robots, using whichever tool will best get the job done in any given situation.

between chemical abundance (originating in the form of vapor or particles), physiologic sensitivity of the dog for the chemicals, and whether the dog is trained to detect that odor.

When a detector dog finds the odor of explosives, it will encounter the following parts, which make up a complete odor print:

- *Main odor*: the smell of the explosive the dog is trained to find.
- *Accompanying odor*: the smell of the cartridges or shells that contain the explosives.
- *Human scent*: during training, you use sterile gloves or tools such as tongs to handle explosives to prevent familiar human scents from influencing your dog's search for the scent of an explosive. However, whether on the training field or in a real search, your dog will find at least a trace odor of humans in the area around an explosive.
- *Odor of a disturbed area*: this will mix up the odor print a bit, making it more difficult to pin down.

Figure 3.5 Our current training cases of explosive substances, each clearly marked and packaged to avoid cross-contamination. We have several jars of each explosive to allow us to vary the amount of the substance we ask our dogs to find.

To prevent your training dog from focusing on human scent, accompanying smells, and/or odors of disturbance instead of the odor of explosives, always train your dog in a variety of locations and with a wide variety of objects.

Vapor Pressure

Detection of vapor traces of explosives in the air is a powerful method of revealing the presence of explosive devices. The principle of this detection method is that any explosive will emit a rather small but detectable number of gas-phase molecules.

All solids and liquids emit a certain amount of vapor at all temperatures above absolute zero −459.67°F (−273°C), and at any given temperature, the amount of vapor emitted is characteristic of the particular substance. To illustrate this, consider a piece of solid TNT in a jar with the lid closed. Before the TNT is placed in the jar, there is no TNT vapor present in the jar, but once the explosive is inside with the lid shut, the volume of gas-phase TNT in the jar will increase as vapor molecules are emitted by the solid. Eventually, a state of dynamic equilibrium will be reached, where the number of vapor molecules emitted by the solid per unit time is the same as the number of molecules readsorbed by the solid and walls of the jar. There will then be a constant pressure of TNT gas in the jar, and the quantitative value of this pressure is the vapor pressure of TNT at the prevailing temperature.

Note that the vapor pressure of a chemical at a specific temperature is the maximum pressure of the gas that may exist above a solid or liquid. If the system has not yet reached equilibrium, the actual pressure of the vapor may be less than the vapor pressure, but never more. For convenience, vapor pressures are often expressed as relative concentrations in saturated air rather than in true pressure units. Such concentrations are proportional to the true vapor pressure, and they often provide a clearer picture of the amounts of vapor involved.

Figure 3.6 shows the vapor concentrations in saturated air of several high explosives at room temperature (77°F, 25°C). Note that the vertical axis of Figure 3.6 has an increasing logarithmic scale, so that each higher mark corresponds to a factor-of-ten increase in vapor pressure. The horizontal axis displays the molecular weights of the various compounds and is not important in the following discussion. Clearly the vapor pressures of the explosives shown vary widely. For example, the vapor pressure of ethylene glycol dinitrate (EGDN) is about 10^9 times (one billion times) higher than the vapor pressure of HMX (homocyclonite, or octogen).

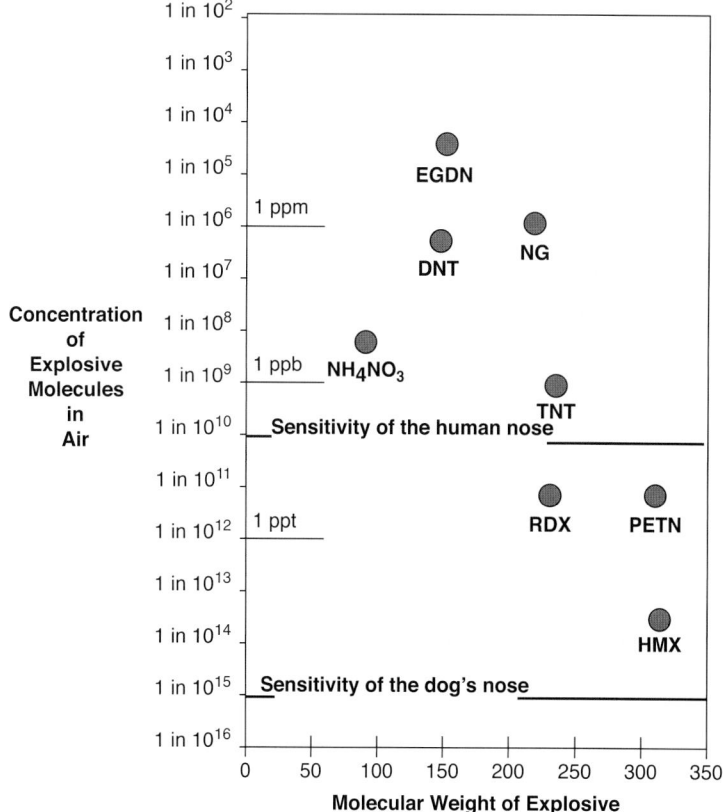

Figure 3.6 Vapor concentrations in saturated air of several high explosives at room temperature (77°F, 25°C).

DETECTION OF VAPOR TRACES

In general, explosives can be broken into three groups based on their vapor pressures. The relative values of these vapor pressures have important implications for the trace detection of explosives. These vapor pressures are for pure materials. Vapor pressures for mixtures containing these explosives may be lower.

- *High vapor pressure explosives* include EGDN, nitroglycerin, and 2,4-dinitrotoluene (DNT). These explosives have saturated vapor concentrations in air close to or greater than one part per million (1 ppm), which means that at equilibrium, there will be roughly one molecule of explosive vapor for every million air molecules. The high vapor pressure explosives are relatively easy for dogs to detect. Thus dynamite, which usually contains EGDN and/or NG as an explosive ingredient, can usually be detected from its vapor.

- *Medium vapor pressure explosives* have saturated vapor concentrations in air near one part per billion (1 ppb), a factor of about 1,000 lower than high vapor pressure explosives. The medium vapor pressure group includes TNT and ammonium nitrate. These explosives can also be easily detected by dogs from their vapor. Ammonium nitrate is particularly easy to find because it is almost always used in large quantities (hundreds or even thousands of pounds) in devices such as car bombs.

- *Low vapor pressure explosives* have saturated vapor concentrations in air near or below the one part per trillion (1 ppt) level. The low vapor pressure group includes HMX, RDX, and PETN. Low vapor pressure explosives do not produce much vapor, but can still be detected by dogs.

EFFECT OF PACKAGING

Packaging also plays an important role in concealing explosives. Effective vapor pressure of explosive devices can be reduced by a factor of 1,000 by sealing the explosive in plastics or other coatings. Vapor concentrations of volatile explosives near a bomb may be two to six times less than their equilibrium vapor pressures due to enclosure in a casing, adsorption to soil particles, and because

Figure 3.7 Train your detector dog to be calm and controlled as it works...

Figure 3.8 ...otherwise there is a chance your dog may explode the object.

mixtures of explosive materials have lower vapor pressures than their pure compounds. When a mine is buried in the soil, it will almost always gradually release explosives or chemical derivatives to the surrounding soil through either leakage from cracks and seams or vapor transport through the mine casing. The soil takes on some explosive scent, but it also acts as a type of packaging to reduce the effective vapor pressure of the explosive.

4

Influences on Searching

The last chapter touched on some of the factors that can influence the odor print of explosives, such as the type of explosive and the casing or covering. Other common factors we'll discuss in this chapter include the quantity of the hidden substance, the age of the cache, explosive complexes, adaptation, weather, temperature, relative humidity, and wind. We'll conclude with a brief look at other factors that can influence a dog's detection work, such as its physical health and handler errors.

Figure 4.1 An explosive ordnance disposal (EOD) team in a mission area detonate explosives.

Quantity

It is logical to assume that the more explosives there are, the greater the perimeter of the dispensed odor. But in fact, differences in *amount* of odor can be perceived by the dog as differences in *kind* of odor. Even if a dog can find a small amount of a substance, it may not automatically be able to find a large amount. So when you are training your dog to recognize an odor, vary the amounts of odor it is trained to find. However, do not expect immediate success. Your dog may perceive that a large amount of an odor is a completely different thing from a smaller amount of the same odor.

Age of the Cache

The longer something is hidden, the greater the odor picture becomes. The odor picture is strongest near the cache and gradually weaker the farther away you get. Over a very long time, the scent of an explosive cache will decrease. In technical jargon, this decrease of scent over time is called the "soaking time." The age of an explosive also determines the strength of its odor. Older explosives have a weaker odor. The explosive location—underground,

Figure 4.2 Know that air movements from helicopters or other sources can complicate the work of detection dogs on the ground.

underwater, open air, inside buildings—also affects the amount of perceptible odor available to your dog. Closed spaces have better odor prints, while spaces exposed to wind, humidity, and other environmental factors have poorer odor prints.

Explosive Complexes

If an explosive is presented alone during training, your dog is more sensitive to its odor than if it is presented as part of a complex of smells. So even if a dog is capable of finding a very small amount of a pure explosive, it may still have problems finding the same amount within a complex of explosives.

Discriminating between complex odors is more difficult than between single odors. Dogs can recognize a single odor in smaller amounts easier than when that same odor is part of a complex compound. It appears that dogs learn complex odors as units. But a dog's previous experience with single components in a complex does seem to speed up the learning of the complex odor. So beginning training with single odors leads to a more rapid learning of the complex compounds containing these single odors. But a dog trained to recognize single odors will not always immediately recognize these odors in complex compounds. In practical terms, this means you must train your dog on both single and complex odors.

Figure 4.3 Casey, an improvised explosive device (IED) detection dog with the US marines searches the side of a road for IEDs.

Adaptation

If a sensory cell in the nose is continuously stimulated in a certain way, it will eventually cease to react to the stimulus. This kind of sensory adaptation can make it impossible for a searching detector dog to locate the source of a smell since the environment it is searching may be saturated with the smell.

The density of explosive odor in a room where a lot of a certain explosive has been hidden, for example, or where a smaller amount has been hidden for a long time, can be very high. In such an environment, a detector dog may have difficulty locating the exact source of the odor, especially if the dog has been in the room for some time. The dog's sensory cells have been stimulated so much that they may have adapted and no longer react to the smell.

Consider the following example. If you enter a room where people are smoking, you notice the smell when you come in, but after a while, you don't notice it any more. If you leave the room and let your nose "rest" for a bit, or you get a breath of fresh air, upon re-entering the room, you will smell the smoke again. Giving your dog's nose a short rest in fresh air can help him in the same way.

> Adjust your training and search methods to take adaptation into account. Allow your dog to rest his nose in case the search area is saturated with scent.

Weather

In K9 detector work, weather factors such as temperature, relative humidity, and wind are very important. Wind disperses the odor print, the sun's warmth increases it, rain reduces it, and snow limits the odor print but does not erase it altogether. Odor can be frozen in ice and will keep; when the weather warms up and the thaw begins, the frozen odor emerges and is again detectable.

If you can correctly assess the weather, you can also correctly assess how weather will influence your dog's search work.

However, human assessments of weather are often based on snap judgments about temperature and wind conditions as we perceive them, higher above the ground than the dog's level of perception. For example, when you experience the temperature as 68°F (20°C), your dog's nose, just above the ground, may be in temperatures over 108°F (40°C). Realizing your dog must work under much more difficult circumstances than you perceive will give you more reason than ever to remark on your dog's amazing abilities!

TEMPERATURE

Up to a point, heat makes odors stronger, allowing odor molecules to rise from the source object and spread out. Cold has the opposite result. Generally speaking,

- a *warm* object in a *cold* environment provides a good odor print;
- a *cold* object in a *cold* environment provides a poor odor print;
- a *warm* object in a *warm* environment provides a poor odor print; and
- a *cold* object in *warm* surroundings provides a good odor print.

Table 4.1 shows the temperature taken on a sunny day at several heights. The temperature at or near ground temperature is much warmer than temperatures just 4 feet (1.2 m) from the surface. Yet after sunset, temperatures at the surface cool more quickly than temperatures higher up. As a dog handler, you need to remember that your dog may be working in higher or lower temperatures than you are experiencing.

Table 4.1 Air Temperatures Near Earth's Surface*

Height above Earth's Surface	Temperature during the Day	Temperature after Sunset
4 ft (1.2 m)	± 68°F (20°C)	Not recorded
12 in (30 cm)	80.6°F (27°C)	84.2°F (29°C)
1 in (2.5 cm)	93.2°F (34°C)	Not recorded
0 in (0 cm)	111.2°F (44°C)	55.4°F (13°C)

*Adapted from the "Marvels of Mini-Weather"

> Working in hot temperatures can easily dry a dog's nose, making its work less effective than normal. Take hot conditions into account and limit the searching time of your dog when necessary.

The solar radiation that reaches Earth's surface is partially absorbed by the surface terrain and converted into heat. The extent of absorption depends on the nature of the terrain. Overgrown and dark areas, such as forests and asphalt, readily absorb radiation; white areas, such as snow and ice fields, bounce it back into the atmosphere. Of the radiation absorbed by the terrain, a small part slowly heats the deeper layers of soil. The rest of the absorbed radiation contributes to evaporation and heats the air just above the surface. The most solar radiation reaches the surface around noon, when the sun is at its highest relative to the area receiving sunlight.

Air temperature is generally measured at a height of 5 feet (1.5 m) above Earth's surface. This air temperature reaches its highest value (maximum) in the afternoon and the lowest value (minimum) shortly after sunrise. Closer to Earth's surface, however, the influence of incoming and outgoing radiation is greater. The temperature close to the ground, therefore, has an exaggerated daily routine compared to that at 5 feet, especially in clear weather. In the afternoon, the air closer to the ground is warmer than it is at 5 feet and at sunrise it is colder.

Another thing to keep in mind when conducting a search with your dog is that temperatures mentioned in most weather reports are not always representative of temperatures in urban areas. Especially in large cities, the difference between the weather forecast and the actual temperature can be significant. Stone and concrete buildings retain much of the sun's radiation during the day and only slowly cool down at night. In addition, people produce a lot of indoor heat in urban areas by heating buildings, cooking, using computers, and so on. This heat may leak outside and further delay the fall of the air temperature at night.

The effect of solar radiation on a cache at the ground surface in high air temperatures and low ground temperatures is interesting. When air temperatures are high near the ground, the scent of hidden explosives rises slowly or not at all because the temperature of the air surrounding the explosives is higher than that of the air in the hiding place, thereby hindering the updraft of the colder, heavier air containing the scent of the explosives. In this situation, only wind can carry the scent.

Earth's surface and the atmosphere continuously absorb and reflect solar radiation. How much depends on the time of day. While the surface at night does not receive direct solar radiation, it continues to radiate heat and absorb radiation from the atmosphere. But that radiation is not enough to stop the nighttime cooling of Earth's surface. Nocturnal cooling is also determined by wind and clouds.

RELATIVE HUMIDITY

What a dog finds in a scan for volatile components clearly depends greatly on the ambient temperature, but also on humidity. Explosive molecules have a tendency to adsorb (adhere) strongly onto surfaces such as wood, plastic, paper, and soil. Moisture plays a key role in how well explosives do this. Water competes with explosive molecules for binding sites on soil particles, so as moisture in the soil increases, more explosive molecules will be released into the vapor space. In the case of landmine detection, both dogs and chemical vapor sensors are more efficient at detection after rain.

But be aware that water can also absorb the scent of hidden explosives, so rain on the surface of a cache acts like a cap, preventing the scent of the explosive from rising. In addition, rain cools the surface of the cache, resulting in the air becoming heavier, which prevents the scent from rising. As soon as it stops raining, however, the situation with the cache will change back to the way it was before the rain began.

Humidity is highest early in the morning and in the early evening; it is low during the day. Indoors, the relative humidity can be

Table 4.2 The Three Categories of Relative Humidity

Dry	0–30%
Normal	30–60%
Moist	60–100%

very low. A low-humidity environment may make the mucus membrane in your dog's nose dry sooner than usual, which will result in poorer-than-normal search performance. Moist nasal mucosa helps bring odor particles through the mucus to the receptor cells in the nose. If you and your dog are working out a search in very dry conditions, bring along a wet towel in a plastic bag that you can use to clean and moisten your dog's nose during the search.

WIND

Because we work with detector dogs, we are interested in gauging the wind near Earth's surface, the bottommost feet of the atmosphere. In this layer of air, wind is strongly influenced by the terrain and small-scale meteorological processes, so it often appears erratic. In general, the wind at human height blows harder than it does just above the ground. The ground surface inhibits the wind. As well, ground formations, vegetation, and buildings also redirect the wind, and even on a windy day, the air may be still behind these obstacles. Consider driving a car as a strong wind hits the vehicle broadside. You have to have a firm hand on the wheel and correct the car to stay on course, but if you drive past a building that blocks the wind or through a forest, the wind no longer pushes you, and again you must correct the car to stay on the road. A dog may also experience these bursts of still air as it investigates a search area and encounters obstacles to the wind at its level.

Wind direction is the direction from which the wind is blowing—so a north wind moves from north to south. Wind speed may vary rapidly, with fluctuations in the order of seconds or minutes. Note that wind direction and speed change relative to the time of day. Just as tides have a daily rhythm, wind responds to the predictable, daily changes in solar radiation and temperature.

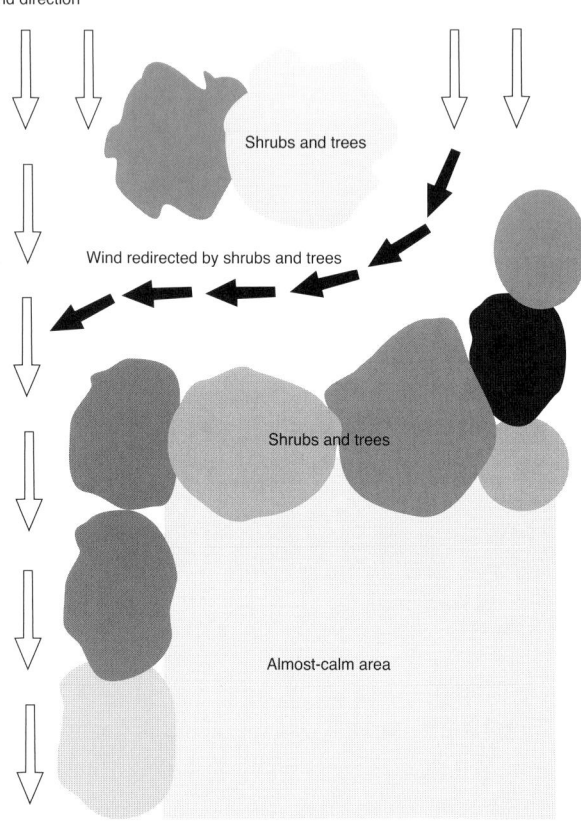

Figure 4.4 An aerial view of a hypothetical outdoor area. Air currents always follow the path of least resistance. Streets and roads, as well as natural features, can channel the wind in different directions. Such air currents, of course, have a great deal of influence on K9 search work.

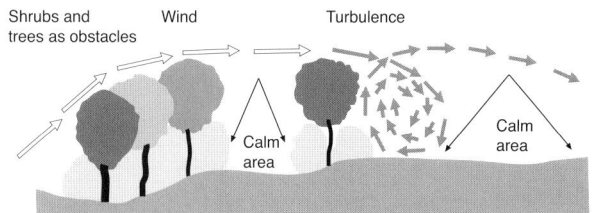

Figure 4.5 The first group of shrubs and trees that the wind encounters in this example (on the far left) create an obstacle, forcing the airflow up and over the second group of shrubs and trees, beyond which there is turbulence. Calm areas occur between the first two groups of trees and shrubs, and after the area of turbulence. When working with your dog outdoors, be aware of how obstacles can affect airflow and your dog's work.

Changing wind conditions are mainly caused by obstacles that impede the flow of air, and these may be more numerous in one place than another. The surfaces of large bodies of water are fairly smooth, for example, so air flows freely over them, meeting few impediments. A grassy plain, however, has a much rougher surface than the lake it surrounds, jarring the flow of air over it. The plain has grasses and scattered, single shrubs and trees, and wind must go over or around these—creating turbulence. The plain becomes a different landscape as it approaches the mountains. Here, there are dense clumps of shrubs and trees, and different sizes of vegetation (in height, width, and length) present in each copse. The airflow is strongly hindered and slowed down among these groupings of trees and shrubs. The towns that dot the plain, replete with buildings, provide even more obstacles to obstruct airflow.

Wind almost always behaves erratically because of surface features: sometimes fluctuations are strong; sometimes they are weak. Swirls of different sizes give wind a whimsical character. The size of swirls varies from a fraction of an inch to tens or even hundreds of yards. The speed with which the vortices move and rotate also varies. For the most part, swirls of air are caused by the wind encountering obstacles on Earth's surface. The rougher the terrain, the greater and more volatile the swirls. Wind turbulence can also be facilitated by locally fluctuating temperatures. The greater the temperature differences over short distances, the more capricious the wind seems.

Wind at Earth's surface almost always fluctuates: the wind is gusty, but how gusty strongly depends on the nature of the terrain in combination with wind speed and the proximity of precipitation. Wind speed is measured according to the Beaufort Scale, shown in Table 4.3. The table also provides descriptions of the visible effects of different strengths of wind.

Handlers don't need to be wind experts, but understanding how conditions affect their dogs' work can help them make their dogs

Table 4.3 The Beaufort Wind-Force Scale and Phenomena Associated with Wind

Beaufort Number	Name	Average km/h	Average mph	Characteristics
0	Calm	< 1	< 1	Smoke rises vertically
1	Light air	1–5	1–3	Direction of wind shown by smoke drift but not by wind vanes
2	Light breeze	6–11	4–7	Wind felt on face; leaves rustle; weather vane moved by wind
3	Gentle breeze	12–19	8–12	Leaves and small twigs in constant motion; wind extends light flags
4	Moderate breeze	20–28	13–18	Small branches on trees move; wind raises dust and loose paper
5	Fresh breeze	29–38	19–24	Small trees in leaf begin to sway; crested wavelets form on water
6	Strong breeze	39–49	25–31	Large branches in motion; whistling heard in overhead wires; umbrellas used with difficulty
7	Near gale	50–61	32–38	Whole trees in motion; inconvenience felt when walking against the wind
8	Gale	62–74	39–46	Twigs break off trees; wind generally impedes movement when walking
9	Strong gale	75–88	47–54	Branches break off trees; slight structural damage occurs, such as roof tiles removed
10	Storm	89–102	55–63	Trees uprooted; considerable structural damage occurs
11	Violent storm	103–117	64–74	Extensive damage to woodlands and buildings
12	Hurricane	> 117	> 75	Almost nothing remains standing

more effective. A handler should, for example, take wind direction and strength into account when deciding whether to proceed with a search at all and, if so, what direction to enter the search area from.

WIND'S EFFECTS ON TEMPERATURE

The wind also influences the temperature near the ground. Wind mixes up the air near Earth's surface and can easily disperse the heat generated by solar radiation during the daytime. At night, when Earth's surface cools down, the wind brings warm air to the surface, counteracting nocturnal cooling. If there is very little wind overnight, Earth's surface can cool considerably. This cooling process is exacerbated in an area with many obstacles that inhibit the wind.

Wind is a major factor in Earth's release of heat into the air. Air itself is a good insulator, so heat is not transferred if the air is not moving. Wind facilitates the transfer of heat (and moisture) from the soil into the atmosphere. The windier it is, the more effective the transfer of heat and moisture from Earth's surface into the atmosphere. During the day, when the sun warms Earth's surface, the wind carries heat off the surface, which means the layers of air closest to Earth can heat up quite a bit. At the same time, the wind promotes evaporation, wicking moisture from the soil.

After sunset, the situation changes. Earth's surface cools by radiating heat upward, but the air just above the surface remains warmer. If the weather is clear and there is little wind, the temperature of Earth's surface drops quickly at night. In winter months in a cold climate, the temperature of Earth's surface may be below freezing. But even during the winter, the air an inch or two above Earth's surface does not cool down as quickly at night. The temperature at 5 feet (1.5 m) or so is still up to 5 degrees warmer than the temperature closer to the ground.

COASTAL WINDS

In coastal areas, the uneven heating of land and sea creates a local wind: during daytime, a sea wind blows, but at night, a land wind blows. During the day, the air above land that has been warmed by the sun rises, creating an area of low pressure. The cooler air over the water, where there is higher pressure, then flows into the lower-pressure area over the land. This sea wind varies in strength, depending on temperature differences between land and sea. But

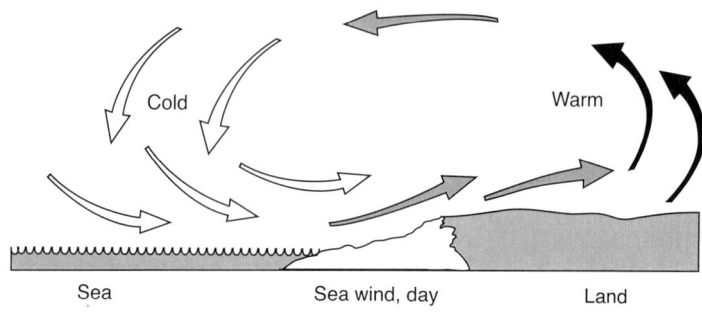

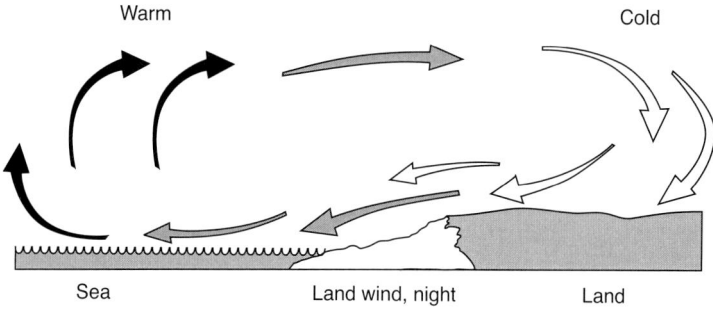

Figure 4.6 During the daytime in coastal areas, the wind blows from over the water, where there is higher pressure, to the lower pressure over the land. This creates the sea wind, which varies in strength depending on temperature differences over the land and sea. At night, there is a change in wind direction as the air over the sea is now warmer than that over the land.

at night, especially when it is cold, the sea is relatively warm compared to the land, and the situation is reversed.

MOUNTAIN WINDS

Mountainous areas also have winds that follow this pattern: mountain and valley winds are local winds that occur as a result of changes in daily temperatures, and thus changes in pressure. The valley wind is a warm wind that blows during the day, uphill from the valley. It arises because the air closest to Earth's surface in the valley is heated more by the sun than the air layers above it. The warm air rises along the mountain slopes.

Mountain winds are the opposite of valley winds. A mountain wind is cold, and it blows downslope toward valleys during

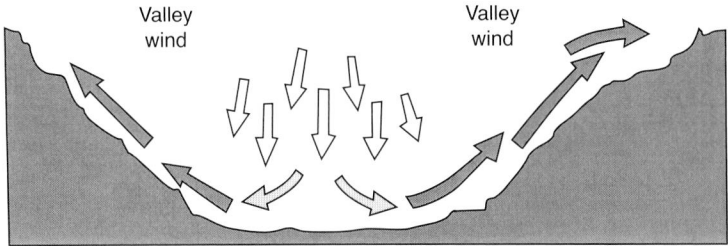

Valley wind created by heated slopes during the daytime

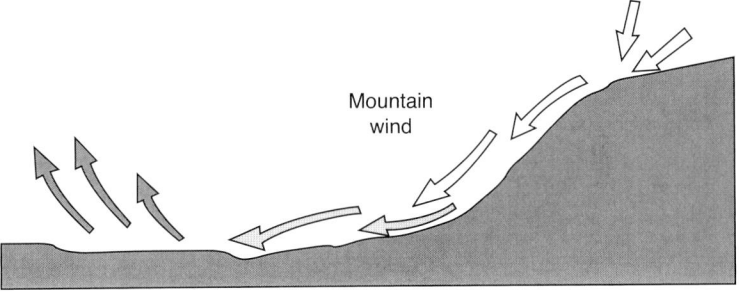

Mountain wind created by cooling at night

Figure 4.7 Mountain and valley winds are local winds that occur as a result of daily fluctuations in temperature. When the valley floor warms during the day, warm air rises up along the mountain slopes, creating the valley wind. In the evening, colder air moves down the mountain sides and collects on the valley floor: a mountain wind.

the evening, at night, and in the early morning. It generally occurs on clear nights. After sunset, the air on mountain slopes cools quicker than the air at the same height just above the valley floor. The colder air on the slopes is denser than warm air and thus slides down to the valley floor. Mountain winds are often stronger late at night and early in the morning: during the night, the air above the valley cools and the temperature difference between the air above the valley and that above the lower, and therefore warmer, ways out of the valley (valley exits) increases. A relatively small area of high pressure forms above the cold valley, and a small area of low pressure forms over the warmer valley exits. Additional air flows from the high- to the low-pressure areas—from the valley floor to the valley exits—resulting in an increase in wind.

WIND AROUND BUILDINGS

Turbulence, where the wind constantly changes direction and strength, is partly a consequence of the wind moving at different heights and correspondingly different speeds above the ground. Right on Earth's surface, air does not move; as altitude increases,

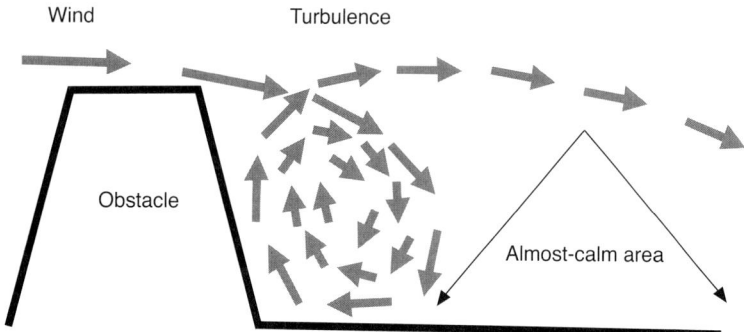

Figure 4.8 Wind speeds over 5–6 miles per hour (9 km/h) create turbulence behind obstacles like walls and buildings. Beyond those areas of turbulence, however, are almost-calm spots.

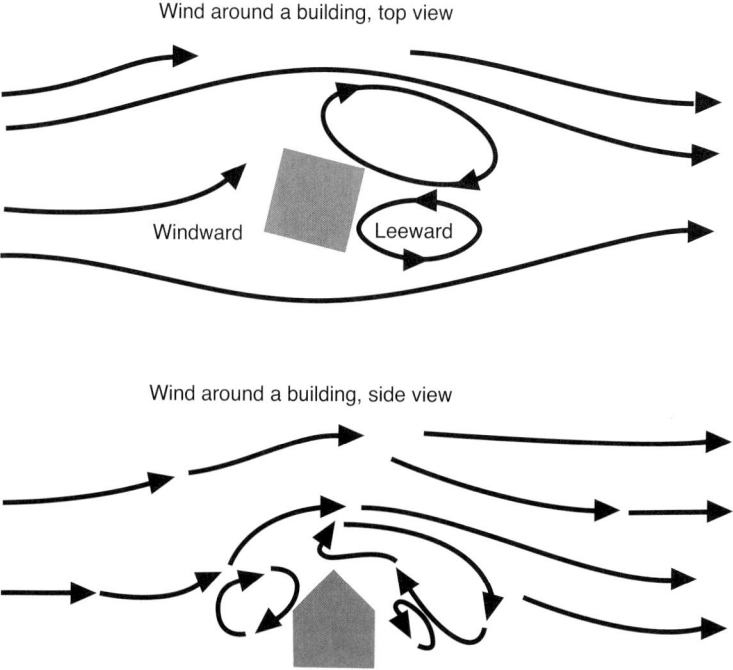

Figure 4.9 When wind blows against an obstacle like a house, a weir effect takes place.

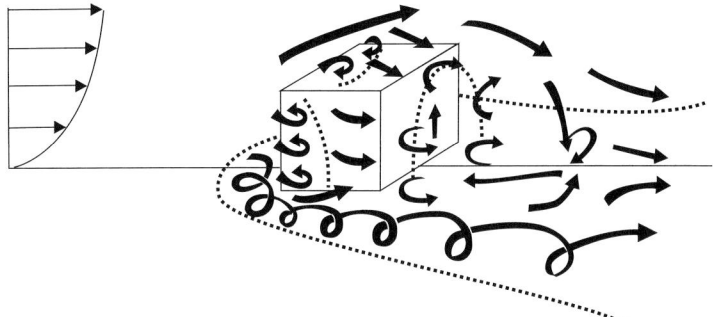

Figure 4.10 Whirling wind around buildings complicates K9 search work. The dotted lines on the drawing represent areas where turbulence is likely.

however, so does the wind's velocity because the influence of friction from Earth's surface decreases the farther up the wind is moving in the atmosphere. This is particularly true for air moving at 33–67 feet (10–20 m) above the ground surface.

As a result of the above principle of air movement, an obstacle in the wind's path (a house or other building) affects the wind at altitudes higher than the top of the obstacle. When the wind blows against the front of the obstacle, a weir effect takes place. This can be seen in the winter when snow blows against the side of a house, for example—the wind causes snow to accumulate against the house. The house blocks the wind, so it is not as windy behind the house, but wind passing beside the house toward the back of it draws air away, forming swirls, so snow can accumulate in the area behind the house. The size of this area where snow can accumulate is about 15 times the height of the obstacle.

Have you ever walked or cycled through a street where apartments or other large buildings stand, and just when you passed a large building you felt a sudden gust of wind? It can be very windy at the base of large buildings. And if a storm is in progress, it can even be dangerous to cycle around large buildings. The wind always blows harder higher up from Earth's surface, and the closer to the Earth's surface a wind blows, the more it is inhibited by surface friction. Tall buildings contend with more wind than low buildings do. When the

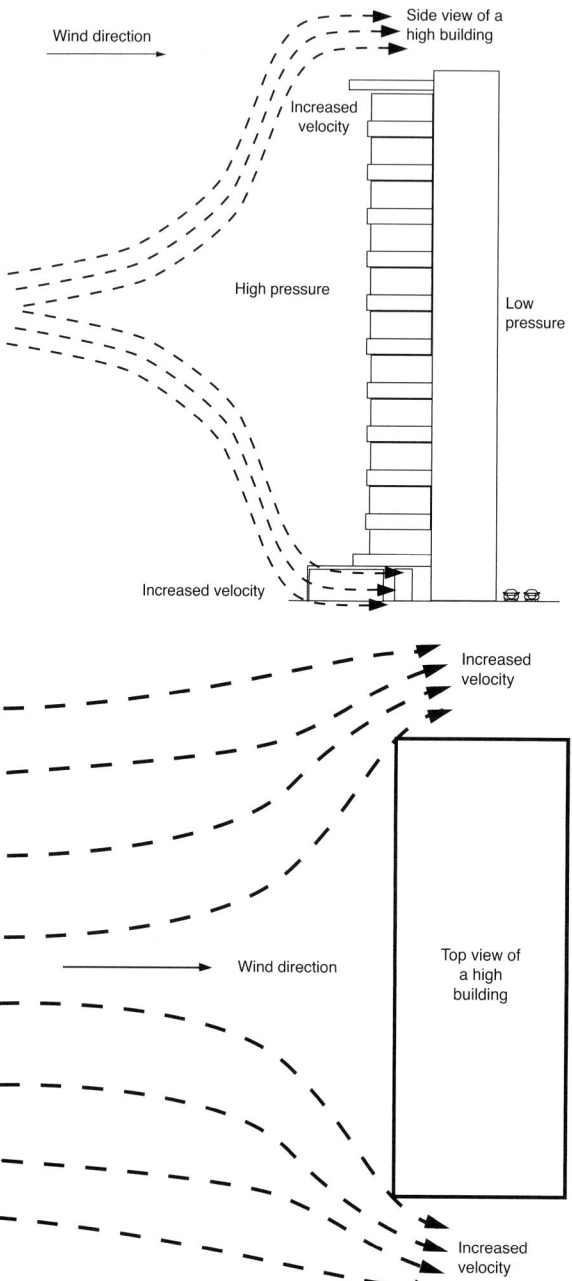

Figure 4.11 When the wind blows against a high building, the airflow is impeded and forced to take different routes in many directions with increased velocity.

wind at high altitudes blows against a high building, the building stops the air and forces it to gust in different directions, including down. This explains why it is often gusty at the base of tall buildings. The windiness around these buildings is even more intense if open areas such as parks or squares—places through which the wind can zip—are located adjacent to the buildings.

Breezes and strong wind gusts that play between neighboring high buildings are also strong. The air, after being redirected downward by the building, is then pressed through a kind of funnel between the buildings, and wind speeds pick up as more air is forced into that funnel. This translates into strong winds and wind gusts moving through the narrow passages between tall buildings and is called the Venturi effect. Keep this effect in mind if you need to conduct a search around tall buildings. As well, consider the less dramatic upwinds and downwinds.

UPWINDS AND DOWNWINDS

At the same temperature, dry air is heavier than humid air and, therefore, dry air sinks and humid air rises. At the same humidity, cold air is heavier than warm air and, therefore, cold air sinks and warm air rises. As a result, there are upward and downward air currents.

Sunshine heating Earth's surface will result in soil heating the air layer directly above it. Because warm air is lighter than cold air,

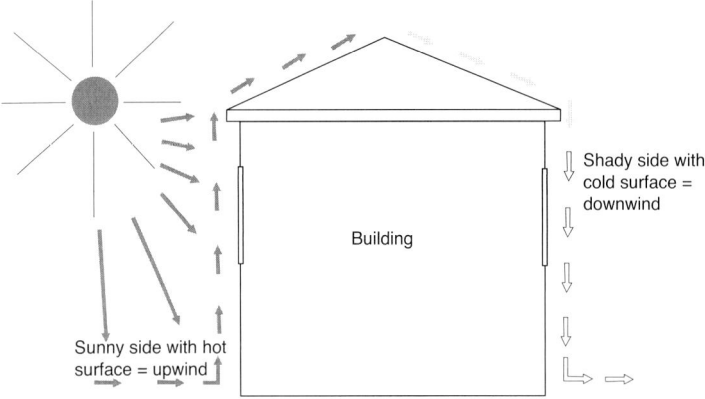

Figure 4.12 The effect of the sun on the outside walls of a building.

this process leads to upwinds. When air cools, it becomes heavier, and that process causes downwinds.

If the temperature of a wall surface is higher than the temperature of the air surrounding it, an upward airflow (buoyancy effect) will result. If the wall's surface is colder than the air, a downward flow of air results. So on the sunny side of a wall or a building, there is an upwind, and on the backside of the same wall or building, in the shade, there is a downwind.

INSIDE BUILDINGS

Rooms inside buildings also experience air currents. The sunny side of a room will have an upward air current, and the shady side will have a downward air current. In effect, the air is rolling inside the room. In large rooms or halls, you may encounter this rolling effect to a greater degree. The sunny side is the primary air roller that, with its upward air current, moves air to the top of the room. At the ceiling on the sunny side to about the middle of the room, the warm air from this current meets colder air from the shady side of the room. The cooler, shady side of the

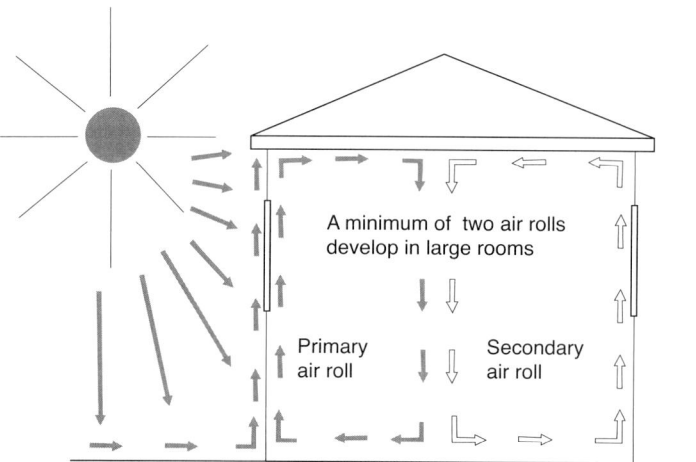

Figure 4.13 The effect of the sun on the inside of a building.

room develops a secondary air roller, with an upward air current along the wall and a downward air current in the middle of the room. As you might guess, your detector dog may find success when searching near walls, but the middle portions of rooms can cause problems.

Even when a building is heated, and warm on the inside, rooms may still have cold walls because of cold outside temperatures; this results in a different pattern of air currents than the one described above. The air travels downward along the cold outside walls, but near the middle of the room the air becomes warmer and so an upward air current develops.

Air always cools off near windows and outside walls when it is very cold outside. This creates greater airflow in a house, even if you can close all vents. An airflow always feels cold; this even applies to a flow of air that is 72°F (22°C), and even more to a stream of cooler air.

When wind blows on a building, it creates pressure on the building's facade. Air is forced through openings into the building on the windward side, and air exits the building through openings

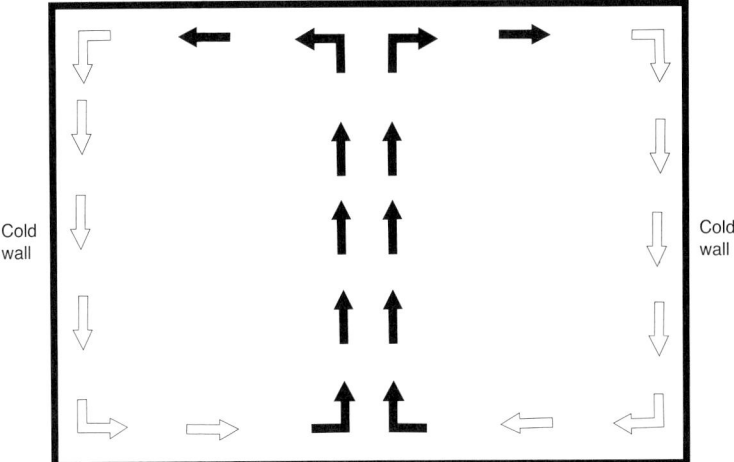

Figure 4.14 Side view of a building showing the effect on airflow of a warm room with cold walls. A downwind forms along cold walls.

Figure 4.15 The airflow in a room.

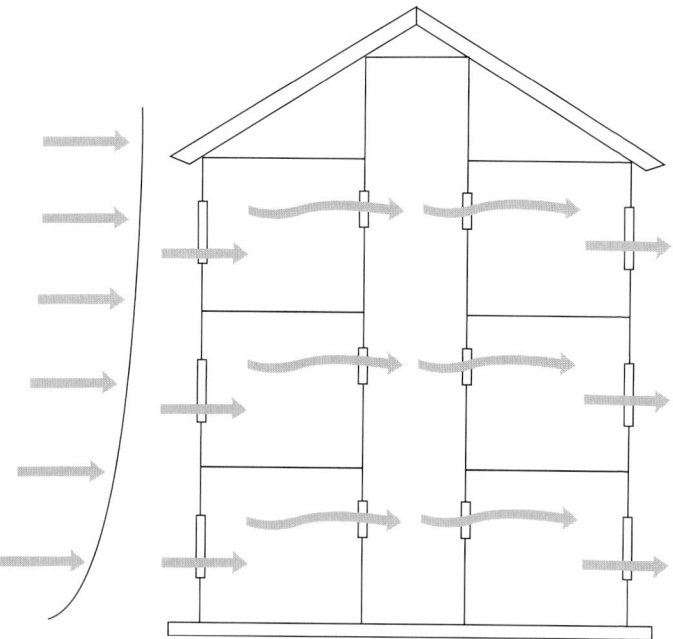

Figure 4.16 Wind flow against a building causes positive pressure (into the building) on the windward side of the building and negative pressure (outward from the building) on the leeward side. This means air enters on the windward side and exits on the leeward side.

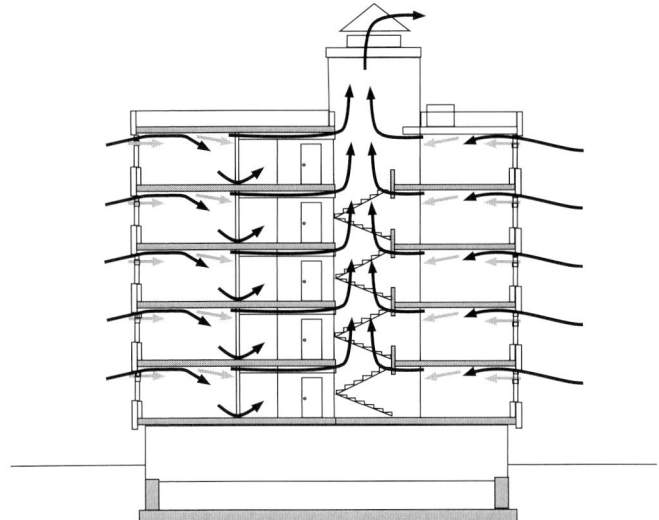

Figure 4.17 Airflow in the stairwell of an apartment building. In this example, the wind is blowing against the left side of a building in which rooms at all levels are connected to a wide central staircase with a vent at the top. The vent sucks the incoming air upward (the chimney effect). This creates a pressure differential, so air flows into the building from both sides.

on the leeward side. Wind flow around a building causes positive pressure (inward) on the windward side and negative pressure (facing out) on the leeward side. This creates a pressure differential across the building and a flow of air is formed. Cross-ventilation occurs when air enters the windward side of the building, flows through the building's interior, and leaves the building again on the other side, the leeward side.

AIR CURRENTS AT THE MICRO-LEVEL

Air currents in buildings also occur at the micro-level. Buildings have many sources of heat, such as people, computers, electrical appliances, and, of course, the sun shining in through the windows. Under the influence of these heat sources, warm air rises and sets air currents in motion. Curtains on windows will influence air currents, too: the layer of air between the window and the curtain is trapped, so it may have a different temperature than that of the rest of the room. The thicker and more insulating the curtain is, the greater this effect.

Figure 4.18 The airstream that results in a room because of various types of heating systems. Top: in-floor heating; middle: radiator heating; bottom: forced-air heating.

Figure 4.19 Special air current tubes can help detect the flow and strength of air currents.

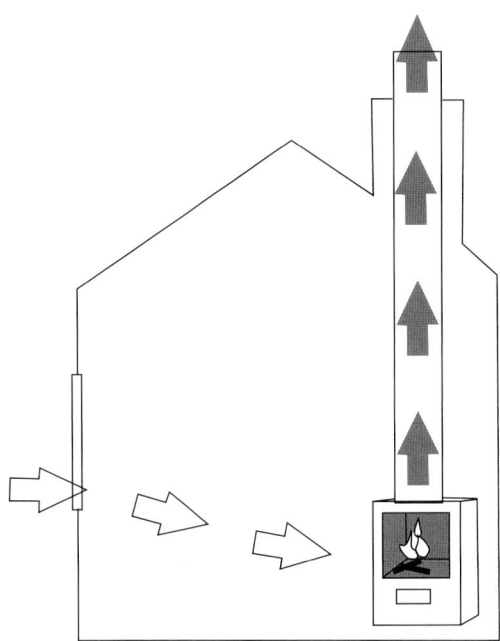

Figure 4.20 If air in a vertical channel, such as a chimney, is heated, it rises. As a result, the air pressure at the bottom of the chimney lowers, and colder air from outside is sucked in from any available opening (windows, cracks in walls or floor, and so on). This is called the chimney effect.

SHAFT VENTILATION

Shaft or chimney ventilation happens because of air pressure. When airflows are produced as a result of temperature differences between inside spaces and outside, the airflow inside moves in a vertical direction along the path of least resistance. Temperature differences cause a difference in air density that leads to motion, with cold air (high density) sinking toward hot air (low density).

Consider the air in a vertical channel, such as a chimney. If it is heated, it rises. As a result, the air pressure at the bottom of the chimney becomes lower, so colder air from outside is sucked in, which keeps the flow of air in motion. This is called the chimney effect. In the winter, where the inside temperature is greater than the outside temperature, the chimney effect is at work inside buildings. This effect can be described by the following seven conditions:

1. The inside temperature is higher than the outside air temperature.
2. Warmer air rises.

3. The upward movement of air causes a negative pressure at the bottom of the air shaft.
4. The top of the shaft has positive pressure.
5. As a result, the warmer air at the top of the building flows out of the building through whatever openings are available.
6. The air underneath the warm air is replaced by colder outside air, sucked in via cracks and seams in wooden floors, along window frames, and from exterior doors.
7. In summer, when the indoor temperature is lower than the outside temperature, the reverse happens.

The chimney effect in a staircase or elevator causes the pressure in the space below to fall. This causes the air to flow back in through existing openings (doors, windows, power outlets, air vents). Wind can increase this phenomenon, and the higher the building, the bigger the updraft.

The airflow in a conservatory, or a greenhouse, during the winter is determined by its glass wall(s). The extent of the cold trap that exists along the glass facade depends on the height of the glass. Near the floor, the airstream deflects toward the center of the conservatory, so that high air velocities at floor level may arise. In a conservatory that is not heated and that has a single glass outer wall, air speeds can reach up to approximately 3.3 feet per second (1 m/s). The high air velocities at floor level can be prevented by placing convectors at the bottom inside of the glass wall.

The airflow in homes and buildings is not constant. Ventilation can change quickly in each room. Also, the rate at which indoor odors release is changeable. Changing ventilation patterns and odor-release rates influence the concentration of odor available to a dog as it investigates an indoor search area. As well, the concentration of the odor in the air depends in part on the volume of the space itself.

Controlled Search

This type of search, in which you, the handler, know the hidden location of the explosives, is conducted during the beginning stages of training an explosive detector dog.

ADVANTAGES

- You can control the search and movements of your dog and can encourage him at the right moments.
- You can learn and begin to recognize your dog's reactions to searching. This allows you to prevent your dog's incorrect responses by reacting at the right moment (e.g., if you see your dog wants to give an incorrect response, you can say, "No" and "Search further" to avoid false alerts).
- You may apply corrective measures without preventing your dog from achieving a positive indication.

DISADVANTAGES

- You may unintentionally indicate where the explosives are located.
- You might be encouraged to stand in one spot, which prevents your dog from learning to search systematically. A good dog handler should walk slowly with the dog and not simply stand in one place.

Blind Search

For you, all searches in real life are conducted "blind." But for the dog, all searches are blind, even during training. When conducting a blind search during training, the helper, instructor, or others who know the locations of the hiding places can be present, but you should not know the locations.

ADVANTAGES

- The blind search helps build the handler–dog team, giving each partner confidence in the other.
- The method refines your concentration.
- It creates a need for the team to search systematically.

DISADVANTAGES

- If used too early in training, you may not notice the dog's search reactions because you are not yet aware of what you have to look for.
- You may allow your dog to do unnecessary work, so your dog may end up searching the same area several times instead of moving on to the next area to search. Sometimes this happens when a handler thinks he has seen a reaction in the dog and so sends it to search an area over and over again.
- You may request confirmation from and encourage your dog at the wrong times, thereby causing confusion and even false indications.

Operational Search

When you conduct an operational search during training, you, the handler, do not know the number of explosive caches hidden in the search area. Indeed, there may be none. When performing an operational search in training, only you and your dog enter the search area. (Your instructor may choose to follow the search by means of a suspended camera or cameras.)

When performing such a search, ensure your dog accurately scans the entire area. Record all possible caches indicated by your dog. Handlers must be able to show the places of the alert(s) afterwards but are not allowed to touch or mark the hidden chemicals. During training, you and your dog should perform more than one operational search in an area where no explosives are hidden.

ADVANTAGES

- You learn to place your trust in your detector dog.
- The method confirms the need to work systematically, including low and high searches.
- The method encourages a busy dog to adapt. A busy dog will only be successful if it slows down and searches intensively.
- Search times increase, which helps develop your dog's concentration and control.

DISADVANTAGES

- You may feel unsteady without backup from colleagues who help you search systematically and observe your dog's behavior.
- Too much search work without success may decrease the bring drive in some dogs.

Equipment

In training, when searching on leash, explosive detector dogs should wear a light plastic or leather collar without metal parts. Make sure your dog's collar fits well—if it's too loose, the collar may come off; if it's too tight, your dog may have trouble breathing, which of course negatively affects training. During a real operational search, explosive detector dogs don't wear any collar or harness—only in training.

Start training with a short leash, also without metal parts. A short leash allows you to correct your dog almost immediately, and so it makes sense that it is mostly used at the beginning of a dog's training. When your dog can adequately perform the training exercises on a short leash, you can transition to a long leash. At this point, use the short leash only when you want your dog to follow you on leash, or in situations where your dog needs to be kept close so it stays out of danger. The length of the long leash (also without metal parts) is mostly a matter of personal preference, but is usually 10–16 feet (3–5 m) long. Because leather long leashes are hard and heavy, we often use a plastic one, which allows for greater maneuverability.

The long leash allows your dog to work more independently than when it is on a short leash, even as the leash allows you a level of control over your dog. The long leash allows you to slowly build distance between you and your dog during search training. As well, you may wish to use a long leash later on, in deployment situations where you feel it is necessary to keep your dog under some degree of control. However, while on a long leash, your dog is always liable to get tangled up in something. As well, the leash may drag through or touch objects in the search area, so make sure you take obstacles into account when conducting searches using this tool.

The Reward

In training as well as in deployment, you should always carry a retrievable reward/motivational item that your dog enjoys. Dogs that are fond of food can be rewarded with a biscuit or piece of cheese hidden in the object; for other dogs, the retrievable object is enough of a reward. Without a reward, your dog will quickly lose the urge to search. Your retrievable object should be easy to handle and a size that your dog cannot swallow. Some examples include a Teflon pipe, rubber or tennis ball, Kong, or Westpaw Hurley. We prefer the Hurley because it doesn't easily roll away.

During training, use the retrievable object as a guard against your dog coming into contact with toxic substances. When training your dog to find the odor of a particular explosive, for example, place your Hurley near the odor in such a way that your dog can never be in direct contact with the explosive but will be able to fetch the Hurley. If you use a Teflon pipe, ensure your explosives are well-packaged and protected from destruction, damage, or loss.

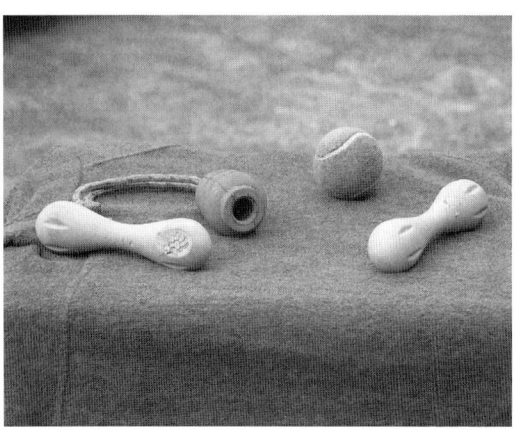

Figure 5.2 Reward tools: on each side, the Westpaw Hurley; in the center, the Kong and a tennis ball.

Rewarding with a training tool at the end of each successful search exercise—finding an odor and giving the correct response—allows your dog to understand that he has completed the command and finished the job. Because the job always ends in a satisfactory way, your dog becomes receptive to further training.

Figure 5.3 A US marine rewards his improvised explosive device (IED) detection dog for accurately finding imitation explosives during training in Afghanistan.

Figure 5.4 A detector dog of the Royal Netherlands Marechaussee (RNLM) likes this tube as a reward. The RNLM serves as a police force for all branches of the Netherlands defense organization: the Royal Netherlands Navy, the Royal Netherlands Army, and the Royal Netherlands Air Force.

Role of the Handler

A dog will only become as good as its handler permits. In other words, the handler–dog combination must be right in order for the team to get positive results. You, the handler, must trust in the quality of your dog and be thoroughly familiar with the principles of dog training. You must also know how to influence your dog and how to read its body language, and you must know about the substances your dog is being trained to detect. Most important, you must be able to work with your dog as a team.

During training, you need to help your dog develop independence so it is not entirely dependent on you as it searches. Such independence can be developed by using the training tool: every time you train, your dog will search more intensively for the tool in order to receive the reward as quickly as possible.

We believe detector dogs should be trained without compulsion or pressure. However, non-compulsive training is successful only if several requirements are met. First, the dog must have a strong bring drive, and second, you must give the dog enough freedom to learn how to work independently.

> **The danger of "helicopter" dog handling is that the dog will pay too much attention to you, depend too much on your cues, and lose concentration on the search work.**

READING YOUR DOG'S BODY LANGUAGE

One of the most important roles of the handler is reading the dog's behavior. The dog is the smelling expert—the handler reads the dog to help find the target substances. To understand your dog's reactions while searching, you must pay close attention to any changes in your dog's behavior. For that, of course, you have to know your dog thoroughly in normal situations, at home as well as during training.

Dogs constantly receive signals through their senses of smell, sight, and hearing, and you, the handler, may not even realize your dog is perceiving something. It is essential for you to understand your dog's behavior and know when it has received signs of an explosive. Because your dog cannot talk, you must encourage it to signal you when something is up. At the same time, you must be careful not to influence your dog into signaling a false response. When handlers fail to recognize behavioral signals, dogs become confused, which in turn results in handlers becoming frustrated and operating on a hit-and-miss basis.

When a dog is searching, you will see the following behaviors:

- *Normal steps:* the movements and pace of the dog during the search before it detects the odor of explosives.
- *Change of attitude:* a difference in tempo and/or behavior; movement of the ears, tail, or a sudden change of direction upon encountering an odor.
- *Lifting the head:* the dog may lift its head and tilt it in a certain direction, or it may stand on its hind legs and raise its head to smell the air when it perceives the smell of explosives.
- *Positive interest:* body movements and behavior that indicate the dog has detected the presence of explosives, but has not yet found the "hot spot." For example, if your dog shows interest and begins to walk forward and back, it probably hasn't found the right place yet. Keep quiet, because the dog may just be orienting herself. Likewise, if your dog tries to alert by sitting or lying down, but immediately stands up and searches the spot again, you might read her behavior as telling you that she is not sure about the smell and hesitates to respond.
- *Response:* the passive (sitting or lying down) alert the dog has been trained to demonstrate when it has found the location of an explosive or explosives.
- *Confirmation:* this is the highest level for well-trained operational dogs. After the dog demonstrates the alert, the handler can confirm that explosives have been found by attempting to lure the dog away (giving additional search commands or trying to gently pull the dog away on leash). If the dog is sure of its find, it will continue to alert and will not leave its place.

Principles of Training

Important to training without pressure are your conscious and unconscious movements, which influence your dog's behaviors. Your body language can give many types of nonverbal commands. For example, you can use body language to draw your dog's attention to a particular place or object. And of course, your voice—all the sounds you use to arouse your dog's curiosity, or to motivate or correct her—is also a critical component of the non-compulsion training method.

Adhere to the following five rules to create a strong foundation from which to train a detector dog:

1. Do not employ strict discipline or harsh commands when training your dog, unless the dog's nature requires it (e.g., the dog does not easily accept instructions from you).
2. Do not use sticks, rocks, or other such objects for fetching, unless you are using them as training tools.
3. Always end the training session with an experience that is pleasurable for your dog—for example, asking it to fetch a favorite toy.
4. Throughout training, do not force your dog to relinquish its toy by giving harsh commands. Instead, encourage it to give up its "prey" by offering treats such as cheese or sausages, or a dog biscuit.
5. Searching, finding, and temporarily retaining an object forms the basis of search-dog training—these activities should always be pleasant for your dog.

INCENTIVE AND ASSOCIATION

The principles of detector-dog training are twofold: incentive and association. To stimulate the bring drive in a dog, you must provide a suitable incentive in the form of an object that your dog wants to fetch. In fact, the first stages of detector training are all about direct retrieving, followed by searching and fetching, and then training of the "alert" or response the dog gives when it has found the odor it is looking for. For an explosive detector dog, this alert is always passive—lying down or sitting. You must teach your dog that it is not allowed to touch any of the odorous substances it finds. The dog must also learn that its reward does not come immediately, as it does in other areas of dog training; it must learn to expect a delayed reward.

The training tool is the incentive; the next step is to associate that tool with the explosive odor. Ensure that every time you give your dog a reward during training, it is associated with an explosive odor. There are a variety of ways to teach your dog the association between the odors and the reward. One of the best ways, in our view, is to ensure the dog perceives the explosive odor alongside the reward at an early stage of training. For example, at first hide the Hurley along with the cache of explosives so your dog can take the reward upon finding the odor. Later on, only hide the explosives. Learning how to find caches in this way will help your dog focus its passions for searching and retrieving on the retrievable object that is also now strongly associated with the odor of explosives.

We use the all-important retrievable object in four different parts of training: as a reward, a drive stimulator, an independence builder, and a way for you, the handler, to learn to read

Figure 5.5 For a positive indication, the dog pinpoints the explosive odor and immediately moves to the trained distance of about 10 inches (25 cm) and sits or lies down.

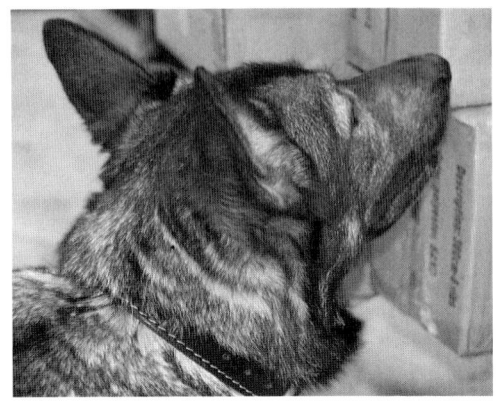

Figure 5.6 After an alert, wait a couple seconds, say "Free," show the dog the reward, and then throw it for the dog to retrieve in the opposite direction from the scent clue. This makes the dog turn away from the explosive to get the reward.

your dog's body language. As you and your dog go through the many stages of search training together, you will come to recognize the meaning behind your dog's behavior and reactions. The retrievable object is a tool that allows you to observe everything your dog does without interruptions; because the dog is driven to independently find the odor of the hidden explosive, you will be able to observe it from a short distance, watching and learning its body language.

Concentration

Because curiosity is part of every dog's nature, during training you need to develop your dog's ability to concentrate on the task at hand and not get distracted by other interesting things. To do this, you have to familiarize your dog with the many different environments in which it might later work. If you train your dog in many different locations, it will become used to a variety of surroundings, sounds, objects, smells, people, and experiences, and this familiarity will prepare it for work as a detector dog. It is impossible to be prepared for every situation. However, in many cases, your dog will experience one type of environment in the same way that it views another. For example, working in aircraft hangars is similar to working in cargo sheds, warehouses, and other large, cavernous buildings.

TYPES OF SEARCH LOCATIONS

Because every situation and environment can potentially be a search area, simulated search areas set up for training purposes should include indoor venues (in-use, empty, and dilapidated buildings; storage areas and basements; large sheds and hangars; public buildings; schools; and offices); open-air environments (parking lots, industrial sites, railways, public meeting spaces, and event grounds); and vehicles (public trains and buses, cars and trucks, aircraft, and water-going vessels).

AGILITY TRAINING

Agility training will help your dog work around obstacles such as boxes, steps, and vehicles. Your dog must eventually be able to take on such obstacles without doubt or fear. If your dog is agile enough to jump over and maneuver around obstacles, either on its own volition or on your command, it will be able to handle any environment without losing concentration. Of course, you must also train your dog not to jump around in a search area needlessly.

TYPES OF DISTRACTIONS

Here we come back to the key idea that dogs concentrate better when they are not distracted. While training your dog, pay close attention to the most obvious distractions and familiarize your dog with them; make the distractions so common as to be unworthy of notice. Through structural repetition (possibly with rewards or corrections), your dog will eventually ignore distractions and accept them as simply part of the search area. Distractions can be of a direct or indirect nature, including the following examples: residual waste and food, unfamiliar situations, wild game or birds, pets, sudden noise or movement, objects that can be retrieved, different weather conditions, flooring or stairways of varying conditions, different types of vegetation, and large crowds of people.

A detector dog should have plenty of perseverance. The more perseverance your dog has, the less distracted it will be. You can help your dog develop this characteristic through delayed rewards during training and operational deployment.

Rules for Hiding Explosives

To avoid disruption during training, as well as contamination and inadvertent planting of clues to hidden explosives, always use sterile tools (forceps or tongs) and/or gloves when handling explosives. If you handle the explosives with bare hands, you will impart your own odor onto the explosive; as well, many explosives are toxic or corrosive and should not be handled without gloves.

Detector dogs are always looking for clues about where an explosive could be hidden. We cannot emphasize this point enough: always work to prevent your dog from reacting to human scent during training. It is of the utmost importance that you never hold or hide explosives without wearing gloves. In addition, make sure all substances are stored separately to prevent cross-contamination. And, of course, be vigilant and watch for tracks you or a helper may have laid in the search area that might lead your dog to the cache. To avoid creating a track that leads directly to the prize, always ask a few people to walk around in a training search area before asking your dog to find the explosives.

SORTING TEST

During training, you will need to regularly make sure your dog is not finding the hidden substance by searching for a human scent or any odors that might accompany the substance in question; the dog must find the explosives it is searching for by finding the odor of the explosives themselves. To do this, perform the sorting test. Hide an object (one that does not contain any explosives or has not been in contact with explosives) replete with human odor—perhaps your own or that of a helper—near but not too close to some hidden explosives. Usually 6–10 feet (2–3 m) is about right, but in some situations and with some dogs, less can be fine (but not under 3 feet, 1 m). Then test your dog's odor-recognition skills by asking it to find the explosives, not the other hidden object. Only reward your dog if it demonstrates it can find the hidden explosives.

Generally speaking, during training, hidden explosives should be packaged in vials, bottles, plastics, or the like. But during the sorting test, you may need to remove the packaging from the explosives to decrease the likelihood of your dog sniffing for an accompanying smell (sometimes called an emitter) instead of the smell of the explosives themselves. In later training, the explosives or the explosive odor carriers must be hidden without any foreign objects. If this is not done, the dog may learn to indicate for the smell of, for example, a plastic bag. If you need to remove the explosive substances from their packaging, make sure you hide the explosives in a place where they are detectable but also where your dog cannot reach them (e.g., in a closed suitcase or box). Also remember not to hide the explosives in plain sight; dogs can become used to responding to visual characteristics associated with "hidden" explosive caches.

GENERAL RULES FOR HIDING EXPLOSIVES

Five other rules you should follow when hiding explosives during training are as follows:

1. Never leave hidden explosives unattended.
2. Always hide explosives in a safe place, or leave the hiding to a competent person, such as a fellow officer or trainer.
3. If you are training your dog to find more than one cache of hidden explosives in an exercise, remember to take note of the locations and number of hiding places to prevent abandoning explosives somewhere.
4. To avoid distracting your dog during search exercises, do not wear or hold anything that might contain explosive substances, such as used gloves.
5. When you begin training your dog to recognize different explosive odors, do not mix different types of explosives together. If working with explosive mixtures for early training, always use the same mixture. Only once the dog knows the odor(s) in training can you change to another explosive odor or another mixture.

TRAINING THE SMELL OF ARMS

When searching for small arms or other weapons, a dog trained to alert for black powder is most useful. Even if modern weapons no longer use black powder, they have similar odor components. At the beginning of training, and also from time to time in maintenance training, use freshly shot weapons (e.g., alarm pistols) and cartridges. The weapons should be regularly cleaned with different weapon oils so that your dog will also be familiar with these odor components. For long-hidden weapons without cartridges, the smell of weapon oil is often the only odor indication the dog can find. Be sure to use small arms and weapons handled by different people to prevent the dog from being influenced too much by the smell of a single person.

Training the First Explosive

Some introduce their dogs to different explosive odors one at a time. As soon as their dogs do well with the first odor, they introduce the next scent alongside the first one. This process (introducing a new scent along with a known sent) continues until the dog has learned all the required scents. It is possible to train your dog to recognize more than one scent at a time, which is a faster method. However, the step-by-step approach is more effective; when training your dog in this way, you can be sure it knows and recognizes each odor. The disadvantage of training each odor one at a time is that it takes longer to train your dog.

Always begin scent training with an explosive scent that is not unpleasant or likely to elicit an adverse response in your dog. For instance, some dogs find that ammonium nitrate stings their nose. But, just as different people experience scents in different ways, you can expect different dogs to have different reactions to the same odor. Try to discover an explosive scent that your dog likes and start with that. Many dogs we have worked with like the scent of TNT.

If your dog sniffs once at a certain explosive and then avoids it, you know the dog doesn't like the explosive's smell because it is repulsive, stings the nose, or is otherwise too strong. If this happens, you would not, of course, use this scent when you begin scent training. Also consider that the first scent you train your dog on should not be one whose odor spreads too quickly in larger areas, such as nitroglycerin (NG) or ethylene glycol dinitrate (EGDN), because it is possible that too many objects in the search area will then take on the odor, making it difficult for your dog to pinpoint the exact hiding place of the explosive.

When you practice searching for different explosives, you need to use pure, clean products. You can reuse substances as long as they are not contaminated with other odors. When you use pure explosives, make sure your dog cannot access them directly and that, for example, powder cannot enter the dog's mouth or nostrils. We have found that re-sealable plastic bags provide fine storage for explosives used in training. As you prepare an explosive cache, enclose the bag of explosives in an unused re-sealable plastic bag, making sure you don't touch either the explosives or bag with your bare hands.

USING SCENT-TRANSFER OBJECTS

If you do not wish to use pure explosives in your search exercises, you may employ scent-transfer objects instead, such as cotton pads or a Teflon pipe with small openings in it. Ensure the scent transfer by placing the scent-transfer object beside well-packaged explosives (the scent source) in a clean glass jar. Leave the sealed glass jar overnight. Shortly before starting the search exercise, use tweezers or tongs to remove the cotton pad or pipe from the jar, making sure you avoid contaminating it with your own odor.

If you use scent-transfer objects, always remember to handle them as carefully as you would handle the original scent source. Cotton pads should be discarded after one use. Scent the training tubes and cotton pads with only one scent at a time. When you have finishing training your dog on a specific scent, you need new, clean jars and tubes for new explosive odors. Do not reuse the jars for other scents because of risk of contamination. For instance, glass jars that have stored TNT, even overnight, can be reused only for TNT; washing and sterilizing them will not render them "clean" for other odors.

Training the Passive Response

The response your dog gives you when it has found the odor it is looking for is important. If your dog has a well-developed drive to find the odors it is trained to find, you can always rely on the dog's response. In explosive detector dog training, we only use passive responses. Which type of passive response you teach should suit your dog's behavior and character.

Passive alerts include sitting, standing, or lying down near the scent clue. Barking, scratching, or other active responses are not allowed. The passive response may be accompanied by the dog pointing its nose at the spot that has the most concentrated explosive odor. Dogs are not allowed to go too close to or on top of the indicated explosive substance, nor are they allowed to scratch or try to move the covering with their nose. The best distance for the dog to indicate an explosive substance from is about 10 inches (25 cm). For a positive indication, the dog pinpoints and immediately moves to the trained distance and sits or lies down. We have found that dogs like the passive response in searches when they are trained correctly and rewarded the moment they lie down or sit at the correct distance from the odor of explosives.

Training Preparation

First, teach your dog to play fetch with the training tool (a tennis ball, Hurley, or other retrievable object). Then, put together three or four boxes about 12 inches wide, 12 inches long, and 8 inches high (30 × 30 × 20 cm). The boxes should all be the same shape and made of the same material. The top side of the boxes should have an opening into which you can fit the training tool. Always use the same box for the odor substances. Keep the other boxes scent free; otherwise, all your boxes will acquire the same scent, and your dog will end up alerting for every box. Now you can begin training the first scent.

EXPLOSIVE DETECTION TRAINING

Figure 5.7 Begin passive response training with a box that holds the odor of the explosive you are training your dog to recognize. The lid of the box should have an opening through which you can place a reward tool.

Figure 5.8 In the first step of training, your dog should be able to see you putting the reward into the box.

Training Schedule

STEP 1

Place one training box containing one explosive (or four separately packaged explosives if you are using the concurrent method) in a quiet place that is free from distractions. Ask your dog to sit somewhat away from but in front of the box. Now, making sure your dog can see what you are doing, insert the training tool into the top opening of the box. Because your dog is crazy about the toy, he will go straight to the box to try to get it, sticking his nose right into the opening on top. Do not allow him to scratch at it or touch it; instead, say, "Sit" or "Down." If he doesn't take that position, command him again and quietly bring him into position about 10 inches (25 cm) away from the box, telling him he is a good boy.

Wait a couple seconds, say "Free," and at the same time throw a different training tool for him to retrieve in the opposite direction of the box, so the dog has to turn away from the box to get it. Make sure your dog does not turn away from the box before you throw the ball or Hurley. If your dog pays more attention to you than to the box, try the following: after your dog lies down for a few seconds, go to the box, open the lid, take the training tool out, and throw it away from the box, saying, "Free."

After repeating this exercise many times over many training sessions, deepen the exercise. This time, don't place the training tool in the box but keep the explosive scent or scents in there. Immediately after your dog sniffs and sits or lies down, throw her ball to retrieve and praise her for the good work. Or, using the other method, keep the training tool hidden in your hand (not visible to the dog), go to the box, open the lid, and pretend to take out the training tool and throw it away.

Figure 5.9 If the dog wants to sit or lie down with his nose right at the box, show him a second training tool and move the reward above his head backward so he will creep or crawl back to the right position. Once he's in position, reward him immediately.

Slowly increase the amount of time your dog has to alert by sitting or lying down from 3 to 10 seconds (or even more) before you throw the reward.

STEP 2

If your dog seems to understand that he has to sit or lie down in front of the box, it is time for a test. Place a second box without the scent of explosives in a row with the other box. Lead your dog to the boxes, ensuring that the first box he meets is the empty box. Now you will see if you have trained your dog properly. If the dog sits or lies down at the first box, you will have to go back to the initial training because the dog does not yet understand that it is not supposed to alert to just any box, but only boxes with the smell of an explosive or explosives. Start initial training again, but do things a little differently to be sure the dog understands what to do. For example, you might use an empty box sometimes with no reward.

If the dog worked out the mini-lineup well—it sniffed the first box and then moved on to the second, where it sniffed and sat or lay down, reward the dog by throwing the training tool. Perform the two-box lineup over several training sessions.

STEP 3

Bring in more empty boxes and regularly change the position of the scented box in the lineups you create. You can use all types of boxes for your lineups as long as all are of the same material and shape.

Figure 5.10 This dog is learning how to investigate a scent-identification lineup. One of the boxes holds the scent of the explosive the dog is looking for.

Figure 5.11 The dog smells the odor of the explosive...

Figure 5.12 ...and reacts with a correct response at a distance from the box.

STEP 4

Start training your dog to recognize the scent of a second explosive, hidden together with the first explosive in the box. Repeat Step 1 several times until you can take out the first explosive, and the dog still alerts well for the second odor. If the dog can alert for the second odor about 10 times, you are ready to move on. Then continue with steps 2 and 3 for the second odor. If you are training four different scents at a time, begin training your dog to recognize a new series of four explosives in the box.

STEP 5

Pair a new, third explosive with the first or the second explosive in the box, making sure you use the explosive that was the easiest for your dog to find as the familiar scent. Go through Steps 1 through 3. Complete the training in the same way with all sorts of explosives. Each time your dog completes the exercise properly, make sure you provide the reward by throwing the training tool away from the box.

STEP 6

Put a box containing one type of explosive (or four kinds, depending on your training method) in the corner of a room. Let your dog now search for the box and alert by sitting or lying down. If this goes well, you can progress to putting several boxes in various places around the room and asking your dog to search for the correct box and alert.

If your dog does this correctly, hide the explosive without the box in about the same spot it was the last time you practiced. Ensure the explosive is detectable, but not accessible. Your dog should approach the place where it can smell the hidden scent, and it should sniff and sit or lie down. Do this step with all the explosives your dog has been trained to search, find, and alert for.

STEP 7

From this point on, hide the different explosives in increasingly difficult spots—low and high, in vehicles, in someone's coat, and so on. Always reward your dog for good work by throwing the

Figure 5.13 A scent identification lineup with plastic containers.

Figure 5.14 In explosive-detector dog training, we only use passive responses.

training tool, hidden in your hand, away from the hiding place. Practice in different rooms and types of locations, using a great variety of hiding places: in houses, cars, outbuildings, and other places where your dog will have to work in his career as an explosive detector dog. Always build up the training slowly, making sure your dog understands each exercise, until it can find the substances anywhere and give a correct, passive response every time.

6

Search Actions

Preparation for Deployment

Every search action starts by defining the task. Is it, for example, a search action for the protection of one or more people, or is it the inspection of a space, room, or vehicle? Of course it is also important to clarify the degree of risk: is the search preventive or is there a specific threat? The latter affects the manner of searching substantially.

Preparation for deployment includes assessing the operational capability of the dog and ensuring you have all the equipment required. Develop and use a checklist as part of your standard routine.

Figure 6.1 A US soldier and Bono, a tactical explosive detector dog, inspect an Afghan truck for explosives.

Begin with your dog, because only a healthy and regularly trained dog will be able to meet the demands of deployment. Here the ambitions of a dog handler are absolutely out of place and can be life threatening. A good dog handler notices when his dog is not 100 percent fit and will decline the mission.

Never perform a search action alone; always have a colleague with you as backup. So preparation also includes the selection of the person who is to accompany the detector dog team; it is beneficial if the backup person has already worked with the team during training. With a backup on site, the handler can fully concentrate on his dog and the task. The backup can establish contact with others on site, such as the caretaker or another person familiar with the site, to find out about any objects that do not fit into the environment, such as wastebaskets, fire extinguishers, flowerpots, suitcases, and abnormalities in any vehicles present (changes in vehicles, unfamiliar vehicles, etc.). The backup can communicate search priorities to the handler.

For all risky situations, it can also be good to have at least two search dogs available, so one dog can work while the other dog has a break. If time pressures are extreme, both dogs can search the area simultaneously. Furthermore, you can use one dog to confirm the alerts or suspicious behavior of the other.

Figure 6.2 Rush, a US marine improvised explosive device (IED) detector dog, searches for explosives during a patrol in Afghanistan in 2014.

BOMB THREAT BY TELEPHONE

In case of a bomb threat by telephone, try to get answers to the questions below to plan the search action with your dog. Staff, especially receptionists, should be trained to respond to a bomb threat. They should remain calm and try to get as much information as possible:

- When is the bomb going to explode?
- Where is the bomb?
- What does it look like?
- What kind of bomb is it?
- What will cause it to explode?
- Did you place the bomb?
- Why?
- Where are you calling from?
- What is your address?
- What is your name?
- Make note of callers voice. Was it:

    - Calm
    - Stuttering
    - Giggling
    - Stressed
    - Disguised
    - Slow
    - Deep
    - Accented
    - Nasal
    - Sincere

    - Crying
    - Loud
    - Angry
    - Lisping
    - Squeaky
    - Slurred
    - Broken
    - Rapid
    - Excited
    - Normal

- Was the voice familiar? If so, who did it sound like?
- Was there any background noise?
- Note the exact words of the caller as much as possible, plus:

    - Exact time of call
    - Telephone number the call was received at

    - Name of person receiving call
    - Date/place the call was received

THE INITIAL SURVEY

Before starting a search, you should first obtain all relevant information about the object or area, allowing you to plan your dog's search action properly. Survey the object or area with the following points in mind:

- Ascertain whether or not searching the object with your dog (a) is possible and (b) has a chance of success.
- Decide, in consultation with your backup, whether or not to deploy your dog.
- If several dogs are available, decide which dog is most suited to the job.
- Determine the appropriate method for the search.
- Ensure you are fully equipped.
- Assess the weather conditions and wind direction.
- Ascertain where inside the building or area air movement or currents might potentially be misleading or where they might help your dog find a hidden cache.
- Let your dog lie down and relax so it gets used to the situation or becomes accustomed to the object it needs to search.
- The final decision about whether or not to use a K9 to search rests with you, the handler. If you go ahead, stick to the planned search method for the situation.
- If possible, ask a colleague to film the search action. The video can be useful in investigations and later can be used in training situations.
- As you progress, confirm with your backup about what has been searched and what has not to ensure the search is thorough.

> **Create the best possible search environment for the dog with as few distractions as possible.**

No matter how good a detector dog is, it can be successful only when used according to its needs and character, and with the right method. Through careful planning, you should be able to minimize the risks for your dog and at the same time carry out the investigation successfully.

Search Methods

Because so many different situations occur during search actions, you must be able to use a variety of search methods and employ the most appropriate one according to the situation.

FREE SEARCH

Free search is a method commonly used indoors or in a confined area before beginning systematic searching. During a free search, the dog is not really working according to a controlled system and is encouraged to cover as large an area as possible. This is also called a "quick scan." Its purpose is to see if the dog can immediately locate a substance so a detailed search might not be necessary.

SYSTEMATIC SEARCH

Systematic search, as the name implies, is used to perform a search action in a systematic way. With voice and body language, you encourage your dog to sniff and investigate an area in a controlled and thorough manner. A successful systematic search includes four steps.

1. Choose a fixed point to start and always search in a clockwise direction.
2. Search from low to high.

Figure 6.3 A Belgian dog handler lets his dog carefully search a suspicious location leading to the hold of a ship.

3. Whenever and wherever possible, let your dog investigate high places in the search area with your help.
4. If your dog moves off the search pattern to investigate something, let it do so and then start again from the point where it left off.

THE LEASH

In both free and systematic searches, the dog works without a leash and collar. The removal of the collar serves as a conditioned ritual that signals the imminent start of the search to the dog. But this is not the only reason: most importantly, collars can pose a hazard when searching. A dog can hang, for example, if its collar gets hooked on something, but an even a bigger danger is that a collar with metal parts may cause an explosion by triggering a magnetic ignition system.

Searching with a long leash (as long as there are no metal parts on the leash or collar) is a method used if you conclude that your dog should work at some distance from you, but should still be physically under your control. In these situations, use a long line. You should know how to handle a long leash so your dog does not get tangled up or become otherwise restricted. You may need to motivate your dog when you use this method.

Searching with a short leash (as long as there are no metal parts on the leash or collar) can be used for a systematic search action in which your dog must be kept under full control. Keep the leash in your left hand and lead with your right, moving your dog along the objects that need to be scanned.

The proper application of a method of investigation can determine the difference between a search action's success or failure. Remember that the methods mentioned above are merely the tools for searching, to which you must apply your correct assessment of and appropriate reaction to the specific situation at hand.

SEARCHING OPEN-AIR LOCATIONS

You might use this method to find lost or discarded weapons, or while searching for cartridge cases or explosives hidden under the

Figure 6.4 The tEODor is a heavy explosives robot used by explosive ordnance disposal (EOD) teams in the Netherlands. It can investigate, observe, and identify suspicious packages; make buildings, vehicles, and closed spaces accessible; transport, position, and remote control measuring equipment; find hidden booby traps and explosives; and disable IEDs such as roadside and car bombs. Its little brother, the Telemax, has the ability to operate in mass transit systems such as airplanes, trains, buses, and subway systems.

surface, but not for mine detection. Mines require a special method of searching (see chapter 8: Mine Detector Dogs).

Searching open terrain is not easy. Open-air locations can have many disturbances, such as wind and weather. Start with areas open to the public (which are easier for bombers to access), and then move to areas closed to the public. Search manholes, garbage bins, containers, shrubs, planters, bike sheds, external mailboxes, telephone booths, and so on. If there is no danger for booby traps, and if it is possible, you can start an investigation with a free search, wherein your dog moves through the area quickly to find any suspicious odors. After that, the total search area should be divided into sectors that your dog will search in detail, slowly inspecting all locations in each sector, including the following:

- Beside, under, and up in trees
- Under shrubs and other plants
- In and around sheds or other buildings
- In and around lampposts and flagpoles
- Around billboards

Do not let your dog step on the doormat without first searching it thoroughly. Then search the air gap between the bottom of the door and the sill. Once these places have been thoroughly searched, move to higher openings on the door, such as keyholes, the door knob, the doorbell, mail slots, and along the side of the door and frame. Be sure your dog does not touch or lean on the door. Have your dog lean on your arm to search the higher places.

If the dog, after carefully searching the door, doesn't give any sign of recognizing an explosive odor, the handler and dog should step back and stay behind the wall. The person who opens the door should also stand alongside the wall, next to the door, not directly in the doorway. If there is an undiscovered booby trap that is triggered when the door opens, then the pressure wave will push the door through the area, but the dog and officers will be protected by the wall.

After opening the door, use a wedge (if needed) to keep the door open while searching inside. You may need to leave quickly, or your dog might want to leave briefly to get a fresh nose before continuing the search.

Figure 6.8 A Springer spaniel with a perfect sitting alert.

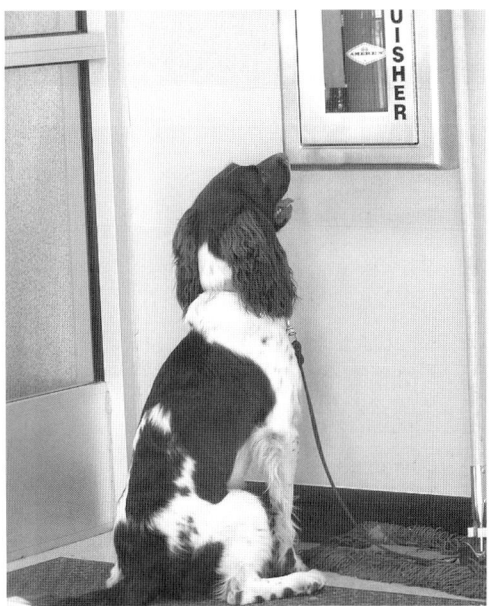

SEARCHING HOUSES AND BUILDINGS

Before starting your search action, remember the following:
- Work systematically.
- If possible, you and your dog should be allowed to become familiar with the surroundings and odors of a building before starting.
- Air currents are extremely difficult to assess when working indoors. Drafts, cross-ventilation, and heating and air-conditioning units all affect existing scent patterns. Try to control these conditions as much as possible by switching off air conditioners and heaters.
- You may need to allow your dog to go outside the room or even outside the building to get a breath of fresh air.

Houses and other buildings are always searched from outside to inside. Inside the building, begin with the ground floor and work your way up. Special attention is necessary for public spaces such as the lobby, the reception desk, rooms for cleaners or housekeeping, and washrooms. Also pay special attention to any shipping and receiving locations, such as mailrooms and loading docks. These locations are a priority because of the number of people coming and going and because new objects or packages can go unnoticed for some time.

Before entering a new search area, have your dog first search the doorway or entranceway thoroughly. Then inspect the area or room visually. If possible, perform this inspection from the entrance or another area that has been searched and found to be free of explosives. Look for possible dangers and note search priorities, such as aberrant objects or slots/gaps, which may release odor molecules from hidden explosives. Other search priorities inside buildings include the following:

- Strips, skirting boards, cable ducts, air ducts
- Unsecured bays for electricity, water, or sanitation
- Air-conditioning or heating systems
- Loose ceiling systems and false ceilings
- Fresh changes to walls
- Switches, sockets

- Under posters, paintings, picture frames, and mirrors
- Furniture, such as chairs, sofas, and tables, as well as the objects sitting on top of them
- Fire extinguishers and firehoses
- Flower pots, recycling bins, and document shredders
- Waste containers and under the plastic bag in such containers
- Electronic devices
- Suitcases, bags, boxes, and other luggage
- Holes, spaces, and gaps of any kind (check closets, drawers, walls, doors, window panes, tables, between furniture, between the floor or walls and furniture, heating vents, under blankets and tarpaulins, etc.)

It's impossible to list all possible search priorities, so this list is suggestive, not exhaustive. During your visual inspection, also determine the best search route for the dog that will help maintain an optimal search rhythm. You want the dog to concentrate and work as free from interruptions as possible.

Work through each room and level of the building and don't forget the elevator shaft. Search the stairwells as you move to the next levels. Don't forget to search, if they are accessible, the attic and flat roofs. For buildings with many floors and a basement, start with the floor where the entrance is. In certain situations, you must keep the dog leashed in order to work safely. For example, some roofs are only reachable by narrow stairs or gratings that might pose a falling risk for your dog.

Each controlled area should be marked to indicate that it has been checked. This marking can consist of a cross made with chalk or a sticker on the door.

SEARCHING A ROOM

Before entering a room, first do your visual survey of the situation and determine any search priorities. If necessary, divide the room into different zones to facilitate a systematic search. This time also allows you and your dog to get used to the prevailing sounds, smells, and light strength. If the room is dark, use a flashlight. Do not turn on overhead light fixtures or other lights until they've been cleared.

Do not let the dog go inside before checking the inside doormat and other mats or carpeting. Never pull the entire rug to the side. Instead, roll it gently, piece by piece, while letting your dog search its length. If the entire underlying floor surface is controlled, the mat or carpet can be removed. Then search the floor for hatches or loose boards, planks, tiles, or other floor parts. After the floor, look at the ceiling for false or loose modular components. If anything looks suspicious, use a table or other platform that has been inspected to get your dog closer so it can search.

In principle there are two main methods for searching a room, depending on how carefully and fast the dog can search and, of course, the situation inside the room. In the first method, a free search, the dog will be sent in the room for a quick scan before beginning systematic searching. With a free search, the dog is encouraged to cover as large an area as possible. During this quick scan, the handler, if possible, just observes the dog from the doorway. If the dog searches the area and shows no suspicious behavior, you can enter the room for a systematic search.

In the second method, we don't let the dog do a quick scan and instead immediately begin with a systematic search. Start at the wall to the left side of the door and work around the perimeter of the room in a clockwise direction until you reach the right side of the door. As you move, instruct the dog to search the walls, any furniture or objects placed along the walls, spaces behind furniture or cupboards, window sills, radiators, curtains, and the waste baskets—in short, anything along the walls of the room. Each object or piece of furniture should be searched completely from low to high before moving on. After the perimeter search, go to the furniture in the middle of the space.

If there is almost no furniture in the room, then the room can also be divided into different search heights as a way of organizing your work:
- From the floor to your waist
- From your waist to your eye level
- From your eye level to the ceiling
- The ceiling

First let the dog search all low-lying objects to your waist level around the room in a clockwise direction. This method doesn't disturb the dog's search rhythm, ensuring everything will be searched well by the dog. If there are any objects that the dog has not searched properly by the time it finishes its route around the room, bring the dog back to the object again to be sure.

If the search work to the level of your waist is done, begin work at the higher-lying areas from your hip to eye level. Here the dog must often stand on its hind legs to search behind objects such as mirrors or paintings. For this situation, the dog sometimes needs help by leaning with its front legs or paws on the forearm of the dog handler. If only some slots or gaps to search are at this level, you can help your dog search these in the first search around the room.

The search from eye level to the ceiling and the ceiling itself are tasks for the handler, although if a dog stands at a wall sniffing up, you can sometimes use furniture such as a table to bring the dog to a higher level.

Even if a dog does not give an alert, it is difficult for a handler to guarantee that the room is free of explosives. Even a great dog can miss an odor. If a dog has shown no suspicious behavior, the entire responsibility for declaring an area free rests on the dog

Figure 6.9 Have your dog lean on your arm to search higher places.

Figure 6.10 Leaning the dog on your arm prevents the dog from touching and possibly moving shelves or other objects.

Figure 6.11 A chair helps this Springer spaniel search a higher place more intensively.

handler—a heavy responsibility. You may want to inspect some places yourself, such as higher areas that the dog may have trouble reaching. For example, if you find a cupboard with a pile of clothes, blankets, or towels, work layer by layer to investigate the contents. In this situation, remove each layer as you check it until you have checked the entire stack. Or if a bookcase should be examined, look at the books one by one, removing each carefully so the rest of the books cannot fall.

If you have to inspect a chest or cabinet of drawers, first have your dog search the outside of the cabinet thoroughly. After that, gently pull the top drawer toward you until you see a tiny gap between the front of the drawer and the cabinet. Carefully check the gap and under the drawer for string, wire, tape, foil, or other unusual material. If all looks okay, open the drawer a little further and examine it again. Keep moving in this way until you have checked the entire drawer. If you can remove the drawer, do so. Usually this can be done by pulling out the drawer completely and lifting. Inspect the drawer contents carefully. Letters or papers can be removed for inspection, but boxes in the drawer should be inspected carefully before moving them. Now you'll have a good view of the contents of the second drawer. In this way, continue to check the rest of the drawers, one by one.

It is critical to keep track of where you have searched with your dog and where you have not. If several rooms in a house or building have to be searched, always follow the same search procedure. After the room is completely searched and no suspicious objects are detected, make a mark on the door and close, but do not lock it.

SEARCHING LETTERS AND PARCELS

A room in an office, shop, or even house that needs special attention is the mailroom, the place were mail is brought inside. There we have to search for letter bombs—also called parcel bombs, mail bombs, or post bombs—which are IEDs in letters or packages sent through normal postal services. The letter bomb or package is usually created to explode when the letter or package is opened. Before this time, the shipment is subjected to mail processing, transportation by vehicles, vessels, and/or aircraft, and various loadings and unloadings. All this time, the letter or package stays intact. Yet it explodes immediately upon opening with the intention to kill, injure, or intimidate the recipient.

It is difficult to differentiate a letter or parcel bomb from a normal letter or standard package, but letter bombs are sometimes identified by the following clues:

- The letter or package is extra thick, stiff, or too heavy in relation to its size.
- The weight of the package is unevenly distributed.
- The word "personal" is noted on the outside.
- The package has a greasy or oily stain (exudation of the explosive substance).
- The package has messy, odd, or grammatically incorrect addressing, or an incomplete or abnormal address.
- The package may be sent from abroad.
- The item has excessive postage.
- The shipment is unexpected or is received at an unusual time.
- The address of the sender is unknown, does not exist, is absent, or is illegible.
- The letter or package has a strange smell.

A well-trained explosive detector dog can detect explosives in a suspicious shipment. If the letters and packages on a table are too high for the dog to search, make a lineup of mail on the floor. Leave a space of at least 12 inches (30 cm) between each letter and package. Your dog can investigate this type of lineup either inside or outside. During sorting, have your dog conduct a "slow scan," in which it smells all the objects at a leisurely pace. This can be done by letting your dog search off leash, using signals to direct it to the different objects in the row.

> **It is important that everything in the lineup is carefully searched. Keep in mind that one object could be contaminated through contact with odor from another object.**

As long as a suspicious letter or package is not opened, you can be reasonably sure it will not explode. However, if a suspicious shipment is recognized, it is best not to touch it, although some companies move suspicious mail to a special room or area away from people. This room or space should be easily accessible, it should be dry, not damp, and it should have the same temperature as the mailroom. Other safety and protective measures include the following:

- Touch the suspect shipment as little as possible.
- Never bend or squeeze the suspect letter or parcel. Such actions could convert switches or bring two substances together, resulting in a reaction.
- Never immerse a letter bomb or parcel in water, which might cause a chemical reaction or close an electrical circuit.
- Never open or puncture a suspect letter or package. Many letter bombs are set off by two foil layers that touch each other when the package is opened. Piercing can also cause the metal layers to touch, setting off an explosion.

SEARCHING VEHICLES

Searching vehicles is a difficult job because there are many different types of vehicles and a lot of spaces inside in which to hide an explosive device. Begin by asking the owner of the suspect vehicle (if reliable) when the vehicle was last used, or when it was missed and seen again. It is important to know how long a vehicle has been unattended or missing because the longer a vehicle was in possession of the bomb maker, the more time there was to build a more sophisticated bomb and to hide the explosive. However, "under car" bombs with magnets can be placed in seconds, so time for the bomb maker is not always a major factor.

To get as much information as possible before starting your search, try to get the following questions answered:

- Who manages the keys to the vehicle?
- Is the vehicle normally locked?
- When was the vehicle last used?
- To where was the last ride?
- Where and by whom was the vehicle last refueled?
- What kind of repair was last executed and when?

- When was the vehicle missed and when was it seen again?
- How long has the vehicle been parked there?
- What reasons might someone have to put a bomb in the vehicle?
- Was it known when the vehicle would be used again and by whom?

Searching vehicles on a public road is considerably hampered because the vehicle is usually near a populated or otherwise vital location, such as an apartment, a shopping mall, a hospital, an office building, or a gas station. Before approaching the vehicle, first observe it from a distance to see if it tilts or leans back. If the vehicle sits low on its suspension, you can assume that there is something heavy inside. Vehicle bombs with large explosive contents, some more than 400 pounds (200 kg), are sometimes placed with the intention of blowing up all or part of a building near its parking spot. This tactic is used primarily for buildings with tight security that prevent the bomb maker from planting a bomb inside. The fuel inside the vehicle presents a secondary risk.

Vehicle explosives can be activated by several normal operations:
- Locking or unlocking a door, including remote door locks
- Opening a door
- Sitting in the driver's seat
- Turning on the ignition or starting the engine
- Putting on the seat belt
- Turning on the lights, radio/navigation, or similar device
- Driving away

SEARCHING OUTSIDE A VEHICLE

After observing the vehicle from a distance, first check (without your dog) the area around the vehicle for any suspicious material such as safety pins, adhesive remnants, or pieces of wire. Look for any signs of forced entry to windows or doors. Don't open the vehicle, but look inside through the windows for anything suspicious.

Keep in mind that even if you immediately see something that looks suspicious, this does not mean that it is the only danger present—the vehicle may have more than one explosive device or more than one type of explosive device. Look to see if the vehicle is locked. An unlocked vehicle may be a sign that it has been tampered with. Be sure you do not lean on the vehicle while searching.

After your visual check, you can begin the dog's search. In approaching the vehicle with your dog, take wind direction into account. Try to approach with a head wind, so your dog can get the odor of the vehicle from a distance first. When searching vehicles, you must exercise firm control on your dog at all times. It can be easy to read a false alert because vehicles have so much extraneous scent in and around them. Human- and animal-associated odors may confuse your dog and distract it from the search.

The search action described here is for a passenger vehicle with left-hand drive. Start at the front of the vehicle with a quick scan by the dog around the perimeter (counterclockwise for a left-drive vehicle and clockwise for a right-drive vehicle). Pay special attention to the openings and underside of the vehicle. After that, begin a more systematic, fine search, with the following sequence for a left-drive vehicle:

FRONT SEARCH
- The front of the vehicle
- The space behind the front license plate
- The outside of the grill
- The front bumper and the inside of the bumper

LEFT-SIDE VEHICLE SEARCH
- The front lights on the left side
- The left front wheel and the wheel arch
- The lights and the mirror on the left side
- The edges and interstices of the left front and rear doors
- The door handles (without opening the door!)

- The cap of the fuel tank (if on this side)
- The left rear wheel and wheel arch
- The rear lights on the left side

REAR SEARCH

- The rear bumper and the inside of the bumper
- The space behind the rear license plate
- The spare wheel, if available and visible
- The edges and interstices of the rear door or trunk
- The exhaust system

RIGHT-SIDE VEHICLE SEARCH

- The rear lights on the right side
- The right rear wheel and wheel arch
- The cap of the fuel tank (if on this side)
- The edges and interstices of the right rear and front doors
- The door handles (without opening the door!)
- The lights and the mirror on the right side
- The front lights on the right side

For right-hand drive vehicles, adjust the search order accordingly by moving to the right side after the front search.

SEARCHING INSIDE

Put your dog at a safe distance before opening the door of the vehicle. If necessary, fix the position of the vehicle with a jack or wedges to prevent tilting. If the doors are locked, use a remote control to open them (if possible). If the owner or driver is present, you might ask him to open the doors of the vehicle as a test; if the driver is the suspected bomber, he will probably refuse strenuously! Open the door carefully, much as you would a drawer, searching the gap as you open the door a little at a time.

Never let your dog just jump into a vehicle to begin the inside search. Have your dog stand outside the vehicle to first inspect the seats and all reachable spaces under and around the seats, including the mats and pedals. The driver's seat deserves special attention. For higher vehicles, place a stable platform or table next to the vehicle to bring the dog to a better position to search the seats. The backseat in taxis, armored cars, security vehicles, and other VIP vehicles also needs special attention. After the seats, search the inside of the front and rear doors and all the door pockets. Luggage may be removed from the interior of the vehicle and searched separately.

PASSENGER COMPARTMENT

After searching the seats and all spaces under and around the seats from outside, we can further inspect the inside part of the vehicle. For that ask the dog to systematically search the following:

- The bottom left side of the dashboard
- At and under the driver's seat, including the safety belts
- The console between the driver's and passenger's seats
- The covering of the roof on the inside front of the car
- The mirror and sun visors
- The bottom right side of the dashboard, including the glove box
- The passenger's seat and under it, including the safety belts
- The front and top of the rear seat
- The back sides of the front passenger seat and driver's seat
- The covering on the inside top of the roof in the back of the car

TRUNK SPACE

Be very careful in opening the trunk or luggage compartment of the vehicle. Use a remote trunk opener if one is available. First let the dog smell the trunk compartment as thoroughly as possible while standing outside. Then the dog can go inside the trunk and search the following:

- The trunk lid or tailgate
- The luggage compartment lighting
- The suitcases and luggage. After an initial search, luggage may be carefully removed from the trunk and searched separately. This search might have to take place in stages, with the dog

sniffing each bag in turn before it is removed and searched more thoroughly. Continue to search until the trunk is empty.
- The tool kit, first aid kit, and the like
- Any hidden spaces or storage compartments
- The spare tire and space under and around the tire
- The back side of the backseat, including the floor under the seat

ENGINE COMPARTMENT

Again like the drawer search, open the hood inch by inch. First look for the presence of additional wiring and unusual or unnecessary components. If the engine is still warm, put a piece of carpet over it before letting the dog jump up. The carpet gives your dog a comfortable place to stand. Ask the dog to search the hood, battery, ignition coil, alternator, air cleaner, radiator grill, and all other spaces inside the engine compartment. Also control the washer fluid, oil, and other reservoirs.

SEARCHING MOBILE HOMES, RVS, AND TRAILERS

When searching mobile homes, RVs, and trailers, first look for potential hazards such as gas or fuel tanks. Shut off the gas and briefly scan the vehicle. Then move to a quick scan by the dog around the vehicle, paying attention to the following:
- Walls and externally accessible spaces
- Doors and entrances
- Under the vehicle
- Around the axles
- The drawbar (on trailers)

When searching the inside of a mobile home, RV, or trailer, always first examine the space from the entrance. Look at all seats, tables, cabinets, and beds for anything suspicious. Then carefully search everything with the dog:
- Drawers
- Windows and frames
- Seats, tables, cabinets, beds

- Kitchen, toilet, and shower
- Lamps and other fixtures on the walls and ceiling
- Walls and ceiling: also knock on the walls and ceiling and listen for cavities
- The floor
- The driver and passenger area (in RVs)

SEARCHING VESSELS

You may be called upon to search a vessel for explosives as a preventive measure, but you may also be searching after a bomb threat. In the face of a specific threat, you might know the name of a specific ship or only its destination.

Ships are vulnerable to explosive or incendiary devices in a variety of places:

- In passenger cars, freight vehicles, or coaches
- In misdeclared cargo—keep cargo distribution papers handy
- Carried on board by current passengers, or those from a previous sailing leaving a timed device
- In luggage placed in a baggage trolley
- In the ship's stores

Figure 6.12 While searching this ship, explosive detector dogs found a chest with arms.

- In the post
- Carried on board by shore workers in port or by contractor's personnel

So the first questions have to be: Do you have any information about the location of the explosive device? How many people are on board? Is there any dangerous cargo on board? Is this cargo near a fuel source?

It can be difficult to take control of a ship or ferry to conduct a search, mostly because vessels are large and complex. There are a lot of hiding places, rooms, cabins, and passages, and it's difficult to stay oriented and remember where your dog has already searched. Passing through all of a ship's spaces is often hard going and requires some adjustment and special efforts on the part of you and your dog. Having to crawl under and over pipes, walk on open stairs, and negotiate insecure footing and cramped working conditions may create problems for your dog. In addition, ships don't stay still. Your dog may need a little time to get used to the movement. Such conditions can be overcome only by concentration, patience, repetition, and your encouragement.

During a search action on ships, recruit a crew member, such as a mechanic, an engineer, or the captain—someone who knows the subdivision of the ship and also what belongs to the ship (and what does not). Especially with larger vessels (tankers, freighters, and ferries), you simply cannot work without the help of crew members since those ships have lots of hard-to-reach areas and potential hiding places.

A search of a large vessel will take a lot of time, so you may decide that several search teams should be put to work. Start your investigation at the most easily accessible deck and move up to the top deck. Then search the rest of the ship from the most easily accessible deck to the bottom of the ship. Make sure you have a system to your search route. We suggest using a map to make sure you've searched every room. Mark each controlled area on your map, and note the route you walked through the ship.

> **We highly recommend the deployment of more than one explosive detector dog team when conducting a large vessel search.**

Examples of places to search include the following:

DECK

- Ledges on deck housing, electrical switch rooms, winch control panels
- Lifeboat storage compartments, under coiled rope, in deck storage rooms
- Paint cans, cargo holds, battery rooms, chain lockers

COMPANIONWAYS

- Ducts
- Wire harnesses
- Railings
- Fire extinguishers
- Fire hoses and compartments
- Access panels in floors, walls, and ceilings
- Behind or inside water coolers and vending machines

CABINS

- Beneath bunks (e.g., taped to the bunk frame under a mattress)
- Back sides and underneath drawers
- Between bottom drawers and the deck
- Under washbasins
- Behind removable medicine chests
- Inside radios, video recorders, etc.
- In ventilator ducts
- Inside heating units
- Above or behind light fixtures
- Above ceiling and wall panels
- Inside cutouts behind bulkheads, pictures, etc.
- Under false-bottom clothes closets and within hanging clothes
- Inside wooden clothes hangers

- Inside rolled socks, spare socks
- In hollowed-out molding

WASHROOMS AND SHOWERS
- Behind and under washbasins
- Behind toilets
- In ventilation ducts and heaters
- In toilet tissue rollers, towel dispensers, and supply lockers
- Taped to shower curtains, exposed piping, and light fixtures
- Behind access panels in the floors, walls, and ceiling

GALLEYS AND STEWARDS' STORES
- In flour bins and dry stores
- Inside vegetable sacks, on canned foods (re-glued labels)
- Under or behind refrigerators
- Inside fish or sides of beef in freezers
- In bonded store lockers, slop chests, storage rooms

ENGINE ROOM
- Under deck plates
- In cofferdams, machinery pedestals, bilges
- In journal bearing shrouds and sumps on propeller shafts
- Under catwalks, in the shaft alley
- On escape ladders and ascending areas
- In ventilation ducts, attached to piping, or in tanks with false gauges
- Inside equipment boxes, emergency steering rooms, storage spaces

If a suspected explosive device is found on a ship at sea, the ship may not be allowed to enter a port. An explosion in the port area poses an obvious safety risk and can damage the fairway if the explosion occurs during entry. If the ship is in port near an oil depot or other secondary danger, officials may consider dragging the ship to a safe place with minimal occupation aboard, after which demining experts can do their job.

SEARCHING AIRPLANES

Some airlines carry out regular preventive searches to ensure their aircraft are safe for passengers and crew. Such preventive searches are best performed immediately after the cleaning crew has left the airplane. Preventive scanning of airplanes by explosive detector teams gives a clear signal that airlines are doing what they can to protect passengers and crews and that would-be bombers are unlikely to be successful. But airlines are also faced with bomb threats, so active search actions are also sometimes necessary.

In a search action in and around a passenger plane on the ground, you will need the help of an airplane mechanic for the relevant type of aircraft. A plane has many hidden and inaccessible areas, so take advantage of the mechanic's knowledge. When examining a plane that is already loaded, ask for the help of a loadmaster. The loadmaster will have cargo lists and will know details about the load in the plane. If there are passengers in the plane, have them disembark and take all their hand luggage with them. This hand luggage can be checked again for the presence of suspicious material, but your focus will be on any belongings left behind.

While passengers are deplaning, start the search with the dog on the outside of the plane at the landing gear and move around the plane to inspect all entrances. Once the outside of the plane is cleared, move to the interior spots. In the investigation of the interior, the aircraft can be divided into compartments:

- Passenger areas, which can in turn be divided into three search levels:
  - From the floor to the seat bottom. This can also be a quick scan.
  - From the seat bottom to the upper side of the windows. Ask the airplane mechanic or another available person to move the armrests located between the seats in an upward position so the dog can easily move.
  - From the upper side of the windows to the ceiling. To check the luggage spaces above the seats, you can use two extendable shelves placed on the headrests down the aisle.

The dog can walk on one and step on the other to search the luggage spaces above the seats.
- Bathrooms
- Kitchen units
- The cockpit
- Baggage compartments

Work from a starting point at the entrance to a specific end point so you leave no space unsearched. Mark each controlled area on a map, and note the route you walked. Your final check of the plane should be in all other hard-to-reach areas.

PARCEL AND LUGGAGE SEARCHES

Railway stations, bus stations, sea ports, and airports are handling centers for large quantities of goods, including shipping containers, boxes, packages, luggage, and handbags and other carry-on luggage. Preventive scanning of cargo by explosive detector dogs gives a clear signal that cargo will be inspected, potentially discouraging bomb makers.

When you need to investigate large cargo, such as shipping containers and pallets, search carefully around the cargo first and let your dog smell all the openings, gaps, and hinges. When searching smaller objects, such as suitcases, bags, parcels, or boxes, ask your dog to search these items on a conveyor belt or sorting lineup on the floor.

If you are creating a lineup, make a row of at least five and up to eight objects, preferably spaced 12 inches (30 cm) apart. Your dog can investigate this type of lineup either inside or outside. During sorting, have the dog conduct a "slow scan," in which it smells all the objects at a leisurely pace. This can be done by letting the dog search off leash, using signals to direct it to the different objects in the row. Everything in the lineup must be carefully searched. In particular, have the dog specifically search the following:

- Fasteners and locks
- Hinges
- Zippers

- Suitcase edges
- Carrying straps
- Support frames, especially those with tube-like structures
- Name tags

As always in situations with many individual objects with various origins (e.g., mail, luggage), keep in mind that one object could be contaminated by contact with odor from another object. If your dog locates a suspicious smell, don't automatically assume everything else is free of danger.

When screening cargo (including express package shipping), containers should be opened for examination. Consolidated shipments should not exceed 50 inches (130 cm) high and wide and should not be deeper than 40 inches (100 cm). The dog must have access to all cargo and be able to smell everything. If the dog alerts or shows interest, and after verification by the handler the item is deemed "suspected positive," the handler and dog should leave the spot and report the finding. It is best if a radius of 330–550 yards (300–500 m) around the object of interest is marked with tape and cleared.

Decide whether you need verification of the find. For verification, the dog is set up again, with the proviso that it now must search in the opposite direction to the first search. The verification can also be carried out by a second explosive detector dog.

If the dog indicates there may be explosive substances present in a pallet or other load, the shipment is broken down to let the dog smell each individual package. If the dog indicates a package with a suspect substance, keep it separate from the rest by searching the other objects near it; if these are clear, they can be removed. Once the rest of the cargo is again sniffed, and if the dog indicates nothing else, the rest of the cargo can be sent on.

Initial Actions After Finding IEDs or Explosives

If an explosive device is found, evacuate the house, building, vessel, or airplane in accordance with an emergency plan, retaining only

Figure 6.13 A US marine and Viky, an IED detector dog, search a compound for hidden threats while conducting counter-insurgency operations in Afghanistan in 2013.

enough staff to provide technical support to security services. The handler or his helper must inform the safety office and responsible EOD team immediately with an accurate description of the object, including its size, color, any attachments, and exact location.

ADDITIONAL CAUTIONS

- Do not put the suspicious object in water or spray water on it as this could short a control circuit and detonate the explosive.
- Do not run in the vicinity of the device.
- Do not use VHF/UHF radios within 10 feet (3 m) of a device.
- Do not handle, touch, shake, open, or move suspected explosives or suspected devices.
- Do not cut or pull wires, fuses, or strings.
- Do not turn on or switch off any electrical device.
- Do not pass metallic tools near the suspected device.
- Do not move switches or release hooks or fastenings.
- Do not smoke nearby.
- Do not investigate too closely.
- Do not move the device away from people—move people away from the device.
- Do not get too close.

7

Examinations and Performance Assessment

Examination for Explosive Detector Dogs of the Dutch Police

Since its reorganization in 2012, law enforcement in the Netherlands has been provided by the National Police Corps (*Korps Nationale Politie*). The Dutch Police Act establishes the role of explosive detector dogs in this force. It states that such dogs' senses are highly useful for investigation and implementation of police tasks in society today. We recommend the examination regulations for Dutch police explosive detector dogs and their handlers to other police forces, other jurisdictions, and government services.

Figure 7.1 The test regulations for Dutch police explosive detector dogs are carefully designed to reflect the practical demands of policing and investigative work.

The regulations stipulate that dogs taking part in the test to become explosive detector dogs must
- have been declared healthy by a licensed veterinarian; and
- have up-to-date vaccinations.

In addition, dogs participating in the test should have good teeth and a good coat and must generally meet the requirements that may be placed on a healthy, well-built dog. Dogs perceptibly suffering from any disease or that are visibly pregnant are not allowed to participate in the test.

The regulations also specify the following:

1. Only police officers who are designated dog handlers can be tested with their dogs.
2. Handlers must first pass a written test for handlers of police explosive detector dogs.
3. Handlers and their dogs are examined together—as a team—to assess their suitability for operational work. The police explosive detector dog is used exclusively for detecting explosives, firearms, and ammunition. Teams are evaluated by an inspection committee formed by police officials with wide experience in the training and deployment of police explosive detector dogs.

Figure 7.2 Police explosive detector dog handlers must have a solid understanding of how a dog's sense of smell works in order to help the dog do its job.

REQUIREMENTS FOR POLICE EXPLOSIVE DETECTOR DOGS

1. All police search dogs must
   - show obedience to the handler;
   - cooperate with the handler;
   - not show aggression toward people or other animals; and
   - be highly agile, with the ability to move over and through all manner of obstacles.
2. In addition, all police explosive detector dogs must
   - show the desire and ability to independently search for explosives, weapons, and ammunition; and
   - have the ability to detect, within a reasonable time, explosives, weapons, and ammunition, and demonstrate the ability to localize these finds.

KNOWLEDGE REQUIREMENTS FOR HANDLERS

Handlers of police explosive detector dogs are examined by the inspection committee to ensure their thorough knowledge of the following:

1. Locations and methods of hiding and packing explosives, arms, and ammunition
2. Methods of storing and transporting explosives
3. Factors affecting the functioning of the police explosive detector dog
4. The content of the Weapons and Ammunition Act and the Hazardous Substances Act
5. Applicable sections of the Code of Criminal Procedure

DETAILED TEST REGULATIONS FOR EXPLOSIVE DETECTOR DOGS

The test regulations for Dutch police explosive detector dogs are carefully designed to reflect the practical demands of policing and investigative work. The exam also tests the handler's ability to usefully employ the dog's sense of smell to further an investigation. The tests are intended to assess combinations of handlers and their dogs for their suitability as a team to be used in operations.

I. GENERAL

The test regulations contain several general requirements that a handler and dog must meet.

1. OBJECTIVES

The test regulations ensure that after a certificate in the name of the handler and his police explosives detector dog is achieved,

- the dog and handler as a combination can be deployed for detection tasks of the police;
- there is a sufficient guarantee that the dog will fulfill the commands given by the handler; and
- the risk of making mistakes is as low as possible.

2. CERTIFICATE

The handler–dog team have a core task for which it is certified. The main assessment criteria for achievement of the certificate include

- the handler's theoretical knowledge;
- the dog's obedience and dexterity;
- the skill of the team at searching for and identifying explosives, firearms, and ammunition; and
- the dog and handler's ability to work cooperatively as a team.

Teams should be prepared to perform in rural or urban locations, in daytime or evening. The final choice of time and place for the exam is determined by the inspection committee, taking into account the circumstances in which the handler and dog will have to work in operational service.

Figure 7.3 Here the dog alerts by sitting and the handler must clearly indicate the location of the find to the inspection committee.

II. THEORY

Police explosive detector dog handlers must have a thorough knowledge of the legislation affecting their work and types of explosives, as well as a solid understanding of dog training and how a dog's sense of smell works.

The written exam for dog handlers includes 37 questions, each of which is worth up to 5 points. Topics include

- elements of the Code of Criminal Procedure that are important for the performance of duty;
- knowledge of the Dutch Arms and Ammunition Act, the Hazardous Substances Act, and related regulations;
- knowledge of the preparation of explosives;
- knowledge about handling explosives;
- knowledge of the health and safety concerns of handling explosives;
- knowledge of the requirements with respect to working conditions;
- knowledge about illegal firearms and explosives trafficking, as well as an understanding of efforts to combat this illegal trade;
- knowledge of the history and recent developments of international terrorism;

- an understanding of the search capabilities of police explosive detector dogs;
- knowledge of the training of police explosive detector dogs;
- an understanding of how to employ police explosive detector dogs in investigations; and
- knowledge related to bomb detection.

The maximum number of points is 185. Handlers must score a minimum of 111 points (60 percent) to pass the written test.

III. OBEDIENCE AND DEXTERITY EXERCISES

During the execution of obedience and dexterity exercises, the dog must unconditionally follow the commands of the handler and show that it has the skill necessary for police work. The handler must have the necessary authority to control the dog.

OBEDIENCE EXERCISES

Objective: The dog must show docility toward its handler.

Execution: The handler walks with his dog in a straight line over a distance of about 54 yards (50 m). The dog must walk next to the handler with a slack (bent) leash. There are five different obedience exercises:

1. Heeling on leash at normal pace: The handler walks with the dog on leash in a straight line over a distance of about 54 yards. The dog walks with a slack leash next to the handler.

2. Heeling on leash in a run: The handler runs with the dog on leash in a straight line covering a distance of about 54 yards. The dog must run during this exercise on a bent leash next to the handler.

3. Heeling without a leash at normal pace: The handler walks at normal pace, with his dog unleashed, in a straight line over a distance of about 54 yards. The dog must walk next to the handler.

4. Heeling on the right and left side: The handler walks with his dog without a leash over a distance of 54 yards; at designated markings, the handler commands the dog to his other side. Commands must be audible to the inspection

committee and the dog should not deviate too much in moving to the other side of the handler. The dog not moving on command is rated as a refusal.

5. Heeling on leash next to a bicycle: The handler moves with his dog on leash to a bike. Once there, the dog must, whether or not given a command by the handler, go to the right-hand side of the bicycle. After this, the handler with his dog on leash cycles a distance of about 54 yards. The dog should walk with its head approximately level with the axis of the front wheel.

Assessment

For each of the obedience exercises, the following points can be gained:

1. Heeling on leash at normal pace: 5 points
2. Heeling on leash in a run: 5 points
3. Heeling without a leash at normal pace: 5 points
4. Heeling on the right and left side: 5 points
5. Heeling on leash next to a bicycle: 5 points

The maximum number of points for obedience is thus 25. The evaluation committee watches for the following and may issue deductions when necessary:

- The handler has to keep the leash in the hand on the side the dog is located.
- The leash should hang in a curve, and the dog must walk next to the handler.
- The handler may not threaten the dog in any way.
- During the obedience exercises, the handler may not give signs or additional commands to the dog.
- During off-leash exercises, the leash should not be visible.
- When off leash, the dog may wear only a plain collar, not a chain or other collar that exerts undue control over the animal.
- With every incorrect completion of the specified requirement (walk to far side, walk in front, fall back, etc.), 1 point is deducted from the component.

LIE DOWN EXERCISE

Objective: The dog must lie down for three minutes in the absence of the handler.

Execution: After one of the obedience exercises, at the choice of the inspection committee, the dog has to lie down on command of the handler, after which the handler has to move out of sight of the dog. The dog must remain off leash and in the same spot for three minutes while paying attention to its surroundings. At a sign from the inspection committee, the handler can return to the dog.

Assessment

The maximum number of points for this exercise is 5.

The evaluation committee watches for the following and may issue deductions when necessary:

- The dog must be attentive.
- The dog may not move, sit, stand, or the like. If the dog moves more than 16 feet (5 m) from the place where it was given the command to lie down, no points are awarded.

DEXTERITY EXERCISES

Objective: The handler must show that his dog can move over various obstacles.

Execution: After a sign from the inspection committee, the handler and dog independently work their way through six obstacles. They should take a short break after each obstacle. The dog's dexterity is demonstrated by the following:

1. Walking an open staircase: The handler takes position at the bottom of an open staircase of at least 12 steps. He then sends his dog up the stairs. Only the uphill walk is assessed.

2. Moving independently on and off a beam: A beam or plank of approximately 20 inches wide and at least 16 feet long (50 cm x 5 m) should be placed at a height of about 6.5 feet (2 m) on a scaffold from which the dog can independently move on and off the beam.

   The handler takes a position at the start of the scaffold and sends his dog onto the beam or plank. The handler may walk with his dog to the other end of the scaffold, where the dog leaves it again. The dog's performance on the straight (horizontal) part of the beam or plank is assessed.

3. Crawling through a tube: The handler sends his dog inside a tube with a diameter about 20 inches (50 cm) and whose end is not visible (so that, for the dog, it is dark inside). The handler may then walk to the end where the dog will leave the pipe.
4. Climbing a fence: The fence should be 6–6.5 feet (1.8–2 m) high with, at the back side, a sloping board or wooden partition. The handler and his dog take position in front of the fence. On command from the handler, the dog must jump or climb over the fence and move down the back side via the sloping board or wooden partition.
5. Jumping a pit or ditch: The pit must be at least 7 feet (2.25 m) wide and may include a sloping jump board about 3 feet (1 m) wide and about 20 inches (50 cm) above the ditch. The handler and his dog take position in front of the ditch or pit. On command of the handler, the dog must make a free jump over the ditch or pit.
6. Jumping over a crush barrier fence with bars, which is used as a crowd control barricade. The handler and his dog take their place in front of the fence. On command of the handler, the dog must jump free over the fence.

Assessment

A dog and handler can earn up to 5 points for each exercise, thus a total of 30 points in the dexterity exercises. The maximum number of points is achieved when the dog performs the exercise independently. For an incorrectly executed objective, up to 3 points can be achieved. After a failure or refusal, each exercise may be repeated once. A maximum of 2 points can be obtained if the handler helps the dog or the dog successfully repeats an exercise.

ASSESSMENT: OBEDIENCE AND DEXTERITY EXERCISES

The maximum number of points for the obedience and dexterity exercises is 60 points. A minimum of 36 points (60 percent) is required to pass.

Figure 7.4 Dexterity exercises. Left: Walking an open staircase; right top: Moving independently on and off a beam; middle: Jumping over a crush barrier fence with bars; below: Jumping a pit or ditch.

IV. THE SEARCH FOR EXPLOSIVES, FIREARMS, AND AMMUNITION

In these exercises, the handler must show that he knows his dog well and can make the best possible use of the dog's olfactory organ. The dog must respond to smells of explosives, and the handler must correctly interpret the dog's behavior.

SEARCH FOR EXPLOSIVES, A GUN, AND CARTRIDGE CASES

Objective: At randomly chosen locations, the dog has to search for and find eight different types of explosive devices, plus one firearm and one or more cartridge cases.

Execution: At several types of locations (see "Search Exercises," page 170), eight preparations with explosives are hidden. In addition, at a simulated crime scene, a firearm and one or more cartridge cases will be hidden. This gun and the cartridge case or cases should have been shot not more than one hour before starting the test. In the case of multiple cartridge cases, they will be hidden in an area of no more than one half a square yard (0.5 m²). The hiding places of the firearm and cartridges should at least 33 feet (10 m) apart.

The handler may enter the simulated crime scene. If the firearm is hidden in an indoor location, the cartridges will be discarded outside (in an area not greater than 50 feet by 50 feet, 15 × 15 m). No hidden object should be visible to the dog and handler. The dog and handler team must locate all the explosive preparations, firearms, and the hidden cartridge case or cases. The dog may make only one false alert (response).

Assessment

For their method of searching, teams are awarded 5 points for each found preparation or article. For the method of alert or response, teams are awarded another 5 points for each found preparation or article.

A total of 100 points can be achieved. Teams must receive at least 60 points (60 percent) to obtain a certificate. Deductions are given when the dog does anything not belonging to the search work. Biting or retrieving an explosive or firearm results in an automatic failure.

SEARCH EXERCISES

Objective: The dog must find and alert for various explosives, a firearm, and one or more cartridge cases at the following locations:

- in a house, ship, or airplane;
- in a factory, office, restaurant, canteen, workshop, hangar, church, or the like;
- in a tram, bus, truck, or car; and
- in a park, garden, or other outdoor location.

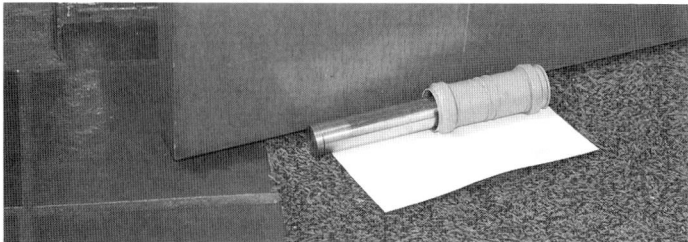

Figure 7.5 To place an explosive behind a door in a training or a test, put the explosive on a piece of paper that extends on both sides of the door and, after closing the door, pull the paper outside. The explosive will now be right behind the closed door.

Execution

1. In a house, ship, or aircraft: Approximately one hour before the start of the examination, hide one to four explosive preparations in a house, ship, or aircraft. The preparations should be in different packages and must be hidden in a realistic scenario reflecting real-life operations. None may be visible to the search teams. The inspection committee will decide where the handler and his dog should begin. If it brings no risk to the handler, he may first explore the test area without the dog. The handler may accompany his dog during the

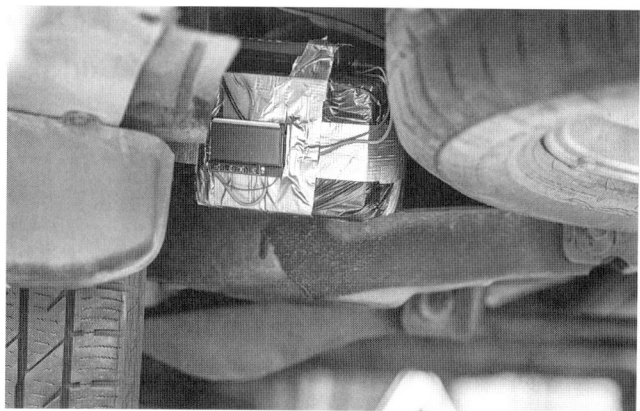

Figure 7.6 A bomb with radio control and a digital countdown timer hidden under a car.

Figure 7.7 The same bomb with radio control placed near the wheel of the car in a terrorism concept.

whole search at a short distance and may encourage the dog to search. It is preferred, however, that the dog searches independently as much as possible. If the dog alerts for the explosive or article—by sitting, standing, or lying down—the handler must clearly indicate to the inspection committee the location of the find. The handler may, if the dog's search drive is low, ask the inspection committee for a break. After the break, the handler must indicate that he is ready to finish the search of the location, with or without a find; if he doesn't, the investigation may be terminated by the inspection committee. The committee may also terminate the investigation if it sees that the dog is no longer searching.

2. In a factory, office, restaurant, canteen, workshop, hangar, church, or the like: The exercise is prepared and should be performed as specified in the search of a house, ship, or aircraft.

3. In a tram, bus, truck, or car: The exercise is prepared and should be performed as specified in the search of a house, ship, or aircraft. The explosive substances can be hidden both **in** and **on** the vehicle.

4. In a park, garden, or other outdoor location: The exercise is prepared and should be performed as specified in the search of a house, ship, or aircraft. However, in this exercise, at least one explosive substance must be hidden under the ground surface. It should be placed underground about three hours before the start of the search action. The preparation should weigh at least 1 pound (500 g) and not be buried deeper than 12 inches (30 cm).

Figure 7.8 A US marine directs Falco, an explosive detection dog, through a training area with odors associated with improvised explosive devices.

EXAMINATIONS AND PERFORMANCE ASSESSMENT

Assessment

A maximum of 100 points can be obtained from this section. A score of at least 60 points (60 percent) must be awarded to obtain a certificate. Deductions are taken

- if the dog does things that do not belong to the search work;
- if the dog moves away from a preparation, but later alerts for it; and
- when the dog is uncontrolled, jumps around, or unnecessarily touches objects.

V. FORMING A TEAM

The handler will be assessed on his skill, tact, and search tactics with regard to the handling and deployment of his dog. The dog is judged on its suitability to support tasks of the police service. In particular, the dog will be judged on willingness to work, reliability, obedience, intelligence, skill, character, and courage.

Execution: The quality of the handler–dog team is judged in all exercises that are done jointly (all except the Lie Down Exercise). This means that in addition to the assessment of the exercise itself (e.g., obedience, dexterity), the handler and dog are also evaluated for how well they work together. For each exercise, the team will achieve between 0 and 5 points.

Handler grades are awarded as follows:

- 5 points for excellence in relationship formation with the dog, excellent insights into the dog's behavior, and excellent search tactics
- 4 points for good work
- 3 points for relatively good work
- 2 points for insufficient work
- 1 point for bad work
- 0 for work not performed

Figure 7.9 Maci, a tactical explosive detector dog (TEDD), sniffs out explosives while his handler remains at a safe distance during training in California in 2011.

Figure 7.10 Boogy, an improvised explosive device (IED) detector dog, searches for traces of explosives during training exercises.

Dog grades are awarded as follows:

- 5 points for excellent work in executing the handler's commands
- 4 points for good work
- 3 points for relatively good work
- 2 points for insufficient work
- 1 point for bad work
- 0 for work not performed

Assessment

A maximum of 120 points can be obtained from this section:

- Two exercises in obedience and dexterity: each 10 points = 20 points
- Ten exercises in searching and alerting for explosives: each 10 points = 100 points

Total: 120 points. The minimum requirement to pass is 72 points (60 percent).

General Guidelines for the Tests

SETTING UP THE TESTS

The inspection committee will decide where the preparations are to be hidden, but they will usually use a helper who will hide the preparations and articles. The preparations, including a firearm, must be hidden in such a way that they can be found by a dog's nose. This usually means hiding two preparations low (near the ground), two at about elbow height (on shelves, etc.), two 3 feet (1 m) high, and two higher up (but for the dog's nose still locatable).

Figure 7.11 In the Dutch police dog test, explosives are hidden at various heights to reflect real-life scenarios.

If the dog has smelled a preparation and shows interest but then walks away for any other reason than to be able to approach the preparation from another side, then each time 1 point will be deducted for the "method of alert or response." After three such a walks away, the handler–dog team will be rejected.

If the inspection committee believes that a dog isn't searching anymore, it can terminate the search.

FALSE ALERT

A false alert occurs when the handler notifies the committee of a dog's alert by raising his hand and saying the word "alert" or "response" in a location where there is no explosive preparation (or firearm or cartridge case) present.

Only one false report is permitted, with 5 points deducted for "method of alert or response" from the total number of points. With a second false alert, the handler–dog team is rejected.

OTHER DETAILS

- During the test, only smooth collars and leashes may be used.
- Each exercise begins with a sign from a member of the inspection committee.
- In certain dangerous situations, the handler can ask the inspection committee to work with the dog on leash.
- "Unleashed" means with collar and without leash.
- All individuals present at the test site should strictly adhere to the rules and instructions of the members of the inspection committee.
- As soon as possible after the test, the inspection committee should issue a report (including list of points) to the handler of each participating team. The report should be signed by the members of the inspection committee.
- Certificates must include the name of the handler and the explosive detector dog and are valid for two years and three months. The date on which the validity ends is noted on the certificate.

- Teams that do not pass the exam can be retested in accordance with regulations.

Certification of Civilian Handlers and Explosive Detector Dogs

In the Netherlands, care is also taken to ensure civilian handler–dog teams are adequately skilled in the detection of explosives. The NBDH (*Nederlandse Bond voor de Diensthond*), the Dutch Association for the Service Dog, certifies service dogs employed by private security and special investigating services, and also certifies civilian handlers and explosive detector dogs in close consultation with the Ministry of Safety and Justice.

Certification ensures that civilian dog–handler teams have been assessed by independent judges and that qualifying dogs are able to detect all different kinds of explosives. The dog must indicate finds passively. The dog may not touch anything and may not produce any sound. The certificate consists of the following components:

PART 1
- Heeling on leash
- Remaining lying down
- Resisting sound
- Not acting aggressively
- Unaffected in traffic
- Taking hurdles

PART 2
- Method of searching
- Way of indicating
- Number of found explosives and weapons
- The way the handler lets the dog search

The handler must be a member of the NBDH or must be employed by members of the association. Handlers must present their dogs at least once a year for the test. If a dog no longer meets the requirements of the inspection regulations, the team has the chance to attend the next inspection. If again the minimum points are not achieved, the certificate is revoked.

Certificates specify the types of explosives the dog has been found qualified to detect. During a review, a handler may ask to search for additional types of explosives or types of fired weapons. If successful, the dog's ability to find additional explosives is recorded on the certificate. A certified explosive detector dog may only be used for the detection of the explosives specifically written on the certificate.

Performance Assessment

A certified dog handler is, with his explosive detector dog, part of a team that in a safe and efficient manner can respond to a bomb threat, bomb alert, or the discovery of a potential explosive. The explosive detector dog handler always works with a backup (a helper or a second handler) and also functions as a backup when the second dog handler with his dog is used as a control to verify the search object.

The handler should always make a quick survey of the site without a dog and will then decide whether or not to deploy the dog. It's possible that a handler may perform a complete survey of a site without a dog. When the dog is used, the handler decides which search method should be applied. If a suspected explosive object is found, he must take primary protection measures and ensure the reporting of the search.

> **During all searches, the handler must make security for his dog and other individuals in the area a priority.**

Below are stages in and aspects of an in-service evaluation for dog handlers. A handler's response to and actions during each stage can be assessed using the detailed discussion that follows.

1. Receive command
2. Arrival at crime scene

3. Search method and planning
4. First exploration with backup and without a dog
5. Search action with dog and backup
6. Safety
7. Measures after finding a suspicious object
8. Settlement incident
9. Appearance and behavior

1. RECEIVE COMMAND

THE HANDLER

- verifies the information received about the assignment;
- instructs the backup;
- consults with others as needed to plan the best route to the search site;
- takes all necessary equipment along; and
- lets the dog relieve itself before starting.

2. ARRIVAL AT SCENE

THE HANDLER

- parks his vehicle in a suitable place;
- reports to the responsible person;
- asks when the suspicious object was discovered or reported;
- asks whether it is known when the bomb might explode;
- asks if it is known where the bomb could be or what object should be searched; and
- evaluates the possible route to the area or object to be searched.

3. SEARCH METHOD AND PLANNING

THE HANDLER

- determines the end time of exploration (if it is known when the detonation will occur);
- determines the route for the exploration;
- determines the search method for the first exploration;

- determines whether or not to search with the dog;
- defines the search method with the dog;
- determines the wind direction and drafts;
- makes a choice of all necessary equipment for search with the dog; and
- plans where to start the search with the dog.

4. FIRST EXPLORATION WITH BACKUP AND WITHOUT A DOG

THE HANDLER

- is accompanied by the backup and a person with local knowledge (if possible);
- enquires about the reliability of the local person;
- looks, listens, smells, and gets used to the light in new rooms of the search area;
- looks for items that do not seem to belong;
- looks for signs of forced entry;
- notes pins, wire, tape, and the like;
- reports to the backup any enclosed spaces that will need special attention—the backup will help the handler remember which locations are a priority for the search so nothing gets missed;
- checks the floor and surroundings for potential safety and security issues for the dog;
- removes, if necessary, small obstacles once they have been controlled (e.g., a chair that blocks a door or cupboard);
- adheres to the route planned in step 3; and
- stops at the predetermined end time of his exploration.

5. SEARCH ACTION WITH DOG AND BACKUP

THE HANDLER

- lets the dog lie down and get used to the situation;
- determines the start and end (both in terms of route and timing);
- controls his dog through verbal cues and body movement;

- motivates the dog (if necessary) during the search;
- does not interfere with the dog during the search work;
- takes distractions into account;
- takes drift of the odor print into account;
- lets the dog rest when tired;
- makes use of a second dog, if necessary (e.g., if the first dog is really interested in a particular spot but does not give an alert and the handler cannot see any reason for the dog's interest); and
- reads the dog properly and recognizes reactions accurately.

6. MEASURES AFTER FINDING A SUSPICIOUS OBJECT

THE HANDLER

- brings the dog to a safe place;
- quickly takes time to review the situation with the backup;
- warns other team members;
- stops further search work near the response location;
- clears all people from that spot;
- leaves doors, lighting, heating, and the like just as it was;
- marks the route to the object or location (possibly by unwinding a warning or marking tape while walking back to a safe place);
- uses the same route back; and
- ensures the route to the location stays free by fixing doors open with wedges, if necessary.

7. SETTLEMENT INCIDENT

THE HANDLER

- stays on standby for the bomb clearers;
- records significant data (e.g., kind of bomb or explosive) for the bomb clearers;
- ensures the suspicious object is put under guard from a distance (if, for example, people might approach the object from other directions);

- makes a bomb reconnaissance report (including the place and type of explosive, the time of arrival and search, the dog used, etc.); and
- evaluates the search action with all persons involved.

8. SAFETY

THE HANDLER

- touches nothing before it is checked;
- performs no action on a suspicious object, including touching it;
- does not allow the dog to jump uncontrollably in the search site or at a search object;
- leans on nothing until after it's verified;
- doesn't put equipment somewhere before the location is verified;
- doesn't move a suspicious object;
- ensures the leash never drags on the ground or over objects;
- prevents ground vibrations by walking carefully and softly;
- doesn't speak if the dog is near a suspicious object; and
- doesn't reward the dog at the place of an alert or response.

9. APPEARANCE AND BEHAVIOR

THE HANDLER

- behaves professionally and politely;
- respects others;
- is open to advice;
- is not easily irritated;
- does not get too nervous;
- operates almost silently;
- works systematically;
- sets the correct priorities;
- acts decisively;
- keeps his dog under control at all times;
- always shows exemplary behavior to his dog; and
- cares for his dog after the search.

8

Mine Detection Dogs

A mine is an amount of explosive, whether or not in a metal or plastic casing, along with an igniter. Landmines are specially designed to deny access to a certain area, eliminate personnel, or to damage, deactivate, or destroy combat equipment. The igniter in a mine is activated by the target through a time delay or by remote control.

Figure 8.1 A landmine warning sign in the Falklands. Many minefields, and also individual mines, were never recorded as they were set, so people become victims even long after the conflict that prompted the laying of the mines is over.

Figure 8.2 A minefield sign on a barbed wire fence in Hebrew, Arabic, and English. Clearing minefields takes so long that sometimes all communities can do is mark dangerous areas.

Buried landmines are difficult to find because they are designed to be concealed. These small, low-tech devices are constructed with a wide variety of designs and materials and can barely be differentiated from stones, roots, and scrap material on the ground. Sometimes mine locations are recorded while they are being laid to facilitate their clearance at a later stage. However, many minefields, and also individual mines, were never recorded, and so people become victims even long after the conflict that prompted the laying of the mines is over.

There are two main types of landmines:
- Anti-personnel mines
- Anti-tank mines

Anti-Personnel Mines

Anti-personnel mines are designed to wound, not necessarily kill, soldiers who step on them or set them off by tripwire. Modern, sophisticated mines have self-destruct mechanisms or a mechanism that makes the mine safe after a certain period. However, millions of mines currently in place do not have this feature. Worldwide, there are approximately 110 million anti-personnel mines in 68 countries under the ground and another 250 million stored in depots. Most of these mines are located in developing nations. There are four sub-types of anti-personnel mines.

- *Blast mines:* will wound people that step on them through a blast of the detonating high explosive (HE). Blast mines have a thin housing with between less than 1 to almost 8 ounces (25 to 225 g) of HE inside. The mines are placed on the surface or buried just below the surface. Less than 7 ounces (200 g) of pressure can activate them.
- *Fragmentation mines:* will wound people with flying fragments after they detonate. Fragmentation mines have a thick casing that can be pre-fragmented. They are placed above the surface and are usually detonated by tripwires. Their effective radius is about 65–80 feet (20–25 m).
- *Bounding fragmentation mines:* also wound people with fragments after they detonate. The difference is that bounding fragmentation mines are buried below the surface and are launched about 3 feet (1 m) high before they detonate.
- *Directional fragmentation mines:* produce fragments only in a certain direction. They are placed above the surface and are operated by tripwire or electrical contact.

Figure 8.3 A directional anti-personnel mine.

Every year, thousands of people are injured or killed by mines. Landmines are "blind" weapons. They do not distinguish between soldiers, playing children, or women gathering firewood. Hidden under the ground or in the grass, they wait, sometimes years, to be set off. The explosion may not be fatal, but it can take off a leg or arm. Designed to slow the march of military opponents, the mines pose a great danger to people clearing them. Such work is time-consuming and dangerous.

Figure 8.4 A rusty anti-tank mine in grass.

Figure 8.5 A Thai engineer removes a landmine cable.

Anti-Tank Mines

Anti-tank mines are meant to destroy vehicles and will therefore not normally detonate if a person steps on them. There are three sub-types of anti-tank mines:

- *Blast mines:* have 11–22 pounds (5–10 kg) of HE in them and are set off by a pressure of more than 275 pounds (125 kg).
- *Off-route mines:* are basically heat rocket launchers that are placed 33–82 feet (10–25 m) from the route of a tank or other vehicle. They will fire a heat rocket when the tank passes and activates the mine.
- *Plate mines:* contain 4–11 pounds (2–5 kg) of HE. When the mine is set off, it fires a high-velocity, convex-shaped projectile that penetrates the belly of a tank or vehicle.

Figure 8.6 An anti-tank mine.

Figure 8.7 A mine installed in the grass next to a road.

Figure 8.8 An old-fashioned type of landmine.

A Short History of Mines

The type of mines we know today were first used in the American Civil War (1861–1865) by digging corridors and tunnels beneath the fortified positions of the enemy, placing explosive charges, and then letting them explode. This type of mining was also used at the beginning of World War I, but after the development of the tank, mines changed with the new function of stopping enemy tanks. Due to the quick increase in the number and diversity of types of tanks, the production of anti-tank mines also increased. In this initial stage, anti-tank mines were improvised from artillery shells. Then anti-personnel mines were developed. The first anti-personnel mines consisted of an explosive load with a wrapping attached to barbed wire. They were used to repel the nocturnal actions of the enemy. Ignition was through tensile or tripwires (tensile wires can be placed higher than tripwires).

In the period between the two world wars, the tank as an offensive weapon was further developed, as well as a wide variety of mines. These developments mainly took place in Germany, and so the Germans had a big lead in landmine technology when World War II broke out. During that war, the Germans and Russians both used mines extensively. By the end of the war, the Germans had about 40 different types of mines, while the Russians had more than 50 models.

Today, landmines are widely used in small wars of liberation, mainly because the mines are relatively inexpensive to produce. However, the many unexploded mines left in fields after a period of war is a global problem. They are deadly remnants of wars that are sometimes long over. Post-conflict, most victims are civilians. Mine clearance is a time-consuming affair because it requires many security procedures.

One issue is that no one usually knows exactly where any given minefield begins and ends, so a large area must be searched. Many searches find nothing. Manual searching for mines with metal detectors has become increasingly difficult because new types of mines contain less metal casing. Plastic is now often used to construct the devices, so a metal detector cannot find them. However, because the explosive materials are the same, dogs can search for even plastic mines.

Searching with dogs is much faster at locating a minefield than manual searching. The purpose of a mine detector dog is to locate a minefield, not to clear it.

Figure 8.9 A US soldier describes visible signs that can be used to spot improvised explosive devices during a training session for Afghan National Security Forces in 2013.

Figure 8.10 Dutch engineers check a route for explosives in Afghanistan.

Figure 8.11 An anti-tank mine in the sand.

Characteristics of a Mine Detector Dog

According to the Geneva International Centre for Humanitarian Demining, the most essential characteristics of a mine detector dog are the following:

- The dog's nose is always on the hunt for the odors it has been trained to find. If the odors are highly volatile, they might be more readily available in the air above the ground than at the surface. Or the odors might be more accessible on vegetation (due perhaps to being transported from underground through the plant's roots and vascular transport system). Through its experience searching for those odors, the dog will have learned where they are most likely to be found.

- The dog's intensity of focus is high. The dog concentrates on the sensory input to its nose and may snuffle or huff to improve the flow of air through its nose. Mine detector dogs must search for a critical, but small odor among a massive background of sensory input. They do not know which square inch of soil contains the odor searched for, so each inch must be scrutinized carefully. Any loss of concentration increases the chance that the important odor will be missed, even though the ground is apparently being covered. Thus the dog must be able to concentrate intensely, even though it may only rarely encounter the sought-for odor.

- The dog must be able to do a job that involves constant repetition of a simple task in a rigorously controlled way. The actions required of mine detector dogs are highly repetitive (usually involving walking a carefully prescribed, narrow path). Safety concerns, and the need to ensure that all of the ground is covered, require the dog to move in a predictable manner. An important benefit of a repetitive search pattern is that the dog becomes conditioned to undertaking the work in a very precise way—including high levels of search intensity and focus.

- Reliability. A mine detector dog can perform a series of actions (including staying on command) with 100 percent reliability.

Figure 8.12 Mine detector dogs must search for a critical, but small odor among a massive background of sensory input.

> **Any dog that behaves with less than 100 percent reliability in a minefield is a danger to itself and to its handler.**

- To search effectively, the dog must move slowly by reducing its gait to a walk, or even a slow walk. Dogs that do so naturally are likely to be better mine detector dogs than dogs that prefer to move quickly.
- The dog wants to work—it is enthusiastic about the job. Any creature undertaking a physically demanding and repetitive activity is likely to work more effectively and for longer periods if it enjoys what it is doing. Most training with mine detector dogs turns the search activity into a game in which the dog works for a highly desired reward (usually a toy).

To train as a mine detector dog, a dog must
- have an excellent nose;
- preferably belong to one of the following breeds or crossbreeds: Malinois, German or Dutch shepherd, Labrador or spaniel;
- show social behavior toward humans and other animals;

- demonstrate a high degree of retrieval (bring) drive;
- be trainable;
- be stress resistant;
- have good health, high natural fitness, and good endurance;
- be able to tolerate local environmental conditions and resist local diseases; and
- show exemplary basic obedience.

Handler Responsibilities

The mine detector dog handler has the final responsibility for decisions about a mine detector dog's training and use in operations. The handler has the following tasks and obligations:

- Assess the mine detector dog according to his organization's standard operating procedures (SOPs) before entering the area of training or operation. The SOPs should include:
  - Checking whether the mine detector dog is capable that day of assessing the area of training or operation.
  - Checking that the mine detector dog's condition and well-being are optimal.
- Stop the search if the mine detector dog is suffering from heat exhaustion, dehydration, or an illness. In this case, the dog should be taken out of the area of operation for treatment and recuperation.
- Provide the mine detector dog with shade and regular access to water during hot weather and during rest periods after training or rotation of the dogs.
- Ensure the mine detector dog is well fed and taken care of when out of the area of operation.
- Be responsible for the health and welfare of the mine detector dog.

Field Training

There are four search methods for mine detector dogs:

1. *Off leash*: the ideal method, to be used with highly experienced dogs.

2. *Short leash*: sometimes used, but usually it results in the dog handler being too close to the dog to adequately observe its behavior.
3. *Long leash*: in general, the most-used method for operational mine detection.
4. *Remote explosive scent tracing (REST)*: in this method, the dog is not active in the field. Instead, the dog smells odor samples from the soil in a scent lineup performed off site. Details on this method are described on page 200.

SEARCH SUBSTANCES

Before training a mine detector dog, check the dog's scent recognition for the following explosive substances:

- TNT
- PETN
- RDX
- Tetryl
- Composite explosives
- Other explosive materials common in the area of operation, such as mines, unexploded ordnances (UXOs), unexploded bombs (UXBs), or explosive remnants of war (ERWs)

You can train your dog for these odors using the same methods used for all explosive detector dogs (see chapter 3). However, mine detector dogs must learn two specific search procedures: the box system and the lane system. First teach the box system and then the lane system, to be used both for mine and UXO or UXB indication. Both methods employ a long leash to handle the dogs. The leash is usually 20–50 feet (6–15 m) long.

The Box System

The box system can be used for training mine detector dogs and in operational situations. A square box of 32 × 32 feet (10 × 10 m) is marked with wooden or plastic sticks at each corner. The whole perimeter of the area is then surrounded by clearly visible red (or red and white) tape. The box is then surrounded by a safe lane with a width of 3–6.5 feet (1–2 m) for safe entry into the box. The whole box has to be visible at one time to the handler and dog. If the handler is not able to oversee the area or observe the mine detector dog due to vegetation, obstacles, rocks, or so forth, the larger box should be divided into several smaller boxes to be sure the whole search area will eventually be covered in a safe search.

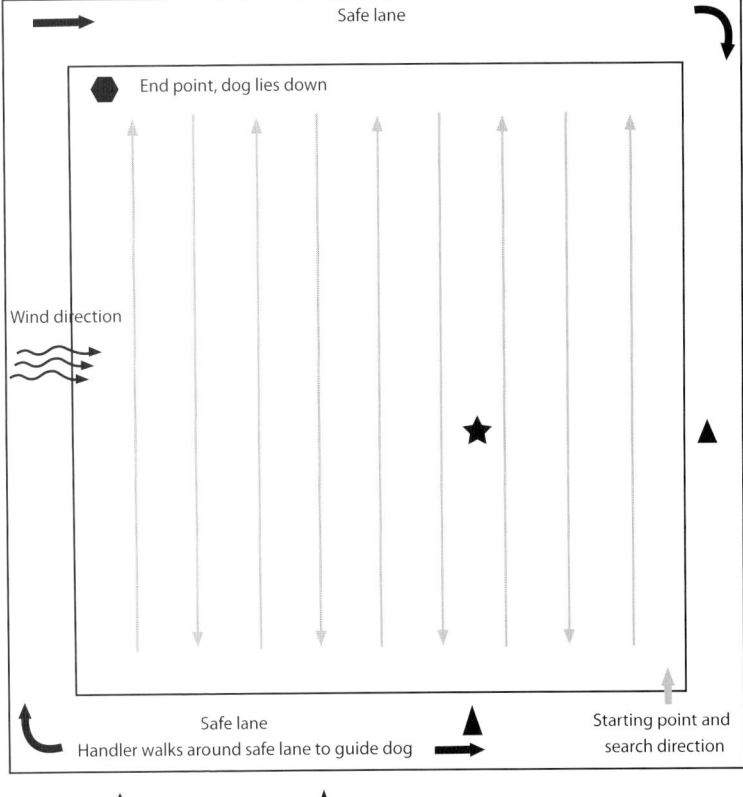

Figure 8.13 Layout of the box system. For training purposes, the box is divided into lanes with tape to help the dog get used to working systematically across the box. In operations, the dog should also be able to work using unmarked lanes. In the box system, the handler stays in the safe zone around the perimeter of the box. Indications are marked with two flags on the perimeter.

Figure 8.14 First teach the box system and then the lane system, to be used both for mine and UXO or UXB indication. Both methods use a long leash to handle the dogs.

Figure 8.15 The dog rounds the end of the box and returns over the next lane.

SAFE LANES

To provide safe access to the area of operation for the mine detector dog, handler, and other personnel, deminers prepare safe lanes using metal detectors or via areas already searched by dogs. The safe lanes are also used as start lines for the dog and handler. The width of a safe lane is a minimum of 3 feet (1 m) up to the ideal width of 6.5 feet (2 m). The safe lanes are marked with tape (usually red or red and white), which is attached to wooden or plastic sticks. Since the box is also marked this way, this mean the entire area (box and safe lane) are marked in tape showing two boxes, one (the search box) inside the other (outer border of the safe lane). It's normal during training not to mark the outer edge of the safe zone with tape since you know the area is safe. During operations, however, both boxes can be marked to ensure the safe zone is clearly identified.

Figure 8.16 A soldier walking in a safe lane marked with danger tape.

The mine detector dog will search the box in lanes, each about a foot and a half (0.5 m) wide. At the beginning of training, you'll mark these lanes with tape to get the dog used to working systematically, back and forth across the whole area of the box. Once the dog is used to the search pattern, you'll sometimes not mark them so the dog will be able to independently search the box using unmarked lanes. In operations, you won't often have the time to mark the lanes with tape, or you may not be able to mark them due to the setting or hardness of the soil.

Where to start depends on the wind. The handler should ideally set up to begin searching so the dog has a side wind. The dog then searches in lines in front of the handler, going forward to the end of the box and returning over the next lane. While the dog is checking the box, the handler moves slowly in the safe lane from the start point to the end of the box, providing a reference point for the dog moving forward and back until all lanes in the box are searched.

If the dog smells a target vapor and moves out of the lane, the handler lets the dog follow the scent. At the same time, the handler stays in place, awaiting the reaction of the dog. If the dog doesn't alert, the handler calls the dog back and sets it up for searching again from the perimeter of the box, in the same lane where the dog left off before following the scent track.

To guide the mine detector dog to cover all parts of the box, the handler can move anywhere around the box in the safe lane. When the dog reaches the end of the box, it will lie down, awaiting the command to come out of the box. During an operation, if a dog doesn't find any explosive materials, a second dog will check the box again, but will search lanes at an angle of 90 degrees to the lanes the primary mine detector dog followed.

MARKINGS

If a dog indicates the presence of an explosive substance, the handler calls the dog to come back to him to receive a reward. The handler must ensure that the dog does not walk over an uncleared area. Then the handler marks the cross lines of the targeted substance on the perimeter of the box from inside the safe lane. There are special colored flags for this purpose. After an indication, the box will be declared a contaminated area and the mine will be identified and then cleared by manual demining teams.

When a box is searched and considered free of mines and UXOs, the corner markers can be removed. On the project map, the exact location of each box is recorded and described to permit quality control or post-clearance sampling. Which boxes were cleared by which handler and dogs are also recorded in case of an accident investigation.

The Lane System

The lane system is also used for mine and UXO indication. It's mainly used in areas of operation where no boxes can be laid out due to environmental circumstances, as when clearing a road or working in small areas. The length of a lane depends on the layout of the project, but usually straight lanes of 1.6 feet (0.5 m) wide and if possible about 32 feet (10 m) long can be made. The first lane has an open end and every second lane has an open beginning of 1.5 feet (0.4 m) for the mine detector dog to pass through and continue searching the next lane.

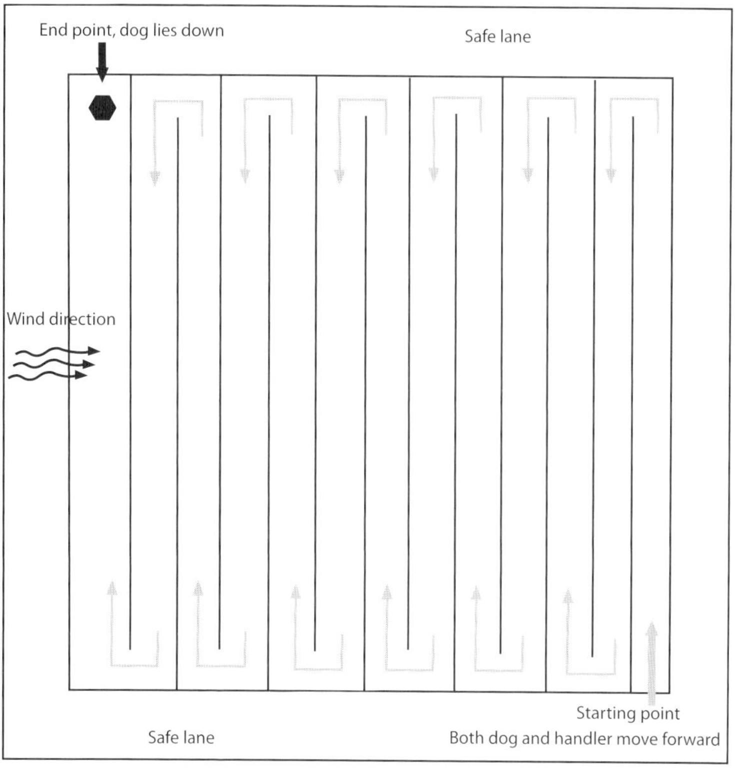

MINE DETECTION DOGS

Figure 8.17 Layout of the lane system. Unlike the box system, in the lane system each lane is marked and the handler follows the dog through the lane.

Figure 8.18 The lane system is mainly used in areas where no boxes can be made.

The mine detector dog's search starts from a safe lane. The dog searches straight forward from the handler, at a 90 degree angle from the base line it started from, and returns back over the next lane. Normally the handler follows his dog in the search lane. If a mine detector dog scents a target odor in another lane, it's allowed to cross the lane(s) to detect the source of the scent. If nothing is found, the handler sets up the dog in the lane where it left off.

MARKINGS

If the dog indicates a target substance, the handler places a marking stick near the indicated location, about 1.5 feet (0.5 m) from the target. A cross bearing is made when the handler cannot place the marking sticks because the ground is too hard or rocky.

The REST System

Remote explosive scent tracing (REST) involves transferring a target odor to a specially designed filter. The filters are created at the suspect site by vacuuming air through them. Any target substances from mines are collected by suction of air and dust particles from the ground surface using a portable vacuum pump in a light cart or carried in a backpack. (For obvious reasons, this procedure is used mainly for anti-tank mines, not anti-personnel mines.) Filter cartridges for the pump should be held close to the ground during scent trapping to ensure the collection of maximum contamination. Detecting landmines using this method involves vacuuming an area of land suspected to contain mines. The detector dog then performs a scent identification lineup on the filters in a laboratory environment. Dogs employed in this method are trained to detect very low concentrations of target odors. The test involves several internal controls to ensure reliability.

The REST method was developed by the South African government, through Mechem Consultants, at the end of the 1980s. The method was first called MEDDS (Mechem Explosives and Drug Detection System). It has subsequently been called the EVD (Explosives Vapor Detection) system by Norwegian People's Aid (NPA) in Angola. The method is used to detect drugs, explosives, and weapons at border checkpoints. In these cases, the vehicle or cargo is vacuumed and then the dogs sniff the filters. The system has been used at border checkpoints between South Africa and Swaziland and Lesotho, but also at other main border crossings. Experience has shown that the system has the capacity to check a significant number of vehicles, train carriages, and other cargo in a short time with a minimum number of personnel.

Indication and Rewarding

A mine detector dog gives a positive identification by lying down close to a target substance—ideally about 10 inches (0.25 m) away. They are not allowed to go too close to or on top of the indicated explosive substance, scratch the soil, or try to move the soil with their nose. In a positive indication, the mine detector dog should pinpoint briefly and then immediately back up 10 inches and lie down.

Rewarding procedures during training and retraining (after a dog has made a mistake) can be different from rewarding procedures during operations. In training and quality control tests (see "Check First Test," page 204), the mine detector dog can be rewarded near the targeted substance, after pinpointing the target substance and being taken out of the box or lane by the handler for more motivation by, for example, retrieving the reward item several times or eating some more dog biscuits. It's up to the handler how and when the dog will be rewarded during training, retraining, and quality control tests. However, it should always be a delayed reward; a trained mine detector dog has to focus on the target substance for several seconds before receiving the reward item.

After an indication in an operational situation, the handler calls the dog to come to him to receive the reward. The dog is not allowed to move over an uncleared area. Rewarding the dog can happen with a ball or Hurley—giving or throwing it to the dog in a safe area such as the safe lane or an area that's been cleared. We like using the Hurley to have better control over where the object lands. If a mine detector dog gives a positive identification and manual inspection verifies the presence of a mine or UXO, the dog must be withdrawn from that area of operation until the mine has been cleared. After the deminer has done his job by removing or exploding the mine, the dog can go on searching from the point where it left off.

Search Time and Rotation of Dogs

In ideal conditions, the maximum search time for a mine detector dog is 20 minutes in one stretch to be sure of quality scent recognition. This suggested time limit comes from data from quality control tests, and in training and retraining, when mine detector dogs are evaluated on their search time and stamina in different temperatures, humidity, and environments. Out of these evaluations comes an average time of 20 minutes in which most mine detector dogs are capable of detecting all target odors, although they will likely show signs of fatigue by the end of this period.

To ensure the quick recuperation of a mine detector dog after a shift, the handler should switch dogs every 20 minutes, unless the search will allow breaks. During a rest period in an operation, the dog should be kenneled in the handler's vehicle, or at another place in the shade, out of sight of the other dog and its handler, to ensure adequate rest and recuperation. If the dog is rested in a vehicle, it must be parked in the shade with open windows and, if necessary, open doors, or even better be ventilated by an electric fan in the roof of the vehicle to provide the dog with fresh, cool air. The dog should also be provided with fresh water.

Since the mine detector dogs in a team are both used as primary and secondary search dogs, the order of dogs searching must be rotated on a daily basis to prevent one dog from getting used to following the scent trail of the other dog. When a mine detector dog within the team develops such a habit, it must be removed from service for retraining and another dog must take its place.

Effects of Temperature and Humidity

Temperature greatly influences a mine detector dog's search. A low temperature makes detecting the vapor of the target substances more difficult because the vapor diminishes. When the temperature is near freezing, the vapor of the target substances is almost undetectable. Operating a search in such cold temperatures can cause mine detector dogs to fail in their task, so no search should take place in temperatures below 41°F (5°C).

High temperatures cause the target scent to rise and expand, making the scents easier for the dog to smell. But search quality and scent recognition can decrease in hot temperatures because the dog has to constantly scent hot air coming from hot soil, which can cause heat exhaustion. Therefore, in extremely hot temperatures, a handler should rotate his dogs more than usual. In temperatures above 77°F (25°C), mine detector dogs can quickly lose their scent recognition when they are searching up to their normal time limit. Shorter search times are therefore advised.

Dew or water from a light rain on the soil surface and vegetation near the ground can enhance vapor detection when the temperature rises and the odor of the target substances rise. Low humidity or dry conditions, combined with dry air, will result in little evaporation of the target odors. With dry soil, dry air, and high temperatures, detecting target substances becomes extremely difficult and only mine detector dogs with a proven record of clearance in such circumstances should be allowed to operate.

In general, mine detector dogs cannot work well in snow and rain. Snow covers the target scent, while rain washes it away. We advise waiting two days after rain to deploy mine detector dogs in the area. With snow, we advise waiting until the snow melts and the soil temperature rises.

> No search for mines should take place with a temperature below 41°F (5°C), except with mine detector dogs with a proven record of training, testing, and operational assignments in which they were able to detect target explosive substances at such temperatures.

Effects of Wind

During the initial survey of a search area, factors influencing the search must be identified and incorporated into planning. Still, weather conditions can change from day to day; because of this, the handler should check temperature, wind direction, and humidity daily. Even during a search, the handler should stay aware of changing conditions.

> **GUIDELINES CONCERNING WIND DIRECTION AND VELOCITY**
>
> - Ideally, mine detector dogs will perform their search with a side wind.
> - Searching with a light head wind is acceptable.
> - Searching with a tail wind is not permitted because the target substance may not be recognized until after the dog has passed its location. This rule can be ignored as long as the wind is no stronger than 3–6 feet per second (1–2 m/s).
> - Strong wind from any direction will influence a mine detector dog's search because the target odor will be spread over a wide area. To avoid missing a target substance, it's prohibited to search with mine detector dogs when the wind speed at ground level is more than 60 feet per second (18 m/s). When the ground is dusty and dry, searching is prohibited if the wind speed is more than 23 feet per second (7 m/s).

Check First Test

The "check first test" assesses whether a mine detector dog is capable of detecting the target substances it was trained to detect (i.e., target substances and devices). The test must be performed each time a team is deployed in an operational search. This test can also be used as training, as a warm-up, and as quality control. The test affirms that the dog is healthy and well trained, enhancing the handler's trust and confidence in his dog's abilities.

Box 1

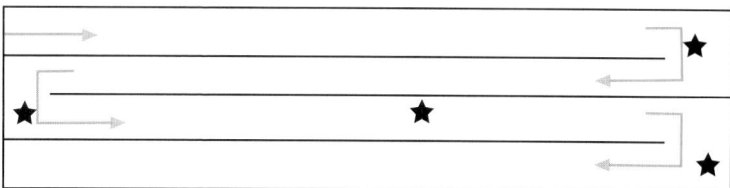

Box 2

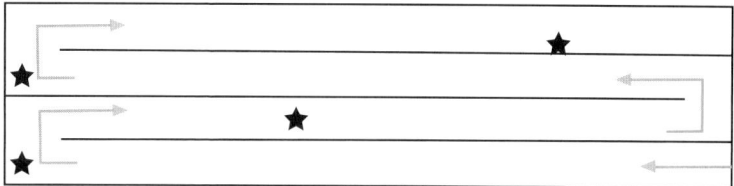

Box 3

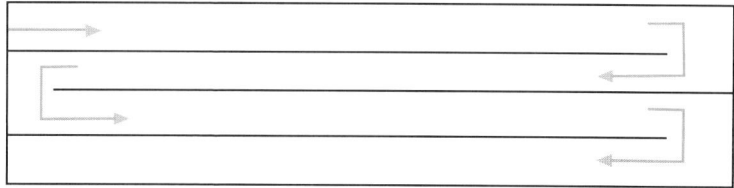

Legend ★ Target substance

Figure 8.19 Layout of three test boxes for a check first test. Each box is 33 feet long and 10 feet wide (10 m x 3 m). The lanes in each box should be about 40 inches (1 m) wide and are marked with tape. The mine detector dog searches the boxes for indication of the target substances. Box 3 has no target odors and should be rotated every time as the first, second, or last box to be searched.

When possible, the test boxes are prepared one or more days before testing takes place so there aren't visible signs of where the target substances are hidden.

REQUIREMENTS FOR TEST SITES

- It can be used only once and then not again for few days to allow any residual smells to dissipate. Waiting four or five days is usually sufficient.
- It should preferably be flat to give you a good overview of the area.

- It must have minimal vegetation.
- The soil should have a normal structure (no clay, aqueous, or rocky soils).
- It should be free from explosive residues.
- It must be free of metal and other scrap.
- The wind should be minimal.
- It must be situated in a quiet area.
- The distance between test boxes must be at least 10 feet (3 m), although 16 feet (5 m) is preferable.
- Along with explosive substances, the test site should contain parts of (or whole) UXOs, anti-personnel mines, and/or anti-tank mines—all, of course, without ignitions.

Each substance or item should be placed about 8 inches (20 cm) below the surface and covered with soil, leaves, and/or other vegetation. You might hide more than one type of explosive in a box. Some spots in the lanes should also be disturbed without hiding anything. Handle the target substances and contaminated test items with sterile gloves (only to be used once) or special pliers, only to be used for one target substance and cleaned at the end of every day.

Figure 8.20 A Dutch military dog handler with his mine detector dog.

Before testing the nose work of the mine detector dog, the check first test looks at practical general obedience, such as short heel work, retrieving, and staying at a distance upon command of the handler. Testing the dog's searching abilities consists of observing his motivation, concentration, obedience, and the ability to detect the target substances and test items by giving a correct indication for every test item or substance. This can happen by check first test alone or by remote explosive scent tracing (REST) in a scent lineup and after that searching one or more lanes.

After the team has finished the check first test, the handler, instructor, and team leader discuss whether the dog should go on an operational search that day, but ultimately it is the handler who decides whether the dog will search or not search.

FAILING THE CHECK FIRST TEST

A mine detector dog fails the check first test and has to be taken out of deployment if it

- touches an object in an alert;
- does not indicate an hidden explosive;
- searches too fast; and
- searches with its head too high. How high a dog's head should be will depend on humidity and weather, but normally the head should be as close to the ground as possible.

A mine detector dog that fails must go back to training. After retraining, if the dog again fails a check first test, then it may have to be taken out of deployment permanently.

Deployment

Before entering an area of operation, the handler must study the boxes, lanes, or area he is assigned to. He must also get the latest information about the operation from the site manager. With this information, the handler develops a plan for entry to the area of operation. This assessment and planning stage should include the following steps and information:

- Draw the boxes or lanes on a map of the area.
- Look for search priorities in the area.
- For a road, search from one end of the road to the other in a zigzag pattern to be sure all parts of the road are searched. With two mine detector dogs, they can search from both ends of the road toward the middle.
- Learn the sort of mines that can be expected in the area.
- Use reliable weather and wind data. Usually you would set up your own weather station near the search area.
- Incorporate the number of available mine detector dogs.
- Assess the reliability of the safe areas (e.g., were the areas made by a professional or resident?)
- Choose the access route.
- Set up the search lanes.

Figure 8.21 Searching for hidden explosives in the road with a metal detector or ground penetrating radar (GPR).

Figure 8.22 A landmine.

EFFECT OF VEGETATION ON BURIED EXPLOSIVES

The handler should assess the temperature and humidity to see how they might impact the search. For example, on extremely dry days, the scent released from the soil may be significantly diminished. Flowers, grass, and bushes, however, will continue to release humidity and thus emit the target scent. As a result, if mine detector dogs cannot pick up the target scent from the soil, they might be able pick up scent from breathing the air around plants.

However, while vegetation is generally known to have a positive effect on vapor detection, some dogs have problems working effectively and safely in densely vegetated areas. For this reason, sometimes the vegetation is mechanically cut before a dog's search. Cutting may also disturb the scent picture above mines by increasing the scent of cut plants. But because plants may uptake target substances from soil water through the roots, after cutting, this water from the plant will also vaporize, releasing the target substances.

The result may be increased scent and more favorable conditions for vapor detection, although the scent may be disturbed, making it more difficult for the dog to pinpoint a location with accuracy.

When searching the verges or ditches next to roads, a proven and successful practice is to search from a safe lane established on the road itself. The search lanes are normally angled 90 degrees to the road direction, although wind direction may alter this practice. Clearing verges with mine detector dogs can sometimes be difficult due to steep slopes, fluctuating terrain, and vegetation. If the vegetation is too dense and is cut mechanically before the search, the scent picture may be disturbed. Therefore, it is recommended to wait a minimum of two days after cutting vegetation before searching with mine detector dogs.

IMPORTANT GENERAL POINTS

- Always watch for tripwires.
- Weather conditions should always be considered in planning and carrying out a search.
- Consider the age and condition of the object you are searching for. The odor print of UXOs and mines that lie in the soil for long periods can change over time, so explosives can be very difficult to smell. For long-buried explosives, you will need to allow more time for searching.
- If possible, find out the number of possible mines in a specific area to assess the potential odor saturation of the soil.
- If possible, get information from a local about the typical method of hiding explosives, the typical depth, and the sort of material used.

SEARCHING TWICE

Parts or all of a box or lane should be re-examined if any of the following occur:

- The search tempo of the primary mine detector dog is too fast.
- The dog lifts its head over a distance of 12 inches (30 cm).
- A strong side or head wind blows during the search.

- After each box search in which no explosive materials are detected, a second dog should check the box again, but searching on an angle of 90 degrees to the lane pattern the primary dog followed.
- After each lane search, the lane should be, under the same conditions, controlled by a second dog, so each lane is checked by two dogs. The order of the dogs must be changed as much as possible (e.g., every day) because otherwise the second dog may start to follow the smell of the first dog.
- The handler decides how often and how long each dog at the site gets rest and will be deployed.

Limitations

A dog should **not** be deployed under the following conditions:

- The wind is blowing at a speed of over 60 feet per second (18 m/s).
- On a dry, dusty surface, the wind is more than 23 feet per second (7 m/s).
- There is no way to avoid searching with a tail wind.
- It is raining. After it has rained, wait for two days.
- If it rains after a very dry period, wait for one week.
- Vegetation has just been burned. (In some demining programs, vegetation is routinely burned to get a better overview of the working site.) The burning may, however, have a negative effect on the dog's detection capability. After vegetation has been burned, wait one week with dry weather and wait for at least two days after rain.
- Mine detector dogs can be used as a secondary search or quality control in areas already cleared by mine clearance machines such as flails, tillers, sifters, rollers, and soil millers. In this case, the following limitations govern the use of dogs:
    - If the machine has been used to clear an area with a relatively high density of mines, dogs should not be used since lumps of explosive and bits of mine casing are likely to be spread around the area. This will confuse the dog and make the search less reliable.

- If the machine has disturbed the soil, you must wait at least two days before deploying your dog, provided that it has rained at least one time during the two days. Rainfall will wash away most of the undesired contamination caused by the machinery. Waiting after the disturbance will make the dog's search more accurate and reliable. If it does not rain, however, wait at least one week before bringing your dog in.

Figure 8.23 Neutralization of an anti-personnel mine.

Figure 8.24 A soldier sets a mine in the grass next to the road.

Figure 8.25 Military anti-personnel mine removal.

Route Overwatch Search Dogs

A Route Overwatch Search Dog (ROSD) is trained by the Royal Dutch Military Academy Air Force to independently find and alert for buried explosives. An ROSD has a different specialization than the explosive detector dog (EDD). EDDs search a defined space or object to see if there are hidden explosives. The EDD-handler is usually located near the dog so he can give instructions as the dog works. ROSDs, colloquially called "verge bomb dogs," search at sometimes great distances from their handlers for the smell of explosives. With a camera attached to its head, an ROSD searches for explosives by itself while the dog handler watches the dog's progress on a portable video screen from a distance. The handler can, through a radio in the camera headset, keep in contact with his dog.

Special training is required to become an ROSD. A young dog and its handler first go for 20 weeks to Airbase Woensdrecht in the Netherlands, where the dogs get used to wearing the camera

Figure 8.26 ROSDs get used to wearing a camera and receiving remote instructions from their handler via radio transmitter.

on their head. Training focuses the prey drive of the ROSD on finding explosives in sand and other soils. They are also trained on search methods, scent detection, and the passive alert, but also on team building between the dog and handler. For the alert, the dog must learn to sit or lie down when it finds an explosive. Preferably the dog sits or lies down somewhat away from the explosive. After an indication, the handler and deminers go to the dog so it can be removed and the deminers can get to work. If deminers are not immediately available, the handler will mark the spot the dog lay down before removing the animal from the area.

Teams that pass this training successfully go for three weeks to the military explosive ordnance disposal (EOD) service. There handlers learn how bombs, grenades, mines, and inprovised explosive devices (IEDs) work. They also learn how to recognize, explore for, and safely work near or with explosives, as well as the type of information deminers need to do their job. Following this, teams get practical training for six months.

Figure 8.27 Dogs are not the only animals useful in detecting mines. Left: In Tanzania, a Belgian non-governmental organization called APOPO breeds and trains African Giant Pouched Rats to detect landmines. The rats work on a harness suspended between two handlers and indicate their find by scratching. The rats don't weigh enough to trigger mines. Right: The US marines employ bottlenose dolphins for water mine clearance operations.

Figure 8.28 An APOPO HeroRAT rat getting a food reward after a succesful find.

ROSDs are assigned to Gilze-Rijen and Leeuwarden airbases in the Netherlands. If the Royal Dutch Air Force or another armed service needs an ROSD to search a plot or route at home or abroad, there are always one or more dog and handler teams available.

9

Stress in Operational Service

Physical Condition

All dogs in operational service should see a veterinarian regularly. How often a dog should have a regular medical examination and what sort of tests should be performed are decisions that may vary from vet to vet and from dog to dog. Some vets will recommend only a regular physical orthopedic examination, while others might want X-rays and blood tests. Some vets will perform the same examination on all dogs, while others will focus on breed-specific problems.

Figure 9.1 Evacuation of an airplane after a bomb threat. Now the explosive detector dog can start its work.

In all cases, however, attention must be paid to the total physical condition of the dog, its joints and movement, and its senses, especially the nose, eyes, and ears. Furthermore, it is important that the dog's senses not be influenced by medication.

The vet should be informed of all, even minor, injuries. Before a dog goes back into active service after an even small accident, it needs a medical examination to avoid serious problems later on.

Regular veterinary care can help prevent excess strains on your dog, although the dog handler also plays a key role maintaining an animal's health. The handler's most important job is making sure any dog taken into operational service is well prepared and healthy. The dog has to know what its duty is (in other words, be well trained) and has to be mentally and physically able to perform this duty well.

When this optimal condition is lacking, the dog becomes physically exhausted after only a brief exertion. With poor or insufficient feeding, the dog lacks concentration, has insufficient energy to perform, and shows intense nervousness.

A Daily 10 Point Health Check

Once a day, a dog handler should look at the following 10 points to see if his dog is healthy enough for training or deployment.

1. MOVEMENT

When your dog gets up and walks around, watch the way it moves. Watch for the following:

- Stiffness
- Difficulty getting up or down
- Unwillingness to walk
- Unusual quietness
- Restlessness

2. FECES AND URINE

Keep an eye on the regularity of your dog's waste elimination make sure the feces is consistent. Four indications of concern in the dog's feces:

- Diarrhea
- Constipation
- Mucus
- Blood

Causes for concern in the urine include the following symptoms:

- Darkness
- Cloudiness
- Blood

3. BODY CHECK

Check your dog's body for lumps, cuts, inflammation, and any signs of discomfort. Does the coat feel smooth and healthy? Watch for the following:

- Lumps
- Flinching
- Moisture

4. FEET AND CLAWS

Check the pads of the feet by moving the limbs backward (never to the side). Watch for the following:

- Matted fur
- Discharge
- Signs of damage
- Broken nails
- Foreign objects

5. EARS

Feel with your fingers over the pinna (the flappy parts) and the rest of the ear surface. Then look inside the ear canal. A normal ear should be cool, soft, and pale pink. Wax is normal, but the ear should be generally clean and there shouldn't be a bad odor or swelling. Check for the following:

- Lumps
- Bumps
- Areas of pain
- Moisture
- Unusual discharge

6. EYES

The dog's eyes should be clear and there should be no excessive discharge or signs of irritation. Watch for the following:

- Ingrown eyelashes or hair that can touch the eyes
- Eyes that are not equally open
- Pupils that are not the same size
- Squinting
- A dog's need to rub its eyes
- Bulging
- Foreign objects
- Scratches
- Clouding or discoloration

7. NOSE

Your dog's nose should be moist and cool. Also look for the following:

- Discharge
- Sneezing
- Uneven or obstructed breathing

8. MOUTH AND TEETH

Check the mouth for anything out of the ordinary. Lift the upper lip to observe the color of the gums just above the upper canine teeth. Most dogs have gums that are a healthy, bubblegum or salmon-pink color; however, what is normal can vary from dog to dog. Indications of a problem include the following:

- Darker/redder than normal or pale gums
- Bad breath as an indication of digestive problems
- Growths and lumps inside the mouth
- Cuts and sores on the tongue

For a quick check, lift up the mouth flaps and make sure the teeth are clear and that none are loose. Then take a look inside the mouth. Watch for the following:

- Lumps
- Broken/chipped teeth
- Inflamed areas
- Swelling
- Bleeding gums

9. ANUS

Dogs have anal sacs on either side of the anus that fill with fluid produced by the anal glands. This fluid is assumed to be a scent marker useful for delineating territory. Symptoms of problems with the anal sacs include the following:

- Scooting
- Straining to defecate
- Itching/scratching
- Tail chasing
- Discharge from the anal glands
- Licking and biting around the anus

10. GENITAL AREA

A healthy dog should have no discharge in the genital area, although a small amount of whitish-yellow smegma can accumulate around the preputial opening and is completely normal. The presence of preputial discharge that consists of blood, urine, or pus is more serious and suggests an underlying problem, ranging from a mild, relatively benign disorder to a severe, even life-threatening disease. Watch for the following symptoms:

- Spotting
- Swelling or inflammation
- Excessive licking
- Discharge
- Lethargy
- Fever
- Lack of appetite

Symptoms of a problem with female dogs can include the following:

- Discharge from the vulva
- Spotting of blood
- Scooting the hindquarters
- Attracting males
- Frequent urination
- Frequent licking of the vagina

The Strains of Service

The achievements of dogs in operational service have improved greatly over the past few decades. Reasons for this improvement include better training methods and also better nutrition. Our dogs now perform better, but much more is also requested of them.

Training and operational service place a heavy strain on the dog's body. For example, when a dog jumps, not only are the muscles of its hindquarters and back forced to exert themselves, but also the joints, particularly the forepaws, have to cope with a jarring load when it lands.

Intensive searching requires concentrated muscular movements, often employing an unnaturally stretched and bent posture. This causes an extra load on the joints, and the muscle activity produces pyruvate and lactate (lactic acid) in the muscular tissue (acidification). To prepare the dog's body for such a performance, warm-up exercises are strongly recommended. Without a warm-up, the risk of acute injuries is very high. Warm-ups especially help the muscles, but also the ligaments, tendons, and joints. A cool-down period also helps avoid injuries by allowing the body to more easily recover from the performance.

Figure 9.2 After each correct alert of the explosive detector dog, the explosive ordnance disposal (EOD) team starts the dangerous work of removing or defusing the explosive.

Warm-up Exercises

Warm-up exercises prepare the dog's body for the work it has to do. A dog that begins without a warm-up (i.e., cold) starts its duty in training or operational service with muscles, ligaments, and joints that are insufficiently supplied with blood. Blood flow is needed to transport energy and oxygen to the muscles, and after energy consumption, to carry away the waste products from those muscles.

All muscles hold some glycogen as a small energy source for immediate energy requirements. This energy can be drawn upon without oxygen, so even without a warm-up, the muscles can always function. This glycogen is enough for, at the most, two minutes of activity, which explains why a dog without a warm-up can still, for a short time, move at full speed and put in a great effort. The disadvantage of using this energy source without enough oxygen is that lactate builds up in the tissues, and it yields a fairly minor amount of energy as a consequence of a much less efficient consumption of the glycogen. With enough oxygen, the glycogen could produce eight times more energy, with no lactate buildup.

In the past it was thought that lactate causes muscular pain, but that is not true. Aching muscles are caused by small ruptures in the muscular tissue. Nevertheless, lactate has a negative effect on the muscles. Lactate makes muscular fibers hold fluid and swell. This swelling impedes blood circulation, which in turn leads to decreased oxygen delivery.

Good warm-up exercises mean less glycogen is used, less lactate is formed, and lactate and other waste products are drained away faster. Furthermore, better circulation ensures that not only the muscles, but also the tendons and ligaments, resist overstretching, reducing the possibility of ruptures to these tissues (so a load will not become an overload). The reason for this is not completely clear, but ruptures to tissues are the biggest danger for "cold" dogs doing operational work.

Figure 9.3 The Royal Netherlands Marechaussee is responsible for border control. They use explosive detection dogs to check suspicious shipments or vehicles for explosives.

Figure 9.4 A suitcase abandoned at Amsterdam Airport Schiphol will bring work for the explosive detector dog of the Royal Netherlands Marechaussee. Dogs will also sniff all luggage bound for certain destinations.

The warm-up also helps the joints. Through regular, easy joint movements during the warm-up, more synovial fluid is produced, which ensures better lubrication and maintenance of the cartilage of the joints both during and after a performance.

SUGGESTIONS FOR AN EFFECTIVE WARM-UP

A safe, effective warm-up consists of three phases:
- Phase 1: Relaxed start-up of the body for two minutes
- Phase 2: Increasing the circulation for three to six minutes
- Phase 3: Strong, muscular exertion and active stretching for one to two minutes

Starting up the body in phase 1 means that the muscles, as well as the heart and vascular system, are slowly activated from rest. This phase can consist of calmly walking with the dog for about one minute, moving on to an easy trot or jog.

This easy trot can be the start of phase 2 by increasing the tempo for two or three minutes into a full trot. Ensure you trot not only in a straight line, but also in circles, through which the muscles that permit sideward movements are activated and supplied with blood. The easiest way to do this is to run with the dog or train it to run beside a bike.

In phase 3, the muscles have to be contracted and stretched actively to be fully prepared for training or active service. Trotting up and down a hill or slope is perfect. The advantage of a hill or slope is that the dog's muscles are stretching at the same time that they are contracting: uphill the hindquarters, downhill the front legs. As an alternative, the dog can run, but ideally not at full speed, so not after a thrown ball. Exercises like the send away and the recall will get your dog to run, although without the benefits of active stretching.

People often use passive stretching for their warm-ups, which is an ideal preparation for endurance sports because passive stretching decreases muscular tension and increases circulation. For dogs, however, passive stretching is not ideal, because a low muscular tension also means muscles are slow to contract. Active stretching keeps muscular tension at a high level.

Other exercises to warm-up the dog include the attended handstand, through which we pick up and gently shake the dog's hindquarters and back loose. It is also possible to teach the dog to make a play bow, through which the dog sags through its front legs. This exercise also helps loosen up the muscles. By encouraging the dog to move in tight circles around our legs (leading it with a dog treat in hand), we help the dog keep its vertebral column flexible, leading to smooth movement.

Training Exercises

Training exercises can also help a dog move with greater agility and help prevent physical injuries from operational service. An excellent exercise is to let the dog walk between the rungs of a ladder lying flat on the ground. This exercise stimulates the co-ordination of the hind legs. Walking on beams of different sizes lying at different heights over the ground, some of them sloping, also helps a dog become aware of its limbs. Walking on beams teaches the dog to look where to place its feet.

Figure 9.5 A Springer spaniel of the Belgian police searching for explosives and hidden arms.

Cool-Down

After training or operational service, do not immediately put your dog in the car or kennel, or play fetching drills with a ball. Instead, lead your dog through a cool-down, which will help ensure a quick recuperation after a performance. The muscles have to top up their glycogen stock; small damages in muscles, tendons, and ligaments have to be repaired; and all waste products have to leave the muscles and then the dog's body.

Muscles can best recuperate if lactate accumulation is reduced soon after a performance to become energy and material for glycogen. Humans often cool down by stretching their muscles. This is good, but only if there are no ruptures in the muscle fibers (as indicated by aching muscles); if there are, the muscles should be stretched until just before the pain barrier. You can't ask your dog if it has aching muscles, but we can assume it has ruptures in its muscle tissue given a high intensity training or work session. However, finding out the dog's pain barrier while stretching these muscles is almost impossible. In view of both problems, stretching is not recommended as the best cool-down for dogs.

Massage can help if our dogs can fully relax and if we know how to massage. Most of the time, this isn't practical, although dogs often enjoy a massage. It has a salutary influence and most dogs fall asleep. What sort of massage has to be given depends on the state of the muscles. Hard muscles (hypertonic) need a soothing massage to encourage relaxation. Flabby muscles (hypotonic) need a stimulating massage.

The most common way to cool down a dog is to go for an easy run. After active service or training, an appropriate cool-down consists of three minutes of trotting easily, followed by two minutes of normal walking. By then, most of the muscles, joints, and ligaments will have had enough circulation to cool down effectively.

Go for an easy run with your dog for about three minutes to allow him to cool down after active service or training.

Mental Condition

The Webster's definition for stress is "any stimulus, such as fear or pain, that disturbs or interferes with the normal physiological equilibrium of an organism." Stress may also be defined as physical, mental, or emotional strain or tension. Both physical and emotional stress may reduce a dog's working potential.

Although most of the time stress is viewed as negative, it is an absolutely natural reaction of an organism toward certain stimuli, challenges, and loads, the so-called stress factors or stressors. Every strong stimulus, no matter what type, will produce the same physical pattern of reactions. The body does not differentiate between positive stress (eustress) or negative stress (distress).

For normal physical and mental development, every animal needs appropriate stressors. These stressors help the animal adapt to the conditions in its environment. The effects of positive stress include optimal preparedness: quick reactions and physical strength and speed because of an increased supply of energy from the body. The effects of negative stress due to chronic or strong stress stimuli include diseases of the immune system or kidneys and gastrointestinal or cardiovascular problems. In dogs, negative stress can also result in a higher aggressive impulse. The threshold for physical or mental damage from stress differs from animal to animal and depends on many different variables, such as hereditary factors, state of health, experiences, and severity of the stress.

So a certain amount of stress is useful and absolutely necessary for an optimum readiness to perform. Every organism can, without damaging itself, compensate for stress, which means it gets used to a certain level of stress. How well the body compensates depends on the degree of stress experienced. If the body compensates for the stress situation, we say it adapts or copes. If coping is not possible or no longer possible, the organism becomes ill and we speak of *distress*.

REACTIONS TO STRESS

Reactions to stress can be divided into three successive phases: alarm, resistance, and exhaustion.

ALARM

In the alarm phase, the interaction between neural impulses and hormonal secretions ensure the animal has an optimal readiness to react. In this phase, normal physiologic equilibrium (homeostasis) is lost. The sympathetic nervous system and secretions of the adrenal medulla—the hormones noradrenalin and adrenalin—fire up. This leads to cortisol secretion from the adrenal cortex. Noradrenalin, adrenalin, and cortisol have the following effects on the body:

- An accelerated pulse rate
- Contraction of the blood vessels, leading to hypertension
- Dilation of the pupils
- Contraction of the skin, leading to bristling of the hairs
- Dilation of the bronchi, resulting in deep breathing
- Release of fatty acids and fatty deposits
- Decelerated gastrointestinal activity
- Increased gastric acid concentration
- Increased blood glucose due to decomposition of glycogen deposits in the liver
- Increased circulation in the muscular system

These effects get the brain and muscles into an optimal state of readiness, and the ability to react peaks. The body reaches a state of the very highest capacity, which is necessary for a "fight or flight" response.

RESISTANCE

In the resistance phase, pulse rate, blood pressure, and blood glucose levels remain high, giving the animal energy. A further production of energy occurs from the release of glucose and fats from the muscular system and liver.

Resistance to the stressor increases in a process of adaptation. However, resistance to other stimuli decreases. When the state of stress is ongoing, the body tries to diminish the alarm reaction and restore normal physiologic equilibrium. The parasympathetic nerve is responsible for that, prompting the contraction of the bronchi, increased salivation, and increased gastrointestinal and bladder activity. The secretion of noradrenalin, adrenalin, and cortisol continues.

Under conditions of continued stress, the production of cortisol could ultimately result in development of hyperadrenocorticism (Cushing's disease). However, the rising plasma concentration of cortisol is somewhat self-limiting, triggering responses in the body to reduce cortisol. However, during severe and prolonged stress, cortisol levels remain at high concentrations, causing various negative physiologic changes. For example, thyroid and sexual functions become weak and inflammation increases. Memory is reduced (amnesia), the ability of the immune system to fight disease drops, and resistance to new stressors declines.

EXHAUSTION

If the stress is continuous or becomes chronic, in spite of the adaptation created by the resistance phase, the dog can no longer maintain its resistance. The symptoms of the alarm reaction become permanent. This continuous high tension can, combined with other risks, lead to illness and, in the extreme, death.

In the exhaustion phase, the dog will have problems with low energy and malfunctions with the growth, reproduction, and immuno-defense processes. The adrenal cortex enlarges, the thymus gland atrophies, and the organism will experience gastrointestinal disturbances and psychosomatic disorders. Long-term effects can include cardiovascular and renal diseases, allergic reactions, inflammatory diseases, and collapse of the immuno-defense system.

TYPES OF STRESS

Stress can occur in all areas and situations of life, as well as at all ages. The experience of stress and the ways an individual copes with stress differs in humans, as in dogs. A situation that one dog experiences calmly can for another dog be a heavy burden. As with humans, there are five main groups of stressors:

1. *External stressors*: inundation with stimuli of the sense organs (e.g., light, noise, odor, heat, cold) or withdrawal of stimuli (deprivation), pain stimuli, and real or simulated dangerous situations.
2. *Stressors that prevent the satisfaction of primary needs*: hindrance of sleep, withdrawal of food or water, no or less bodily contact, undue restriction of movement (chaining up or kenneling).
3. *Performance stressors*: physical overexertion, over- or undertraining, incorrect training methods, excessive demands in training or operational service, inappropriate activity for the breed or dog, tests, possible failures, reprimands, or punishment.
4. *Social stressors*: isolation, less or no contact with other dogs, incorporation into a new dog group, removal from a dog group, change of human partner.
5. *Mental stressors*: conflicts, uncontrollable situations, anxiety, uncertain expectations, inconsistency in the human relationship, noisy surroundings, irregular days, constantly changing environment.

STRESS SYMPTOMS

Below are some of the symptoms that indicate a dog is stressed—often more than one symptom can be observed at the same time. Some of these behaviors, such as panting, may also occur when the dog is not stressed at all (maybe it is a hot day or the dog has been playing). However, knowing the symptoms of stress will help you assess your dog's well-being when you know it has faced stressful stimuli.

- *Panting*: While under stress, the dog has a higher pulse rate and muscular tension, for which more oxygen is used. In addition, increased metabolism means the body produces more heat. Both situations can lead to panting.
- *Salivation*: In some dogs, excessive salivation is seen after agitation or stress, often combined with excessive panting.
- *Self-destruction*: This is often seen in the form of excessive licking and biting of the extremities, tail, and/or genital area. These parts of the dog's body eventually become open and painful wounds. In response to pain stimuli, the body releases endorphins, the body's own painkillers, also called the "feel-good" hormones. By controlling pain and giving the feeling of well-being, endorphins are similar to morphine. That feeling of analgesia and well-being helps the dog endure the stressful situation, but it can come to rely upon it, resulting in a compulsive behavior.
- *Destruction of objects*: This usually occurs with dogs that are left alone for long periods.
- *Exaggerated bark or whimper*: Continuous barking, whimpering, and howling can be symptoms of an overloaded and stressed dog.
- *Trembling*: While under stress, the muscles are tensed; by trembling, the body tries to relax the muscles to avoid muscle cramps.
- *Nervousness*: The dog is easily startled and distracted. At events or in situations in which it normally stays quiet and calm, the dog now reacts with restlessness, agitation, anxiousness, or aggression.
- *Diarrhea and enuresis*: During fear or at a sudden fright, the intestinal tract is activated, resulting in defecation and increased frequency of urination. Prolonged or excessive stress can also result in diarrhea.
- *Lack of appetite*: This is a well-known phenomenon for dogs in stress, often seen in boarding kennels. However, excessive demands in training can also make the dog refuse or spit out food or rewards.

- *Gluttony*: The opposite of the dog refusing to eat in stressful situations is the dog that gorges itself with everything it can find. This sometimes includes inedible objects such as wood, paper, and stones.
- *Lack of concentration*: The dog is distracted and nervous in training or operational service. Well-known situations or exercises seem to be forgotten. The dog may show poor concentration for learning new exercises or in new situations.

ANTI-STRESS ACTIONS

First of all, if the symptoms are unclear, always ask a vet for a check-up to rule out physical illness. If you know your dog is stressed, try to find out the cause or reason for the stress and change the situation. This seems like an easy, obvious step, but most of the time it demands detailed, difficult detection work, as well as a true and honest desire to make changes to help the dog. These changes may not be easy since they often demand that people change their own behavior and way of handling the dog. To ease the dog's situation, physical therapy (massage) or aromatherapy, essential oils, or Bach Flower Remedies can help. Before giving medicine or changing the dog's food program (which can cause stress), always contact a vet.

BACH FLOWER REMEDIES

Bach Flower Remedies are an alternative treatment developed by the English physician and homeopath Edward Bach (1886–1936). He found that certain flowers, other plant parts, and pure spring water contain energy beneficial in preventing various lifestyle diseases. Despite similarities with homeopathy, Bach Flower Remedies are not homeopathic treatments. They include 38 remedies made from infusions of flowers or other plant parts. The Rescue Remedy, which is a blend of five other remedies, is useful as first aid for stress and panic situations. Many users of the Bach flower therapy always carry it with them.

As a handler, try to prevent your dog from becoming overstressed. Give it the opportunity to become a healthy, self-assured dog by providing controlled opportunities to adapt to stress. In all environments, interact with your dog in a careful, quiet, and confident manner, and respect your dog's individual limits.

> A dog whose natural needs are honored, and which from time to time can be "just a dog" without special demands or tasks, will be better able to cope with stressful situations.

Also be sure to allow your dog to regenerate after strain and stress. It must have the opportunity to recuperate from heavy training or operational service. The form of recuperation can be whatever quiet activity your dog enjoys most: a relaxed walk, gentle playtime, the chance to lie down or sleep in a favorite spot, a bone to chew, and so on.

Caring for Older Dogs

Handlers of dogs in operational service have many special responsibilities. Because the dog is incapable of saying what is too much for it, and cannot indicate when it is overworked, the handler has to protect his dog against excesses. That's the only way dogs in operational service are able to do their job for a lifetime.

In today's world of improved nutrition and veterinary care, it is not uncommon for dogs of 9 and 10 years old to provide top performances, both in training and operational service. For many older dogs, maintaining attitude and interest is far more challenging than maintaining good physical condition. Attitude can often be improved by extra days of rest and extra personal attention.

DIET

Handlers should ensure that older dogs are not overweight and that their diet is suited to their age. Most dog food manufacturers produce a senior diet, which is adapted to the degeneration processes of older dogs. It differs from normal dog food because it has a higher percentage of fiber and a lower percentage of energy and phosphate. The extra fiber helps older dogs because their intestines do not work as efficiently as those of younger animals. The presence of fiber activates the intestines and stimulates bowel movements.

The lower percentage of energy is because many older dogs are less active and tend to gain weight. The older dog in operational service doesn't often suffer from obesity, but if not regularly in active service or training, it will use less energy because its muscle mass will decrease. Deciding whether a senior diet has enough energy for a dog in operational service is a matter of testing; results differ from dog to dog. Our experience is that many older dogs find enough energy in the senior food.

The lower percentage of phosphate helps spare the kidneys. As many dogs age, their kidneys fail to properly excrete phosphate, leading to deposits of calcium phosphate in the kidneys. These calcium phosphate deposits in turn push the kidneys toward a faster decline. Deposits can also be found in joints with osteoarthritis. By lowering the percentage of phosphate in the diet, the possibility of these deposits is reduced, postponing age-related health problems.

OLDER DOGS IN OPERATIONAL SERVICE

Many older dogs develop slight stiffness in their legs and back when they first get up or when they come out of their kennel. Care should be taken to limber up these dogs before they start their work, either by massage or warm-up exercises.

In operational service, take care that you don't require too much of older dogs. Older dogs respond differently to performances than younger dogs do, and their recuperation also differs. In general, it can be said that stressful situations are harder on the body of an older dog. Body tissue and cells are more easily upset with heavy loads, and therefore a load that might be handled well by a young dog might overload an older dog.

Understanding how the aging process affects a dog's body will give you a better sense of how to adapt your dog's work. What follows is a look at some of the ways a dog's body changes at around seven years old and then again at around ten years old. These ages are somewhat arbitrary—you will need to observe your own dog to see how age affects it.

OVER SEVEN YEARS OLD

Dogs more than seven years old have a slower recovery from a performance than younger dogs. Due to a decreasing number of hormones in the aging body, especially growth hormone, the dog's muscle mass will decrease. Furthermore, the dog's organs begin to degenerate. In 70 (!) percent of dogs over seven years old, renal function has decreased, and 30 (!) percent have damaged heart valves. Damaged organs are partly a consequence of the aging process, in which waste products accumulate in cells, resulting in a decline of cell quality. In addition, small inflammation processes in the organs, especially in the kidneys and heart valves, begin to cause long-term damage. A slipped disc in older dogs is often the result of degeneration of an organ: the quality of the wall of the disc decreases, which means the nucleus can move and press on the nerve or spinal marrow.

Another significant problem in dogs as they age is arthrosis, or osteoarthritis. During aging, the quality of joint cartilage decreases. This means cartilage doesn't hold water as well, so it becomes damaged through continued use of the joint. This damage results in inflammation: the beginning of arthrosis—pain and stiff joints, along with difficulty moving.

Compounding the natural results of aging is the intensive training explosive detection dogs have undergone over many years. The many micro-traumas to joints caused by this training compound the natural problems in aging joints. Dogs with even mild forms of hip or elbow dysplasia or shoulder problems such as osteochondritis dissecans can already show mild forms of arthrosis at the age of seven. The underlying lack of stability in the joints caused by these conditions, years of irritation through training and operational work, combined with decreasing muscle mass, mean the condition of the joints will decline faster in a detector dog than in other dogs that are not in operational service.

OVER TEN YEARS OLD

After about ten years of age, the degeneration that begins after age seven happens faster. In addition, several other organs at this age begin to fail. Geriatric cataracts and the quality of the retina may cause a dog's sight to decline. Hearing also decreases due to ossification of the auditory ossicles. As a result, a dog may respond less well or not at all to given commands.

Delaying the Aging Process

Many handlers want to know if there are ways to delay the effects of aging in their dogs. Happily, the answer is yes, there are many things you can do.

First, choose special nutrition designed for senior dogs.

Second, help prevent the development of arthrosis by taking care of your dog's joints. A thin lubricant called *synovial fluid* is secreted by joint membranes. This fluid helps keep the joint cartilage healthy and drains away waste products. The more the synovial fluid is refreshed, the better the maintenance of the cartilage and the prevention of micro-traumas. For training or operational service, this means that before starting to work, the joints, and especially the synovia, have to be activated. This is one more reason not to skip the warm-up! In addition, the recovery of the joints and the quality of the cartilage can be developed in training activities that require a minimum of load and a maximum of joint movement, such as swimming and/or walking beside a bike.

Both swimming and walking beside a bike not only refresh the synovia, they also encourage the third way of preventing problems due to aging: the buildup and maintenance of muscle mass. Specific training to increase muscle mass includes interval training consisting of short sprints alternating with rest. This form of activity develops anaerobic energy metabolism in the muscles. The best place to do sprint training (e.g., running after a ball) is on sandy soil, because there the load on the joints is minimal and every take-off requires a lot of power. Such training can be intensified by running the dog uphill and downhill on sandy soil. This interval training can, of course, only take place after a correct warm-up and always has to be finished with a good cool-down to shorten the muscles' recovery period.

In an aging dog, this sort of maintenance training has to take place more often. Our recommended guideline is to do maintenance training twice for every one normal training session or operational task. Such a training regimen can definitely help limit degeneration of the joints and decrease of the muscle mass.

SUPPLEMENTS

Some older dogs may develop mineral or vitamin deficiencies that can be remedied by simple, inexpensive dietary supplements. However, using nutritional supplements is controversial. Some people swear by the use of certain substances, while others attach no credence to them. From a scientific view, many supplements are useless or even dangerous, although a couple can provide some benefits. Discuss any sort of supplements with your vet before giving them to your dog.

L-CARNITINE

L-carnitine stimulates body cells to burn fat, and its use in healthy dogs leads to an increase in muscle mass and more efficient energy consumption. This substance is often found in diet food for ill and convalescent animals and is also sold as a separate food supplement. Some research suggests that working dogs can benefit from supplements of L-carnitine (see Grandjean et al., 1993).

Side-effects of oral L-carnitine supplements may include nausea, vomiting, abdominal cramps, loose stool, diarrhea, and increased body odor. Always provide it to your dog with food to decrease the gastrointestinal side-effects.

GLUCOSAMINE
Glucosamine is a supplement that delivers glycosaminoglycan, a substance that naturally occurs in many body tissues, including the blood, the joints, and the mucus membrane of various organs. Gluosamine supplements are believed to help maintain and repair cartilage, along with chondratin, which helps cartilage retain water. Many people with arthritis and other joint problems take glucosamine, and some give supplements to dogs with joint problems. The effectiveness of these products is somewhat in doubt—they have never been proven to prevent arthritis. Side-effects are uncommon, but can include fatigue, excessive thirst and urination, and diabetes.

MELOXICAM
A 2007 study investigated the different treatments of osteoarthritis in dogs and concluded that meloxicam—a non-steroidal anti-inflammatory drug (NSAID)—provides a clinically sound treatment of osteoarthritis in dogs. Research suggests meloxicam may be the best treatment for pain and inflammation resulting from arthritis. Discuss this treatment with your vet if you think your dog requires it.

Decertification

When do you need to decertify a dog, removing it from operational service? This can be a difficult decision for the handler. A dog's health usually fails gradually, and it can be difficult to see when a dog's performance is no longer acceptable. Signs that it might be time to retire a dog from operational service include the following:

- After every training session or operational service, the dog walks with a slight limp.
- Two or three days after training or operational service, the dog is still sulky and stiff.
- Without medication (analgesic, inflammation inhibitor), the dog can't function in a normal way.
- The dog is often startled by unexpected or loud noises, or by strange objects in a familiar situation.

A dog's degeneration due to age cannot be stopped, but it can be delayed through modifications in operational service and training, a suitable diet, and nutritional supplements. The goal of the handler and staff should be to continue the dog's useful life for as long as possible. Although the mean age of death/euthanasia of all dogs (service and non-service) averages 8.7 years, many service dogs continue to work very well until they are 12 or 14 years old.

RETIREMENT

The decision to decertify a dog from operational life is not easy. But if the dog suffers from each training or operation, removing it from service is the most ethical choice. If the dog lives as a pet following retirement, it may revive and live a good life for several years.

Continue to train your decertified dog, although in an easy, relaxed way. In particular, let the dog practice its specialty every now and then: let it search for explosives, firearms, or cartridge cases or do obedience exercises—whatever activities it enjoys most.

Returning the older dog to the training school to act as an aid for new students is another method of increasing the dog's useful life. The dog can be used by successive classes of students and can be rested when medical problems erupt. A decertified explosive detector dog can also be used to give public demonstrations of detector dog work.

Figure 9.6 Three important EOD elements: human, dog, and robot.

Never completely stop training your dog. Every dog has an occupational drive, and a working dog's drive is higher than most. However old it may be, the dog still wants to make itself useful, and with that feels like a valuable member of the dog–handler community. Therefore, give your dog the opportunity to show you its specialties until its dying day. Your partner, of course, deserves that!

10

First Aid

Working with explosives is a highly dangerous occupation, both for humans and animals. Although naturally the profession calls for a high attention to safety at all times, you may be called upon to assist another person or a dog in an emergency. This chapter has a brief introduction to some of the first aid knowledge and skills you might need to employ during training or in the field. These guidelines are only a starting point. You are advised to ensure your training in first aid and life-saving methods is as up to date as possible. Always carry a first aid kit with you, bring contact information for your dog's vet, and find out the location of the nearest medical and veterinary care in any deployment situation. Make finding this information part of your preparations for deployment so you are ready in the case of emergency.

First Aid for Dogs

IMMEDIATE ACTION FOR INGESTED EXPLOSIVES
If your dog swallows, licks, or otherwise comes in direct contact with explosive substances, you need to act quickly. Even one lick can cause problems because the mouth has many veins

directly beneath the skin. Toxins can easily can get through the skin of the mouth into the veins and from there to the rest of the body through the bloodstream. Ingested explosives generally cause vomiting, diarrhea, bluish gums, convulsions, and difficulty breathing.

Figure 10.1 If your dog swallows, licks, or otherwise comes in direct contact with explosive substances, you need to act quickly.

Figure 10.2 Toxins can easily move through the skin of the mouth into the veins and bloodstream.

First aid—UNLESS the dog has ingested a caustic substance (see page 247 for how to deal with such toxins)—is to immediately induce vomiting. Do not let the dog drink: doing so may dilute the substances so they are more easily absorbed by the body.

Smokeless powders without nitroglycerin are non-toxic. After inducing vomiting, all other treatment can be given by a vet.

Smokeless powders with nitroglycerin, TNT, and dynamite are all nitrate poisons. After vomiting, the dog must be treated with large amounts of activated charcoal. The treatment after this must be carried out by a veterinarian, who will likely administer methylene and prescribe a diet high in calcium and vitamins A and D.

C-4 explosives cause hyperactivity in dogs; in addition to the treatment described above for nitrate poisons, the dog may also require a valium injection.

INDUCING VOMITING WITH APOMORPHINE

The best and fastest way to get a dog to vomit is to administer an injection of apomorphine. This injection can be given into a vein or a muscle.

INTRAVENOUS INJECTION

- Administer 0.03–0.04 milligrams per 2.2 pounds (1 kg) of your dog's body weight.
- Onset of action is 1 to 4 minutes.

INTRAMUSCULAR INJECTION

- Administer 0.04–0.08 milligrams per 2.2 pounds (1 kg) of your dog's body weight.
- Onset of action is usually 5 to 20 minutes.

After receiving an injection of apomorphine into the bloodstream, dogs will vomit about 75 percent of the stomach's contents. If for some reason the recommended dosage does not provide the desired result, do not administer apomorphine again because you might depress your dog's central nervous system.

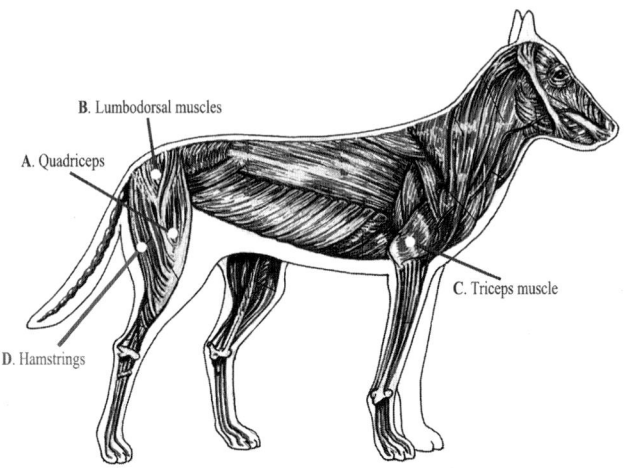

Figure 10.3 The musculature of the dog. Appropriate places for intramuscular injections are (A) the quadriceps (the muscle on the front of the thigh, (B) the lumbodorsal muscles (the muscles on each side of the lumbar spine, (C) the triceps muscle (behind the humerus in the front leg. If you choose to inject medication into the lumbodorsal muscles, always inject away from the spine. Do not inject medication into the hamstrings (D, the muscles at the back of the thigh) to avoid damaging the sciatic nerve, which runs through that area. Place the needle in the muscle and withdraw the plunger slightly to create negative pressure. If no blood is aspirated, give the injection by pushing the plunger gently and steadily. After withdrawing the needle, massage the muscle to help disperse the medicine.

Because the stomach is never completely emptied after emesis, and because some of the substance your dog ingested may have already made its way into the intestines, it is wise to follow up by giving your dog activated carbon, also called activated charcoal or activated coal, which binds many toxins, preventing them from being absorbed by the body. Take your dog to a veterinarian for control and observation. The vet will probably prescribe a laxative specifically formulated for dogs to encourage the body to eliminate any remaining toxin.

OTHER METHODS OF INDUCING VOMITING

If you don't have an apomorphine injection (in some countries, only vets can acquire apomorphine), you can put some table salt in the dog's mouth, on its tongue, or in its throat to induce vomiting. But be careful: there have been cases where dogs have died through administrations of salt.

Hydrogen peroxide (3%) is a safer alternative to table salt. Pour the liquid into your dog's mouth, giving 0.4 teaspoons (2 mL) per 2.2 pounds (1 kg) of body weight, up to 9 teaspoons (45 mL). You can find hydrogen peroxide at the drugstore. Be sure to heed the expiration date on the bottle. When hydrogen peroxide expires, it loses its ability to induce vomiting.

After ingesting hydrogen peroxide, 90 percent of dogs vomit, and, on average, 25 percent of the stomach's contents are regurgitated.

WHEN YOU SHOULD NOT INDUCE VOMITING

If a dog is unconscious, do not try to induce vomiting. Wrap the dog in a blanket and position it so its head is slightly lower than the rest of the body, and immediately contact your vet.

If your dog has ingested a caustic or acidic substance, such as drain cleaner or mineral spirits, or if the dog has ingested broken glass, do not induce vomiting. Vomiting may cause more damage as the caustic substance passes through the esophagus a second time. In these cases, it is best to neutralize the poison or sharp substance and to ease the pain in the throat and stomach.

NEUTRALIZING POISONS IN THE BODY

CAUSTIC SUBSTANCES

Never give milk after eating, licking, or drinking caustic chemicals. Many toxins dissolve very well in milk fat, which helps them enter the bloodstream more quickly. Immediately contact a veterinary clinic and tell them you are on your way; this will allow them to prepare for your arrival. The vet may need to pump the dog's stomach (called "gastric lavage") or administer activated charcoal to bind up any toxins in the stomach. If the dog begins to tremor or convulse, bring it to a safe area where it won't injure itself.

NON-CAUSTIC SUBSTANCES

For non-caustic chemicals, give your dog milk or eggs, or a neutralizing agent containing magnesium. Give the latter at a dose of 1 teaspoon (5 mL) per 5.5 pounds (2.5 kg) of the dog's body weight. If you do not have time to calculate the exact amount, give it just a little to ease the pain. Usually, you will have to administer a neutralizing agent under duress.

TREATING SUBSTANCES IN THE EYES OR ON THE SKIN
If corrosive substances are in your dog's eyes or on its coat or skin, flush the affected area with a lot of water. Never use benzene, turpentine, paint thinner, white spirit, or other such products to remove diesel oil, tar, asphalt, dye, or similar substances from your dog's coat or other parts of his body. Such solvents dissolve the target substance into very small particles that can be absorbed by your dog's skin. After being absorbed, they can enter the bloodstream and cause severe damage, even death.

POISONS
If you suspect your dog has ingested something poisonous, a veterinarian should be consulted immediately. If possible, take a sample of the poison or its packaging with you to the vet. When the vet knows what poison the dog has taken, he or she will know which emergency procedures to apply. First aid can increase the chance of survival, but what to do depends on what the toxin is. Common poisons include the following:

- *Antifreeze:* Induce vomiting. Dogs find this liquid tasty and, if they get the chance, will drink a lot of it. Symptoms are disorientation, vomiting, and faintness.
- *Insecticides:* Induce vomiting. Common products are fly poison, pesticides, and organic organophosphates. Symptoms are excessive salivation, muscle tremors, convulsions, dizziness, vomiting, diarrhea, labored breathing, constricted pupils, fainting, and coma.
- *Rat poison:* Rat poison causes internal bleeding and is therefore extremely dangerous. Induce vomiting and immediately contact a veterinarian. Treatment, including vitamin K, is necessary as soon as possible.

Humans and the Health Dangers of Explosives

The health dangers for people who work with explosive substances depend on various factors, including the type and amount of the substance, as well as the period and manner of exposure. Explosives can be categorized into explosive compounds, powders, and pyrotechnic compositions. We will discuss the toxicity of each of these groups.

EXPLOSIVE COMPOUNDS

Explosive compounds are extremely toxic. Most compounds can be easily absorbed through the skin, which makes handling them very risky. Compounds can also be absorbed orally through insufficient hygiene, or they can be inhaled in vapors, mist, or dust particles. However, the chance of inhaling toxic vapors in harmful concentrations while searching for explosives is relatively small because most explosive substances have a high temperature threshold (more than 194°F or 90°C) before turning from a liquid or solid into a vapor.

Most explosives are nitrogen compounds based on benzene, including TNT (trinitrotoluene), picric acid, and tetryl. Related substances are nitroamines such as hexogen or T4 (RDX) and octogen (HMX). The reaction products released after an explosion or deflagration of nitrate compositions are mainly carbon dioxide, carbon monoxide, and various nitrate vapors, such as nitrogen oxide.

EFFECTS OF NITRO-COMPOUNDS ON THE BODY

Aromatic nitro-compounds cause the human body to create methemoglobin, which leads to methemoglobinemia, a blood disorder. A healthy body uses the hemoglobin in red blood cells to transport oxygen to cells throughout the body; methemoglobin prevents the hemoglobin from performing this function. Methemoglobinemia can lead to central cyanosis (a bluish tinge to the core, lips, and tongue), reduced consciousness, coma, and even death.

With acute nitro-compound poisoning, the following symptoms occur: blue discoloration of the nails (usually first), then skin and lips, nose tip, and the earlobes. In serious cases, all skin can turn blue. Complaints could include headache, dizziness, fatigue, shortness of breath, and quickened heartbeat. A high dose can lead to coma or death.

Not all nitro-compounds are strong enough to cause methemoglobinemia. TNT is fairly weak, for example, although in combination with alcohol, the effects can be strengthened. In practical terms, this means that workers exposed to TNT who have a drink after work increase metheomoglobin creation in their bodies.

EFFECTS OF LONG-TERM EXPOSURE TO NITRO-COMPOUNDS

- Damage to the liver (caused by TNT)
- Damage to the central nervous system (caused by RDX)
- Anemia: shortage of red blood corpuscles (caused by TNT)
- Dermatitis, eczema, and yellow discoloration of the skin (TNT as an irritant and tetryl causing allergic reactions and irritations)

POWDERS

Nitrocellulose and nitroglycerin are in many types of smokeless powder. Pentrite is often used as a main charge or initiation charge.

All powdered explosive substances are toxic—vapors can penetrate the body through the respiratory system; nitroglycerin can also be absorbed through the skin. The reaction products freed during burning (nitrate vapors, carbon monoxide, and carbon dioxide) are the same as from explosive compounds. The most immediate effect of exposure to explosive powders is a widening of the vascular system.

SYMPTOMS OF EXPOSURE TO POWDERED EXPLOSIVES

- Decreased blood pressure
- Heavy, throbbing headache
- Nausea
- Heart palpitations
- Stomachache and vomiting

- Reduced oxygen intake by the blood (from nitroglycerin)
- Dermatitis (from pentrite)

Long-term exposure (several days) can cause acclimatization to the substance. This can then lead to withdrawal symptoms when no longer exposed. After long-term exposure to large quantities, victims can die of heart failure. Death can even occur more than 48 hours after the last exposure. In addition, even after a long period with no exposure, a subsequent exposure could lead to heart failure. That's why it's advisable that people with cardiac problems do not work with explosive powders. Drinking alcohol will also increase health risks when working with powders.

PYROTECHNIC COMPOSITIONS

Pyrotechnic compositions used for aesthetic and entertainment purposes (fireworks) are constructions of cardboard, paper, plastic, and metal containing a low explosive (LE) and/or flammable mixture of chemicals that create effects such as light, sound, smoke, or movement. All pyrotechnic compositions—both fireworks and military—include a variety of chemicals that can cause irritation to the eyes, skin, and respiratory system. Avoid touching or inhaling these substances or their reaction products. If exposure occurs, seek medical attention.

COMMON SUBSTANCES USED IN FIREWORKS
- Materials added for coloration: sodium: yellow; potassium: red/violet; barium: white or green (depending on the composition); strontium: deep red; calcium: brick-red or yellow (depending on the composition); copper: green/blue; or magnesium: white
- Chlorates and perchlorates
- Aluminum, magnesium, and zinc
- Lead and barium
- Black powder (gunpowder)
- Hexachlorobenzene
- Mercury

Figure 10.4 Bodo, a patrol and explosives detection dog, leads US soldiers in Afghanistan.

MILITARY PYROTECHNICS

Military pyrotechnic compositions are used to make smoke, light, tear gas, and detonation simulations (such as a flashbang, also known as a stun grenade or sound bomb).

SMOKE GRENADES

Smoke grenades are bombs that give off thick smoke when they explode. They are used to make a smoke screen or to mark a position for military tactical operations and smoke tests, but also for non-military purposes such as sports and games like airsoft, paintball, and tactical shooting. Smoke grenades are manufactured with a variety of chemicals that can be harmful to human health.

HEXACHLOROETHANE (HCE)

HCE smoke grenades ("HC smoke") are made with roughly equal parts HCE and zinc oxide and approximately 6 percent granular aluminum. HCE and HC smoke are irritating to the eyes, mucus membranes, and respiratory system. They can also cause acute and chronic problems for the nervous system. Symptoms for acute cases include nausea, vomiting, transpiration, headache, and dizziness. Chronic symptoms after months or years of exposure include fatigue, sleeplessness, depression, and slowed (decreased) awareness.

Long-term exposure will also cause dermatitis (skin disease) and damage to the kidneys and liver.

ZINC OXIDE

Zinc oxide is not that toxic, but inhaling zinc oxide powder can result in metal fume fever. Zinc mixed with zinc oxide and HCE produces zinc-chloride, which absorbs moisture to create a whitish-gray smoke. Zinc-chloride is very toxic and caustic to skin, eyes, and the respiratory system. It can cause lung edema and death.

High safety standards are required when handling munitions containing zinc-chloride. A frequent mistake is using the substances in small rooms, which allows the concentration in the air to get too high, causing acute symptoms and death.

PHOSPHOR

Phosphor is a yellowish waxy substance that is insoluble in water and spontaneously combustible when exposed to oxygen. It is often used in combination with explosives such as smoke shells and hand grenades. These grenades have a central filling of explosives surrounded by phosphor. Detonation causes the phosphor to spread over a large area. Reacting with the oxygen in the air, phosphor generates a white smoke (phosphorpentoxide). This vapor is caustic to the nose, throat, and eyes, potentially causing serious damage to the latter. Phosphorpentoxide combined with the moisture of the lungs produces phosphoric acid. Phosphoric acid etches blisters into the lung tissue, damaging them permanently.

Burning, white smoke and a characteristic smell are indications of phosphor. Serious burns can occur through skin contact, with deep wounds that heal poorly. The wounds burn as long as they have contact with oxygen and stop only when the material is burnt up completely or the wound is cut off from the oxygen supply.

White phosphor is sometimes used in smoke bombs and is extremely poisonous. Phosphor absorption can damage the liver and kidneys, and it can cause skin diseases such as dermatitis and eczema. Phosphor also kills off bone tissue, which makes bones porous and easily breakable. The jawbone and teeth are especially susceptible to damage, so people working with phosphor should keep their teeth in good condition. After having a tooth pulled, individuals should wait two months before working with phosphor.

Red phosphor is not dangerous, but it may contain remnants of white phosphor. The reaction products of white and red phosphor (smoke) are caustic to the eyes and the respiratory system; inhalation can cause pulmonary edema and death.

Figure 10.5 If a dog shows interest in an area and begins to walk forward and back, it probably hasn't found the right place and is just trying to get oriented.

Figure 10.6 If a dog tries to alert by sitting or lying down but immediately stands up and searches the spot again, it is showing that it is not sure about the smell and hesitates to respond. This dog in training seems certain about its find.

Figure 10.7 This is a correct alert after smelling an explosive substance.

TEAR GAS COMPOSITIONS

Chloracetophenone or its substitute, phenacyl chloride, was historically used in a riot control agent called CN gas. CN gas is the main component of Mace. The CN tear agent is now known to be carcinogenic and for that reason has been banned from use by NATO. A safer product is chlorobenzylidene malononitrile, which is the main component CS gas, a tear gas often used today. CS gas causes severe reactions, but is not toxic. Concentration should not exceed 5 mg/m^3. Exposure causes a burning sensation and tearing of the eyes so severe that people cannot keep their eyes open. Exposure also causes a burning irritation of the nose, mouth, and throat mucus membranes, resulting in coughing, nasal discharge, disorientation, and difficulty breathing. Skin irritations are also possible. The reactions or symptoms disappear roughly 30 minutes after the last exposure. Although CS gas can be absorbed through the skin, it must be delivered as a vapor or smoke to affect the respiratory system and eyes.

Work Safe: First Aid for Handlers

Exposure to all toxic explosive substances should, of course, be avoided.

BASIC SAFETY PRECAUTIONS

- After work and before eating, drinking, or smoking, wash your hands.
- Use personal safety equipment, such as gloves and protective glasses.
- Wear service clothing; wash clothing once a week in a separate load.
- When (regularly) exposed to phosphor, take care of your teeth.
- People with cardiac problems should not work with pentrite or powders.

DEALING WITH EXPOSURE TO TOXIC SUBSTANCES

When you encounter someone who has been exposed to toxic substances in unacceptable levels, deal with the situation immediately. First assess any continuing dangers of exposure, especially for yourself. After assessing the situation and determining what happened to the victim, take measures to get expert advice and keep the victim calm. Help the victim on location if you can; if needed, transport the individual out of the danger zone into the fresh air.

Poisons can be solid, liquid, gas, or vapor, and toxic substances can penetrate the body in many ways: through the gastric system, the respiratory system, or absorption through the skin.

Acute poisoning occurs when the victim absorbs relatively large quantities of a toxic substance in a short period. This can happen when toxic substances are freed suddenly, as during a fire, leakage, or explosion, and when particles are swallowed. Symptoms can appear immediately or after a couple of hours. When you suspect that someone has been poisoned, you must search for clues (such as packaging material) about what substance caused the poisoning.

This information is of vital importance for proper treatment. If the person vomits, take a sample with you for laboratory investigation.

INTAKE OF CAUSTIC EXPLOSIVE SUBSTANCES

Some explosives, such as picric acid, have caustic properties when absorbed into the body. After swallowing caustic substances, the victim can experience painful damage to the lips, mucus membranes, throat, esophagus, and stomach. The damage can be serious enough to burn a hole in the lining of the esophagus or stomach.

SYMPTOMS

- Intense burning sensation in the mouth, throat, esophagus, and/or stomach
- Tickling cough
- Pain when sighing
- Shortness of breath

TREATMENT

- Let the victim immediately drink two glasses of water to dilute the poison (children should drink one half up to one glass of water).
- Do not encourage the victim to vomit: the caustic substance would again contact damaged tissue, causing more damage.
- Bring the victim to a physician or hospital as quickly as possible.
- Find out what substance caused the poisoning and take this information with you to the physician.

INTAKE OF NON-CAUSTIC SUBSTANCES

Try to get the victim to vomit; this will help lessen the degree of poisoning. The victim can use his or her own fingers to facilitate vomiting. To do this, the pointing and middle fingers should be forced as far into the throat as possible and moved up and down. Except for possible panic reactions, there are usually no immediate effects after the intake of non-caustic poisonous substances.

SYMPTOMS

- Blue skin (lips, earlobes, fingernails, and the point of the nose)
- Headache
- Dizziness
- Fatigue
- Shortness of breath
- Increased heartbeat

Note: Victims usually know they have swallowed something.

TREATMENT

- Encourage the victim to vomit.
- Do not let the victim drink; this causes the substance to be absorbed faster.
- Bring the victim to a physician or hospital as quickly as possible.
- Find out what substance caused the poisoning (if necessary, take some of the victim's vomit with you), and give the information to the treating physician.

INHALED TOXIC GASES OR VAPORS OF EXPLOSIVES

People exposed to toxic gases should immediately visit a physician. Sometimes symptoms don't show up for a couple hours after exposure; don't wait for symptoms to appear. Victims with asthma or other lung diseases will have more intense symptoms.

Gases and vapors that work after absorption in the blood obstruct the transport of oxygen and/or damage body cells (e.g., carbon monoxide). Symptoms for this kind of poisoning include loss of consciousness, nausea, and throbbing headache.

Exposure to some gases produces symptoms immediately; others take a couple of hours. Gases that take immediate effect include tear gas and smoke compositions.

> **Victims who have inhaled irritating gases should be kept as calm as possible so their oxygen consumption is kept as low as possible.**

SYMPTOMS
- Tickling cough
- Pain when sighing
- Shortness of breath
- Shivering
- Tiredness
- Fever

TREATMENT
- Immediately bring the victim outside into fresh air.
- Take care not to inhale any of the toxic gas yourself.
- Sometimes expert assistance (e.g., firefighters) is needed to remove the victim from the danger zone.
- If the victim is conscious, a sitting position is often the most comfortable.
- All victims of toxic gas inhalation should be kept as calm as possible.
- Smoking is forbidden.
- Unconscious victims should be kept in the stable side position (keeping the respiratory system clear of obstacles).
- If respiratory failure occurs, begin emergency revival (mouth-to-mouth resuscitation), as long as there is no danger to you, the rescuer.
- Always get expert advice as quickly as possible, even if no symptoms are yet apparent.

ABSORPTION THROUGH THE SKIN

Some toxic substances can penetrate the skin. One example is nitroglycerin, used in powders and mercury fulminate. Substances that are absorbed through the skin can cause muscle paralysis and serious respiratory complications.

SYMPTOMS
- Muscle paralysis
- Trouble breathing

TREATMENT

- Rescuers should always wear gloves.
- Remove any contaminated clothing without endangering yourself.
- Save the contaminated clothing in a plastic bag for later investigation.
- Rinse the skin with flowing water for at least 30 minutes. Rinsing will often be continued by the medics.
- After rinsing, cover chemical burns with sterile bandages.
- Visit a hospital as soon as possible.

PHOSPHOR ON THE SKIN

Indications that your skin has come into contact with white phosphor include feeling a burning sensation, seeing white smoke, and smelling a peculiar smell. Do not use copper sulfate (also called cupric sulfate) on the wounds. In the past it was used as a compress (bandage) or in liquid form to treat contact with phosphor. However, because of its high toxicity, copper sulfate is no longer used.

SYMPTOMS

- Tickling cough
- Shortness of breath or labored breathing
- Burning, watering eyes
- Deep burns (wounds) in the skin, possibly remnants of phosphor that will keep burning

TREATMENT

- Bring the victim outside into the fresh air.
- Take care not to inhale phosphor vapors yourself.
- Cover the wound with bandages soaked with water, or keep the body part underwater, so that no oxygen from the air can get to the wound.
- Bring the victim to a physician or hospital as quickly as possible.

EYE DAMAGE

After toxic explosive substances get in the eyes, sight is usually impaired, and victims often react with panic. Try to calm victims down, talk to them about the steps to be taken. Treatment should begin by rinsing the eyes to flush out the toxic substance from the ocular area.

SYMPTOMS
- Fear or panic
- Pain in one or both eyes
- Redness of the eyes
- Watering or slatted eyes
- Decreased eyesight

TREATMENT
- Immediately rinse with clean water:
  1. Have the victim lie down on his back.
  2. Keep the eye open with your fingers.
  3. Rinse the eye for 30 minutes or more with gently flowing water. Use lukewarm water if possible. Often the medic will continue rinsing.
- Consult a hospital or eye doctor as quickly as possible.

OCULAR INJURY BY A FLASH FIRE

During an explosion or deflagration of explosives, the eyes could be damaged by a flash fire. In this case, immediately try to cool the eyes as much as possible.

SYMPTOMS
- Fear or panic
- Pain in one or both eyes
- Redness of the eyes
- Watering eyes or eyes closed to slits
- Decreased sight

TREATMENT
- Immediately cool with water:
  1. Help the victim lie down on his back.
  2. Keep the eye open.
  3. Rinse the eye for 10 minutes with gently flowing cool or lukewarm water.
- Consult a hospital or eye doctor as quickly as possible.

CHRONIC POISONING

Chronic poisoning happens when someone has had frequent exposure to small amounts of a toxic substance over a long period. As in all cases of poisoning, symptoms will be worse when the quantities absorbed are larger. Very treacherous are the chronic effects caused by frequent short exposures to highly toxic explosive substances.

It is important to get the victim to a medical facility as soon as possible, even before symptoms appear. Often you might suspect poisoning, but will not be sure what toxic explosive caused it.

SYMPTOMS
- Headache
- Nausea
- Lack of appetite
- Insomnia
- Loss of concentration and learning capabilities
- Early dementia
- Dermatitis
- Anemia (shortage of red blood cells)
- Liver complaints
- Kidney complaints
- Cancer (various explosives are suspected to be carcinogenic)
- Necrosis (bone mortification because of contact with phosphor)

- Brain and nerve disorders
- Cardiac and vascular diseases

TREATMENT
- Search for clues about which substance caused the poisoning, and take this information to the physician treating the victim.

Physical Overload in Your Dog

The demands of training and operational service often strain K9s to the limit. Even with well-trained, healthy dogs, injuries can happen because of the demanding nature of the work.

Explosive detector dogs, for example, often have to work on slippery floors, suddenly change direction, and move in a very bowed or contorted position when searching under chairs and other objects. Their muscles, joints, ligaments, and tendons are often loaded to the maximum. Even dogs in optimal mental and physical condition are in danger of overload. But unfortunately, not all dogs are so healthy. Locomotion problems such as hip or elbow dysplasia, as well as problems with the knee, shoulder, or back, even in their slightest forms, can cause problems in heavy training and operational work.

> Due to the intensity required of them, after searching for about 20 minutes, detector dogs need at least half an hour of rest.

LOCOMOTION INJURIES

Although explosive detector dogs can experience internal diseases such as cardiovascular or metabolic disorders, most injuries are locomotion problems. For example, vertebral fractures or dislocations can result from falls or collisions. Fortunately, these injuries are rare, but when they do happen, they are usually quite serious. Whether a vertebral fracture can be successfully treated or not will depend on whether the spinal marrow is damaged and the available surgical knowledge. If the spinal marrow is cut through or damaged in a way that there are insufficient nerve reactions, there can be no hope for a cure. But if the nervous system is intact, most of the time the dog can be cured, although it will not be able to continue in operational service.

Falls or collisions can also result in open and closed fractures, especially those of the long bones of the forearm (radius and ulna) and lower thigh (tibia and fibula), but also at the wrist and hock (carpus and tarsus), and the front and back pasterns (metacarpus and metatarsus). Depending on the location and extensiveness of the injury, fractures can heal completely or result in permanent locomotion problems.

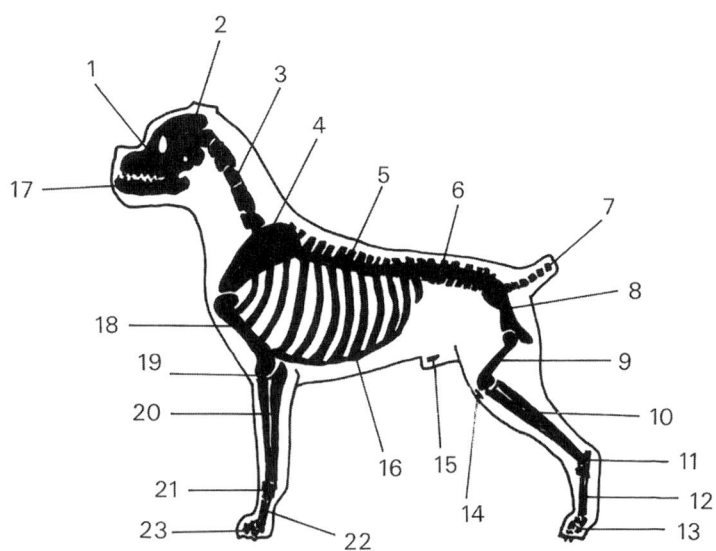

Figure 10.8 The dog's skeleton.

1. Os frontale
2. Os occipitale
3. Cervical vertebrae
4. Scapula without clavicle
5. Thoracic vertebrae
6. Lumbar vertebrae
7. Coccygeal vertebrae
8. Pelvis
9. Femur
10. Tibia and fibula
11. Tarsus with calcaneus
12. Metatarsus
13. Pastern
14. Knee joint with patella
15. Os penis
16. Chest with sternum and ribs
17. Lower jaw (mandible)
18. Humerus
19. Elbow joint
20. Radius and ulna
21. Carpus (wrist)
22. Metacarpus
23. Pastern

Toe fractures are often seen in dogs that run, suddenly turn, or jump (e.g., to catch and fetch balls) over frozen or hard soils, or while stumbling on uneven ground. When professionally treated, most of the time no permanent damage will occur.

OTHER INJURIES

While younger dogs may suffer broken bones from excessive demands on the skeleton, adult dogs tend to have more problem with tightness in the ligaments that stabilize the joints. Sprains, strains, and pulled or torn ligaments are common in adult or older dogs. Examples include torn ligaments of the wrist or hock joints and a torn cruciate ligament of the knee, both of which need to be taken seriously. Injuries to ligaments of the toes can lead to dislocations and can hamper mobility.

Torn tendons or muscles usually occur due to chronic overloading or by skipping warm-ups. With a partial or complete tear of the Achilles tendon, a dog cannot keep its heel angled, so it will walk on its complete pastern instead of the sole of the foot. Surgery and fixation of the affected leg for many weeks, followed by slow and careful rehabilitation, are the necessary treatments.

A tear in the tendon of the bicep near the shoulder of the dog usually begins slowly and gets worse over some weeks. This problem is not easy to diagnose and also needs surgery to correct.

Generally speaking, injuries that occur at the tendons of flexors (at the back and inside of the limbs) are more difficult to treat, need longer rehabilitation, and do not always have as good a prognosis as injuries at the tendons of extensors, which are mainly found at the front and outside of the limbs.

A non-painful, but disturbing contraction of the musculus gracilis in dogs is not always curable. This muscle on the inside of the thigh can gradually change into a shortened, fibrous cord without any elasticity. The dog gradually cannot bring its hind leg into a normal stride length forward, so it will move in short paces with a crouching gait in the hindquarters. Surgical removal of the shortened muscle will once again allow a normal gait, but there can be complications, such as reoccurring symptoms due to shortening of the muscles next to it.

To avoid injuries as much as possible, ensure a careful progression through various levels of training that takes the mental and physical development of the dog into account, doesn't overload the dog, avoids the possibility of injuries, and also promotes its lifelong powerful capability.

Other steps that help avoid injury include maintaining regular training, gently restarting training after a break, and phasing out training gradually before beginning a lengthy period (i.e., weeks) of total rest.

11

Explosives: Past and Present

A Brief History of Explosives

BLACK POWDER

Black powder (gunpowder) is the oldest known explosive mixture, with records showing its use as far back as the ninth century in China. It is made from a mixture of three components—potassium nitrate (a natural, solid source of nitrogen), sulfur, and charcoal. For about one thousand years, it was the only practical propellant. It was being used in fireworks and signals by the tenth century, but was soon used for weapons as well.

Between the tenth and twelfth centuries, the Chinese developed a "fire lance," a short-range proto-gun that channeled the explosive power of gunpowder through a cylinder—initially, a bamboo tube. Upon ignition, projectiles such as arrows or bits of metal would be forcefully ejected along with an impressive flame. In the twelfth and thirteenth centuries, gunpowder was introduced to Arab countries and then to Greece and other European countries.

SMOKELESS POWDERS

Black powder is still widely used today in pyrotechnic systems, mainly because of its great stability. However, for most other uses, including in various firearms, its use has been superceded by several varieties of smokeless powders developed at the end of the nineteenth century (ballistite, cordite, poudre B).

The smokeless powders offered many advantages over the use of black powder on the battlefield. For example, after firing, soldiers using smokeless powder could still see the enemy; those using black powder were engulfed in a cloud of black smoke. Similarly, the location of firing soldiers was not given away by a cloud of smoke. Smokeless powder also had more power than black powder, so bullets could travel farther. Lastly, combustion of black powder generates significant solid residue, which required soldiers to constantly clean their rifles, even in the middle of a battle. Smokeless powders did not require this time-consuming cleaning.

NEW EXPLOSIVES

Around 1800, interest in chemistry increased and new explosives were developed. In 1799, British scientist Edward Howard prepared mercury fulminate, a powerful explosive made by dissolving mercury in nitric acid, then adding ethanol. It was highly sensitive and, in small amounts, was used to initiate the explosion of other less sensitive explosives. However, mercury fulminate weakens as it ages and mercury—especially in times of war—was difficult to get, so lead azide (also highly explosive) largely replaced mercury fulminate. Both mercury fulminate and lead azide were used for many years in detonators, guns, and pistols. In the mid-nineteenth century, potassium perchlorate and other perchlorates were added to mercury fulminate and lead azide as primary or initiating explosives used to detonate other explosives.

In 1845, scientists discovered that by combining cotton with nitric acid, they could create a lightweight, but highly flammable material called nitrocellulose. The inventors soon recognized the military potential of their product and developed a form of nitrocellulose called *guncotton*. This material was used in many types of explosive devices because it produces a large charge with less smoke and heat than gunpowder.

Another advance in explosives occurred with the invention of nitroglycerin around the same time. Nitroglycerin was invented in 1846 by Ascanio Sobrero, an Italian chemist. The unstable liquid caused many deadly accidents until 1867, when Alfred Nobel invented dynamite as a way to use nitroglycerin more safely. Dynamite combined nitroglycerin with diatomaceous earth as a way to stabilize the explosive.

However, both nitroglycerin and guncotton had a problem: they were so sensitive that they sometimes detonated while still in the artillery barrel. Picric acid helped solve that problem. Although scientists had known about picric acid since 1742, it was not until 1871 that they realized it could be used as an explosive. In 1884, Eugène Turpin, a French chemist, found a method to use picric acid in grenades, blasting charges, and shells. After that, many countries used picric acid as a high explosive since it was able to withstand the shock of firing better than either nitroglycerin or guncotton.

Trinitrotoluene (TNT, trotyl) was first prepared in 1863 as a yellow dye. Its explosive properties were discovered in 1891 by German chemist Carl Häussermann. It quickly took over the role of picric acid as an explosive for blasting because it was safer to handle. In addition, whereas shells filled with picric acid tended to explode upon contact, shells filled with TNT could pierce metal armor before exploding, thereby doing much more damage. Today, the blasting abilities of TNT are used as a standard reference by which other explosives are compared, and TNT is still widely used as an explosive.

Today's Explosives

In World War II, three high explosives—tetryl, RDX, and PETN—came into use alongside the older explosives.

- *Tetryl* is the standard booster explosive used today. Booster explosives are used as a bridge between a relatively sensitive detonator explosive and an insensitive explosive charge that is high energy. Tetryl is sufficiently insensitive when it is compressed, and it can be initiated by a flame, by friction, by a shock, and by sparks. It burns quickly, is easier to detonate than TNT, and is about as sensitive as picric acid.

- *RDX* (hexogen) is, next to TNT, one of the most widely used high explosives today. It is often used in mixtures with other explosives and in detonators.
- *PETN* (pentrite) is one of the most powerful military explosives, similar to nitroglycerin. It can detonate at a speed of 4 miles per second (6,400 m/s). Pentrite is widely used in detonating cord, which is a flexible plastic tube that can link explosive charges set at some distance apart. The cord detonates so quickly that the explosives will seem to detonate at the same time.

All explosives have properties that make them more or less useful for certain purposes. For example, some explosives, such as TNT, are less sensitive to shock or friction and can therefore be handled relatively easily and safely. This makes them useful in civilian and some military operations.

Other explosives, such as nitroglycerin, are so sensitive that they can only be used in mixtures with other substances. Often different explosives are mixed to obtain certain properties. For example, a mixture of hexogen with TNT and aluminum, known as "torpex" (**torp**edo **ex**plosive), is used in torpedoes. Underwater, this mixture is 50 percent more potent than TNT alone.

Plastic explosives have become very common in military, civilian, and terrorist operations. Plastic explosives, in general, consist of one or more explosives mixed with oil and other substances until a kneadable mass is obtained. Semtex, a well-known plastic explosive manufactured in the Czech Republic, consists of pentrite, hexogen, paraffin oil, and rubber. Plastic explosives are very brisant: Semtex, for example, is about 30 percent stronger than TNT.

Explosives and Explosive Compositions

Following is a brief description of some of the more common explosives you should know about in your work. Although some have mainly historical uses, you may still encounter them in abandoned or unexploded ordnance.

KEY CHEMISTRY TERMS

HYGROSCOPIC
Substances that attract water vapor from the air and thus become lumpy or even completely liquefy are *hygroscopic*. Many chemicals, including explosive substances, can decompose by hygroscopic effects and become unusable. Hygroscopy is a key factor in the stability of an explosive.

NITRATION
Nitration is the chemical process of adding groups of atoms containing nitrogen to a compound. Nitration reactions create many common explosives, such as the conversion of guanidine to nitroguanidine and toluene to trinitrotoluene.

OXIDATION
An *oxidizer* or *oxidizing agent* is a substance that provides oxygen for chemical reactions in which oxygen atoms are added to another substance. Oxidation reactions are usually very *exothermic*, which means they give off heat. This heat is transferred to the surroundings and can cause fires to burn more fiercely or other materials to combust. An explosive oxidizer is a substance that provides oxygen that combines with fuels or other explosive ingredients to produce explosive energy. Examples include nitrates, chlorates, and perchlorates.

REDUCTION
When a substance is oxidized (takes on oxygen), something else must undergo the opposite reaction and be reduced. *Reducing agents* lose electrons and provide the fuel for oxidation to take place. Strong reducing agents, especially metals, can produce heat and gas. Some react even with water to produce flammable products. This means a fire produced from a strong reducing agent cannot be put out with water.

For example, pyrotechnic compositions include at least one oxidizing agent and one fuel. Typical oxidizing agents in pyrotechnics include nitrates, chlorates, perchlorates, peroxides, chromates, and permanganates. Other oxidizing agents often used in explosives are ammonium nitrate, ammonium perchlorate, and ammonium ditramide.

As fuel (the *reducing agent*), practically all combustible and highly flammable solid materials are used in pyrotechnics (e.g., metals, their alloys, and metal containing compounds). Typical metallic fuels include magnesium, magnesium-aluminum alloys, aluminum, calcium silicide, titanium, zirconium, iron, boron and silicon. Recently, nitrogen-rich compounds have become common as fuel for low-smoke and colorless pyrotechnics. Here hexamethylenetetramine, guanidine nitrate, nitroguanidine, dicyandiamide, and many tetrazolates play an important role.

ACETONE PEROXIDE

Other names: TATP (triacetone triperoxide), TCAP (tricyclic acetone peroxide or tricycloaceton peroxide), peroxyacetone

Raw materials: hydrogen peroxide, acetone, and concentrated sulfuric acid or hydrochloric acid

Properties: a white crytalized powder; smells like bleach

Uses: a primary high explosive used to initiate various industrial reactions; used to bleach flour

Stability: very unstable: heat, friction, impact, or static electricity can cause detonation

Detonation velocity: up to 3.3 miles per second (5,300 m/s)

Special attention: Acetone peroxide sublimates (changes from solid to gas) easily. This property makes it very dangerous to keep the substance in a screw cap jar: the agent can sublimate and precipitate in the jar so that screwing open the cap may lead to detonation.

ALUMINUM POWDER

Raw materials: powdered aluminum

Properties: silvery-white to gray powder

Uses: military equipment, explosives, and solid rocket fuel

Stability: explosive if mixed with bromine, chlorine, carbon tetrachloride, and many other substances, such as chlorinated hydrocarbons, iodine, cyano, hydrogen, carbon monoxide, and carbon dioxide

Special attention: a dust explosion is possible if the powder becomes mixed with air; aluminum powder reacts with water and alcohols and reacts violently with oxidants, strong acids, strong bases, and chlorinated hydrocarbons, causing fire and an explosion hazard

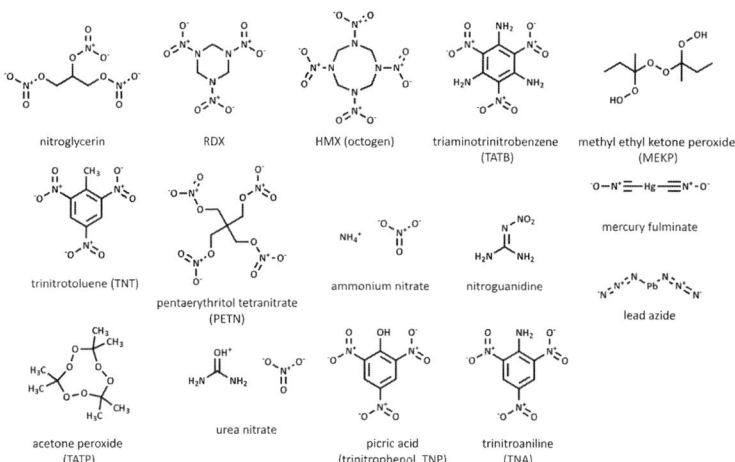

Figure 11.1 Chemical formulas of common explosive compounds.

AMATEX

Raw materials: 51% ammonium nitrate, 40% TNT, 9% RDX
Use: military explosive
Stability: highly stable
Detonation velocity: 4.2 miles per second (6,830 m/s)
Variants: Amatex 20, a pourable mixture that consists of 40% RDX, 40% TNT, and 20% ammonium nitrate

AMATOL

Name: combination of the words **am**monium and **tol**uene (a raw material of TNT)
Raw materials: TNT and ammonium nitrate
Properties: ranges from off-white to pale yellow or pink brown, depending on the mixture used; remains soft, even during long-term storage; creates a cloud of white or gray smoke after detonation
Use: military explosive used in bombs, grenades, and mines during both world wars; rarely encountered today except in abandoned or unexploded ammunition; a form encountered today is called ammonite, which is a less destructive form of amatol used in mining or engineering
Stability: is very hygroscopic, which decreases its explosive properties. To avoid moisture problems, amatol was usually covered with a thin layer of pure molten TNT or bitumens.
Detonation velocity: variable, depending on the mixture:
- 80:20 (very high efficiency; detonation velocity of 4.1 miles per second, 6,570 m/s)

- 60:40 (high efficiency)
- 50:50 (detonation velocity of 3.9 miles per second, 6,290 m/s)
- 20:80 (low efficiency; called ammonite)

Special attention: not stored in containers made from copper or brass, as this could lead to dangerous chemical reactions; often ignited with primary explosives such as powdered mercury fulminate

AMMONAL

Name: combination of the words **ammo**nium **n**itrate and **al**uminum
Raw materials: 72% ammonium nitrate, 25% aluminum powder, and 3% carbon
Uses: non-military (primarily mining) and military (especially in hand grenades and shells)
Stability: ammonium nitrate is highly hygroscopic, so humidity affects its effectiveness and storage
Detonation velocity: 2.7 miles per second (4,400 m/s)
Variants: T-ammonal is created when TNT is added to ammonal so the mixture is brought to explosion easier and faster, and also so its detonation velocity increases significantly; used for military purposes

AMMONIUM NITRATE

Other name: AN
Raw materials: found as a natural mineral, or made from ammonia and nitric acid
Uses: common fertilizer; used in combination with gasoline or with kerosene to create ANFO, which is the most popular industrial explosive in North America
Properties: solid white crystal; highly soluble in water
Detonation velocity: 1.6 miles per second (2,550 m/s)

AMMONIUM PERCHLORATE

Other name: AP
Raw materials: ammonia and perchloric acid
Properties: a colorless to white crystalline powder; readily soluble in water; creates self-sustained combustion when combined with fuel such as powdered aluminum
Use: solid fuel for model rockets, firework rockets, space rockets, and military missiles
Detonation velocity: 3.3 miles per second (5,300 m/s)
Special attention: heat or strong acids may lead to explosion

EXPLOSIVES: PAST AND PRESENT 275

Figure 11.2 Military anti-tank mine removal.

AMMONIUM PICRATE

Other names: Explosive D, Dunnite
Raw materials: picric acid and ammonia; chemically related to TNT
Uses: military explosive; was the first explosive used in an aerial bombing operation in military history; can be used to create TATB, a powerful, but stable explosive
Stability: highly stable
Detonation velocity: 4.1 miles per second (6,650 m/s)

ANFO

Name: acronym of **a**mmonium **n**itrate and **f**uel **o**il
Raw materials: 94% ammonium nitrate and 6% hydrocarbon such as diesel oil (or gasoline, kerosene, heating oil, or even a carbohydrate such as molasses or sugar)
Uses: the most popular industrial explosive in use today; also used in avalanche hazard testing. Because ammonium nitrate can be obtained relatively easily in large quantities as fertilizer, ANFO has been frequently used in war and terrorist attacks.
Stability: tertiary explosive (insensitive and difficult to explode); detonation requires a secondary explosive (dynamite, Tovex, pentolite) and an igniter
Detonation velocity: 3.3 miles per second (5,270 m/s)

Variants: mixing ANFO with aluminum powder increases its sensitivity and explosive energy, but this product is not often manufactured for cost reasons; ammonium nitrate and nitro methane (ANNM) is a type of ANFO described in its own section below

ANNM

Name: acronym of **a**mmonium **n**itrate and **n**itro **m**ethane
Raw materials: nitromethane and ammonium nitrate; is a type of ANFO
Stability: a secondary explosive; the dangerous and sensitive acetone peroxide is often used to ignite it
Detonation velocity: 3.9 miles per second (6,300 m/s)
Variant: KinePak (brand name), a two-part explosive
Special attention: for safety, the components of ANNM are usually stored and transported separately

> **Two-part explosives contain elements that are only explosive when mixed, so they are kept apart until ready to use. They are often used as civilian explosives because they are extra safe.**

ASTROLITE

Name: trade name for a family of two-part liquid explosives
Raw materials: ammonium nitrate and hydrazine rocket fuel
Variants: Astrolite G (most common): a mixture of ammonium nitrate and hydrazine in the weight ratio of 2:1; Astrolite A: a version of Astrolite G with the addition of aluminum powder, making it burn more rapidly and severely
Detonation velocity: Astrolite G: 5.3 miles per second (8,600 m/s); Astrolite A: 4.7 miles per second (7,600 m/s)

AZIDES

Name: group of chemical compounds with various industrial and scientific uses
Variants: lead azide is a shock-sensitive detonator that decomposes to lead and nitrogen; silver azide can detonate from exposure to UV light or impact; sodium azide was used in older airbags, although newer bags use less-sensitive explosives
Properties: lead azide (white to buff powder, not hygroscopic); silver azide (white solid); sodium azide (white salt, soluble in water, highly toxic)

Detonation velocity: lead azide: 2.9 miles per second (4,630 m/s); silver azide: 2.5 miles per second (4,000 m/s); sodium azide: about 2.5 miles per second (4,000 m/s)
Stability: heavy-metal azides are formed when solutions of sodium azide or hydrogen azide vapors come into contact with heavy metals or their salts. Heavy-metal azides can accumulate under certain circumstances, such as in metal pipelines and on the metal components of equipment such as waste pipes, and thus lead to violent explosions.
Special attention: heavy-metal azides are extremely sensitive; lead azide will explode from a drop as small as 6 inches (15 cm)

BALLISTITE

Raw materials: Alfred Nobel patented the formula for ballistite in 1887 as 45% nitroglycerin, 45% nitrocellulose, and 10% camphor (as a stabilizer). However, camphor tends to evaporate over time, leaving a potentially unstable mixture. Ballistite is still manufactured, but now the less volatile but chemically similar diphenylamine is used instead of camphor in the formula: 92% nitroglycerin, 7% nitrocellulose, and 1% diphenylamine.
Uses: the first high-energy smokeless powder for guns—replaced black powder; less-volatile mixture using diphenylamine still used as a solid rocket fuel
Detonation velocity: 5 miles per second (7,970 m/s)
Variants: cordite (58% nitroglycerin, 37% guncotton, and 5% petroleum jelly)—created by the British government in 1889

BARATOL

Raw materials: barium nitrate, 25–33% TNT, plus 1% paraffin
Properties: can be quite dense
Uses: used in early atomic weapons and the Mills bomb, a British hand grenade
Detonation velocity: approximately 3 miles per second (4,900 m/s)

BARIUM NITRATE

Raw materials: barium carbonate and nitric acid, or barium chloride and sodium nitrate
Properties: white/gray crystalline powder or needle-shaped crystals; soluble in water
Uses: various military applications, including thermite grenades and incendiary ammunition; pyrotechnic powders (flame is green if chlorine is present)
Special attention: metal powders can ignite spontaneously when mixed with barium nitrate

BLACK POWDER

Other names: gunpowder, BP, Poudre Noire, Poudre N
Raw materials: saltpeter (the mineral form of potassium nitrate), charcoal, and sulfur combined in the mass ratio of 75:15:10
Properties: a grainy black powder; a low explosive
Uses: the oldest known explosive mixture originating in the ninth century in China, but no longer used in firearms; today still widely used in pyrotechnic mixtures, mainly because of its great stability, so it will not easily ignite after an impact or bumping
Detonation velocity: varies depending on mixture; with 75% potassium nitrate, 19% charcoal, 6% sulfur: 1,969 feet per second (600 m/s)

CELLULOSE NITRATE: *SEE* NITROCELLULOSE.

COMPOSITION A

Name: in the 1940s, the formula "Composition <letter>" was used to name various explosives made with RDX (e.g., Composition A, B, and C)
Raw materials: RDX and wax
Uses: military explosive in land mines and 2.75 and 5 inch (7 and 12.7 cm) rockets
Stability: non-hygroscopic with good storage properties
Detonation velocity: Composition A-3: approximately 5.1 miles per second (8,230 m/s) ; Composition A-5: 5.3 miles per second (8,470 m/s)
Variants: Composition A-3 is a white or buff, wax-coated, granular explosive, consisting of 91% RDX and 9% desensitizing wax. It is not melted or cast, but is instead pressed into projectiles. It is more brisant and powerful than TNT. Composition A-5 consists of 98% RDX and 2% stearic acid.

COMPOSITION B

Other name: Comp B, cyclotol B
Raw materials: 63% RDX, 36% TNT, and 1% wax
Use: military explosive in widespread use from the beginning of World War II until the early 1950s; the standard explosive for detonators in landmines, rockets, hand grenades and artillery; today largely replaced by less sensitive explosives, such as C-4
Detonation velocity: approximately 4.9 miles per second (7,840 m/s)
Variant: Cyclotol B (contains a higher percentage of RDX)

COMPOSITION C-3

Other name: C-3

Raw materials: 77% RDX, 4% TNT, 3% tetryl, 5% 2-nitrotoluene, and 10% 2,4-dinitrotoluene; the latter two substances are oily, ensuring the plasticity of the explosive, which makes it malleable
Properties: a yellow putty
Use: military plastic explosive
Stability: cannot withstand low temperatures, so has largely been replaced today by C-4
Detonation velocity: about 4.7 miles per second (7,600 m/s)

COMPOSITION C-4

Other names: C-4, PE-4 (British version)
Raw materials: different manufacturers use different formulas. The US army uses 90% RDX, 8% polyisobutylene, and 2% dioctyl adipate (1990); the polyisobutylene is a polymer that makes the explosive malleable
Properties: dirty white to brown solid or putty; smells like motor oil; can easily be molded into any desired shape to change the direction of the resulting explosion
Use: used in blasting, especially for military demolitions
Stability: very stable; detonation occurs only with a combination of high temperatures and a shock; commonly set off by firing a detonator into it
Detonation velocity: approximately 5 miles per second (8,092 m/s)
Special attention: C-4 has been used in improvised explosive devices; homemade C-4 is the subject of a chapter in the original edition of *The Anarchist Cookbook*

COMPOSITION H6

Raw materials: 44.0% RDX and nitrocellulose, 29.5% TNT, 21.0% powdered aluminum, 5.0% paraffin wax, and 0.5% calcium chloride
Properties: castable
Use: underwater munitions
Detonation velocity: approximately 4.6 miles per second (7,367 m/s)

CORDITE

Raw materials: 58% nitroglycerin, 37% nitrocellulose, and 5% petroleum jelly
Properties: spaghetti-like rods
Use: a smokeless propellant explosive
Variants: the combustion tempo can be changed by adjusting the surface area of the cordite bars; thin rods (used in small arms) have a relatively high combustion rate, while thicker rods (used in weapons with a long barrel) burn more slowly

CYCLONITE: *SEE* RDX.

CYCLOTOL B: *SEE* COMPOSITION B.

DADNE: AN EXPERIMENTAL, INSENSITIVE HIGH EXPLOSIVE. *SEE* TATB.

DBX

Name: abbreviation of **d**epth **b**omb explosive
Raw materials: 21% RDX, 21% ammonium nitrate, 40% TNT, and 18% powdered aluminum
Properties: gray solid; castable
Use: military explosive primarily used in depth charges
Stability: slightly hygroscopic
Detonation velocity: approximately 4.1 miles per second (6,630 m/s)

DDNP

Name: diazodinitrophenol
Raw materials: nitric acid and picramic acid
Properties: yellow-brown crystallized powder; insoluble in water, but soluble in acetic acid, acetone, and non-polar solvents
Uses: dyes and explosives
Detonation velocity: approximately 4.1 miles per second (6,600 m/s)
Special attention: detonates with a powerful impact or if heated to 356°F (180°C); cannot detonate underwater

DEMOLUX

Raw materials: RDX and EGDN; all ingredients are explosive (i.e., the explosive is free from non-explosive binding agents)
Properties: kneadable, can hold its shape, good adhesive strength
Use: high explosive useful in small spaces when an especially strong explosive force is required (e.g., in steel structures)
Detonation velocity: approximately 4.9 miles per second (7,900 m/s)

DMDNB AND DMNB: A TAGGANT. *SEE* SEMTEX, AND PAGE 71.

DNT

Names: 2-4-dinonitrotoluene, dinitrotoluene, dinitro
Raw materials: toluene and nitric and sulfuric acids; created when manufacturing TNT

Properties: pale yellow crystalline solid
Uses: munitions; mining industry
Variants: 2,4-DNT and 2,6-DNT

DUNNITE: *SEE* AMMONIUM PICRATE.

DYNAMITE

Name: from the Greek word *dýnamis* (power)
Raw materials: nitroglycerin (NG) with diatomaceous earth as absorbent
Properties: orange bars, approximately 1 inch (2.5 cm) in diameter and 8 inches (20 cm) long; waterproof (so can be used for underwater explosions); makes its own oxygen for the explosion
Uses: mining, construction, demolition; sometimes used as initiator for ANFO
Stability: moderately sensitive to shock; dangerous at temperatures higher than 95°F (35°C) because the NG sweats out crystals, making it more shock, friction, and temperature sensitive
Detonation velocity: original (Alfred Nobel's) formula: 75% NG and 23% diatomaceous earth: approximately 4.5 miles per second (7,200 m/s); modern formulas differ from product to product: Dynomix at 2.4 miles per second (3,900 m/s), Unimax at 3.7 miles per second (6,000 m/s)
Special attention: old dynamite is dangerous; the maximum storage time is one year under good storage conditions

EDNA

Other names: Haleite, Explosive H
Raw materials: ethylenedinitramine
Use: powerful military explosive used in World War II
Stability: sensitive; chemically unstable
Detonation velocity: 4.7 miles per second (7,575 m/s)
Variants: See Ednatol

EDNATOL

Raw materials: 60% EDNA and 40% TNT
Properties: yellow color; castable
Uses: military explosive once used as substitute for Composition B; also used in rockets, grenades, and antitank shells; not used today
Stability: stable, non-hygroscopic; can be stored for long periods
Detonation velocity: approximately 4.6 miles per second (7,400 m/s)

EGDN (ETHYLENE GLYCOL DINITRATE): A TAGGANT. *SEE* SEMTEX AND PAGE 72.

EXPLOSIVE D: *SEE* AMMONIUM PICRATE.

EXPLOSIVE H: *SEE* EDNA.

FLASH COTTON, -PAPER, -STRING: *SEE* NITROCELLULOSE.

FOX-7: A POWERFUL EXPERIMENTAL INSENSITIVE HIGH EXPLOSIVE. *SEE* TATB.

GLYCERYL TRINITRATE: *SEE* NITROGLYCERIN.

GUNCOTTON: *SEE* NITROCELLULOSE.

GUNPOWDER: *SEE* BLACK POWDER.

HALEITE: *SEE* EDNA.

HBX

Name: **h**igh **b**last e**x**plosive
Raw materials: HBX-1: 40% RDX plus nitrocellulose, calcium chloride, and calcium silicate, 38% TNT, 17% aluminum powder, and 5% wax plus lecithin as desensitizers
Use: military explosive developed during World War II; replaced torpex for depth bombs and torpedoes
Stability: as powerful as torpex, but less sensitive
Variants: HBX-1, HBX-3, and H-6, which differ in percentage composition
Special attention: HBX produces gas and builds up pressure in the case during storage; adding calcium chloride to the mixture absorbs moisture and eliminates gas production

HEXOGEN: *SEE* RDX.

HMX

Other names: octogen, **h**igh **m**elting e**x**plosive, **H**er **M**ajesty's e**X**plosive, **h**igh-velocity **m**ilitary **x**plosive, or **h**igh-**m**olecular-weight RD**X**, cyclotetramethylene-tetranitramine, tetrahexamine tetranitramine, octahydro-1,3,5,7-tetranitro-1,3,5,7-tetrazocine
Raw materials: nitroamine (chemically related to RDX)
Uses: military explosive created in 1942 as a byproduct when making RDX; detonator in nuclear weapons; solid rocket propellant
Stability: relatively insensitive
Detonation velocity: 5.8 miles per second (9,400 m/s)
Variants: HMX is mixed with TNT and used in castable explosives called octols

Figure 11.3 Dutch engineers look for improvised explosive devices on a road clearance mission in Afghanistan.

KINEPAK: *SEE* ANNM.

LEAD AZIDE: *SEE* AZIDES.

LEAD STYPHNATE

Name: lead 2,4,6-trinitroresorcinate
Raw materials: styphnic acid, methanol, lead oxide
Properties: orange-yellow to dark brown crystals; slightly soluble in water and methyl alcohol
Uses: small-arms ammunition for military and commercial applications; used as a primary explosive with gunpowder and as a component in primer and detonator mixtures for secondary explosives; because of its extreme sensitivity to electrostatic charges is only used mixed with additives, such as tetracene
Stability: non-hygroscopic
Detonation velocity: approximately 3.2 miles per second (5,200 m/s)
Special attention: very sensitive to electrostatic charge. When dry, lead styphnate can readily detonate by static discharge, heat, flame, or shock. It is therefore shipped wet with at least 20% water or a water and denatured ethyl alcohol mixture.

LIQUID AIR EXPLOSIVE: *SEE* OXYLIQUIT.

LIQUID OXYGEN EXPLOSIVE: *SEE* OXYLIQUIT.

LUXITE

Name: trade name of "Sprengsalpéiter" (blast niter), produced between 1907 and 2001 by the company Poudrerie de Luxembourg S.A.

Raw materials: ammonium nitrate, sulfur, brown coal (lignite), wood flour, aluminum powder, and TNT

Properties: hygroscopic, so filled cartridges were wrapped in paper with paraffin so they could be used in humid environments

Use: mining minette, a sedimentary iron ore deposit found in the south of Luxembourg

Variants: Luxite 1, Luxite 3, Luxite 4, Luxite EB, Luxite 18, and Luxite SI. Although production of Luxite reached its peak in the middle of the twentieth century (up to 2,000 tons of civil explosives), it began to decline in the 1980s with the closure of the last iron ore mine in Luxembourg. Production was stopped in 2001.

LYDDITE: *SEE* PICRIC ACID.

MELINITE: *SEE* PICRIC ACID.

MERCURY FULMINATE

Raw materials: produced from the reaction of mercury and nitric acid, plus ethanol

Use: a primary explosive once used as a trigger for other explosives in percussion caps and blasting caps; not used much today in favor of less toxic, more stable chemicals such as lead azide, lead styphnate, and tetrazene derivatives

Stability: non-corrosive, but it is known to weaken with time

Detonation velocity: 2.6 miles per second (4,200 m/s)

O-MNT (ORTHO-MONONITROTOLUENE): A TAGGANT. *SEE* PAGE 71.

P-MNT (PARA-MONONITROTOLUENE): A TAGGANT. *SEE* SEMTEX AND PAGE 72.

NITROCELLULOSE (NC)

Other names: cellulose nitrate, flash paper, flash cotton, guncotton, flash string

Raw materials: cellulose and nitric acid or another powerful nitrating agent (e.g., ammonium nitrate or potassium nitrate)

Use: highly flammable explosive

Stability: sensitive to heat and fire, but not to shock or friction

Detonation velocity: from approximately 4 to 4.5 miles per second (6,400 m/s to 7300 m/s)

NITROGLYCERIN (NG)

Other names: glyceryl trinitrate (GTN), trinitroglycerin (TNG), nitro, and 1,2,3-trinitroxypropane
Raw materials: glycerol and nitric acid
Properties: a colorless, oily, liquid; a "low freezing" explosive ($\pm$ 10°C)
Uses: initially used for tunneling, road construction, and mining; also used in smokeless gunpowders
Stability: unstable; can explode with a relatively small stroke, shock, or friction
Detonation velocity: approximately 5 miles per second (8,100 m/s)

OCTOGEN: *SEE* HMX.

OCTOL

Other names: oktol or oktolit; the name octol combines **octo**gen (HMX) and tro**tyl** (TNT)
Raw materials: cyclotetramethylenetetranitramine (HMX) and trinitrotoluene (TNT)
Properties: solid mixture
Use: generally military (e.g., shaped charges and warheads of missiles, cruise missiles and torpedoes)
Detonation velocity: approximately 5.3 miles per second (8,500 m/s)
Variants: the mixing ratio of HMX:TNT is between 70:30 and 80:20; higher HMX content increases the detonation velocity and reduces stability

OXYLIQUIT

Other names: liquid air explosive, liquid oxygen explosive
Raw materials: mixture of liquid oxygen with a suitable fuel, such as carbon (e.g., lamp black), organic chemicals (e.g., a mixture of soot and naphthalene), wood meal, aluminum powder, or sponge
Uses: civil and military. After initial testing and blasting operations such as the construction of the Simplon Tunnel between Switzerland and Italy in 1899, and in 1900 the German mine Penzberg, the industrial use of liquid air explosives stopped.
Stability: the separate components are relatively safe; liquid air explosives are usually mixed just before use
Detonation velocity: between 1.9 and 3.1 miles per second (3,000 and 5,000 m/s)

PBX

Names: **p**lastic-**b**onded **e**xplosive, **p**olymer-**b**onded **e**xplosive
Raw materials: explosive powder bound together with 5–10% (by weight) synthetic polymer
Use: used for explosive powders that can't safely be melted or otherwise shaped
Stability: rubbery polymers can absorb shocks, making PBX insensitive to accidental detonation; hard polymers produce a PBX that maintains its shape, even under stress; powdered PBX can be pressed and shaped at room

temperature; PBX detonating cord is less sensitive and more waterproof than cords made with PETN

Detonation velocity: depending on the mixture, between 4 and 5.4 miles per second (6,450 m/s and 8,720 m/s)

Variants: PBX 9407: a mix of 95% HMX, 2.5% estane rubber, and 2.5% nitrated plasticizer; other PBX formulas use RDX, PETN, or TATB as the explosive along with binders such as polystyrene plastic, nitrocellulose, polyurethane rubber, or fluoropolymer elastomer

PENTHRITE: *SEE* PETN.

PENTOLITE

Raw materials: TNT and PETN

Uses: high explosive used for military and civilian purposes (e.g., warheads and booster charges)

Detonation velocity: military pentolite: approximately 4.6 miles per second (7,400 m/s); civilian pentolite: approximately 4.8 miles per second (7,800 m/s)

Variants: military pentolite (Pentolite 50/50) mixes 50% PETN phlegmatized with 50% TNT; civilian pentolite uses much less PETN (Pentolite 98/2, Pentolite 95/5, Pentolite 90/10); cast pentolite is used as a primer and booster for blasting agents

PEROXYACETONE: *SEE* ACETONE PEROXIDE.

PETN

Other names: penthrite, PENT, PENTA, TEN, pentaerythritol tetranitrate

Uses: one of the most powerful explosives; first synthesized in 1891; used as an amplifier load and for igniting small-caliber ammunition; also used in detonators in some land mines, in grenades, and as the explosive core of detonating cord

Stability: less resistant to impact and friction than TNT and tetryl; the least stable of the common military explosives

Detonation velocity: approximately 5.2 miles per second (8,350 m/s)

Variants: one of the substances in Semtex

PICRATOL

Name: the name combines ammonium **picra**te and **tro**tyl (TNT)

Raw materials: 52% Dunnite (ammonium picrate and Explosive D) and 48% TNT

Use: exclusively intended for military use; especially popular during World War II

Stability: very insensitive to shock

Detonation velocity: 4.3 miles per second (6,972 m/s)

Special attention: an obsolete explosive, but can be encountered in old munitions and unexploded ordnance

PICRIC ACID

Name: TNP; the name picric acid comes from the Greek *pikros* (bitter), reflecting its bitter taste

Raw materials: 2,4,6-trinitrophenol (TNP); originally made from nitriding natural products such as resin, animal horn, silk, or indigo; later created from phenol (carbolic acid)

Properties: colorless to lemon yellow crystalline solid; poorly soluble in water but quite soluble in ethanol

Uses: munitions; explosives

Stability: more stable than nitroglycerin and guncotton, so widely used in conventional weapons after 1871

Detonation velocity: 4.6 miles per second (7,350 m/s)

Variants: Lyddite, a mixture of picric acid and guncotton created by the British in 1888; about the same time the French called a similar mixture Melinite and the Japanese somewhat changed the mixture and called it Shimose powder; Explosive D (Dunnite) is the ammonium salt of picric acid; it is more powerful but less stable; picramide, formed from picric acid, can be used to produce the highly stable explosive TATB

Special attention: if completely dry, picric acid is shock sensitive and can sublimate in a sealed container, which makes opening the container dangerous; generally stored in glass bottles under a layer of water

Figure 11.4 A Dutch soldier in Afghanistan looking for hidden illegal weapons or explosive devices near a house.

POTASSIUM CHLORATE

Raw materials: chlorine, calcium hydroxide, potassium chloride
Properties: a white crystalline powder; moderately soluble in cold water and readily soluble in hot water
Uses: a key ingredient in percussion caps (primers) for early firearms and is still sometimes used today for this purpose; used in pyrotechnic powders and noisemakers known as "crackers" or "bang snaps"; used in smoke grenades

POTASSIUM NITRATE

Name: belong to a group of compounds called saltpeter
Raw materials: various methods of creating the compound (e.g., combining ammonium nitrate and potassium hydroxide, or ammonium nitrate and potassium chloride, or nitric acid and potassium hydroxide)
Properties: colorless to white crystalline powder; readily soluble in water
Uses: one of the most common oxidizers in fireworks; common fertilizer (source of nitrogen and potassium)
Variants: one of the major components of gunpowder (black powder)

POTASSIUM PERCHLORATE

Raw materials: perchloric acid and potassium hydroxide, or sodium perchlorate and potassium chloride
Properties: white crystals and white crystalline powder
Uses: pyrotechnic powders (flash compositions and sparklers); ammunition percussion caps; explosive primers; and in propellants

POUDRE B

Other names: Poudre Blanche, white powder (to distinguish it from black powder)
Raw materials: two forms of nitrocellulose (collodion and guncotton), plus ethanol and paraffin
Properties: tiny dark greenish-gray flakes
Uses: the first smokeless gun powder to be widely used and adopted; offered tactical advantages on the battlefield
Stability: tends to become unstable over time as the volatile solvents evaporate
Variants: cordite, invented in England in 1889

POUDRE N, POUDRE NOIRE: *SEE* BLACK POWDER.

RDX

Other names: hexogen, cyclonite, cyclotrimethylenetrinitroamine, trinitro-triazacyclohexane, T4. Explanations for the acronym RDX include **R**oyal **d**emolition e**X**plosive and **r**esearch **d**epartment explosive, but the real explanation is that new explosives developed by the British Military got a number preceded by the letters RD for **r**esearch and **d**evelopment. For some reason, RDX could not be assigned a number, so it was provisionally given the letter X, with the intention that the number would be determined later. Although it eventually got assigned a number, it remained known as RDX.

Raw materials: formed by the reaction of nitric acid with hexamine

Properties: a white crystalline solid

Uses: in many military explosives, including common military explosive mixtures with TNT, such as torpex and composition B; also used in Semtex, one of the first plastic explosives; has been used in many terrorist attacks; used for controlled demolitions; is considered one of the most powerful military high explosives

Stability: easily stored, stable at room temperature, detonates only with a detonator, and does not explode even if hit by a projectile from a small firearm

Detonation velocity: 5.4 miles per second (8,750 m/s)

ROBURIT: *SEE* WETTER ENERGIT.

SEMTEX

Name: named after Semtín, a suburb of Pardubice, in the former Czechoslovakia, where the explosive material was first made in 1966 by chemist Stanislav Brebera

Raw materials: PETN and RDX, plus binders and plasticizers

Properties: red or brick-orange (easily distinguished from C-4, which is off-white); waterproof

Uses: a plastic explosive used for demolition, blasting, and military purposes

Stability: usable over a greater temperature range than other plastic explosives since it stays plastic between −22°F and 140°F (−40°C and 60°C)

Detonation velocity: Semtex 1A: approximately 4.8 miles per second (7,670 m/s)

Variants: Semtex 1A (76% PETN, 4.6% RDX, 9.4% binder, and 9% plasticizer) is used for blasting and is based mostly on crystalline PETN; Semtex 1AP and 2P (58% PETN, 23% RDX, 9.2% binder, and 8.45% plasticizer) are used as booster charges

Special attention: Semtex has been linked to several terrorist explosions, including the explosion of a Boeing 747 over Lockerbie, Scotland, in 1988. In response to international pressure, Semtex now has a detection taggant that produces a distinctive vapor signature. First, ethylene glycol dinitrate (EGDN) was used, which was later switched to 2,3-dimethyl-2,3-dinitrobutane (3,4-dinitrohexane, DMDNB) or *p*-mononitrotoluene, which is used currently. According to the manufacturer, Semtex has included a taggant since 1991. The manufacturer says that even pre-1990, untagged Semtex can now be detected.

SHIMOSE POWDER: *SEE* PICRIC ACID.

SILVER AZIDE: *SEE* AZIDES.

SLURRIES: *SEE* WATER-GEL EXPLOSIVES.

SMOKELESS POWDERS: *SEE* POUDRE B, BALLISTITE, AND CORDITE.

SODIUM AZIDE: *SEE* AZIDES.

SODIUM NITRATE

Other names: SN, nitranine, nitratite, soda niter; also called Chile saltpeter or Peru saltpeter to distinguish it from ordinary saltpeter (potassium nitrate)
Raw materials: is mined in Chile and Peru; can be created chemically
Properties: a colorless to white crystalline powder; highly soluble in water
Uses: used industrially to produce fertilizers, pyrotechnics, enamels, smoke bombs, and solid rocket propellant

Figure 11.5 A Dutch soldier on patrol with a metal detector in Afghanistan.

SULFUR

Other names: sulphur; called *brimstone* in the Bible

Properties: a non-metal solid with a bright yellow color; gives off a blue light in combustion; has a distinctive odor; flammable

Uses: matches, insecticides, pyrotechnics; is a component of gunpowder (black powder

Special attention: has long been used for military purposes because of sulfur's flammability and wide availability

T4: *SEE* RDX.

TATB

Name: triaminotrinitrobenzene

Raw materials: 1,3,5-triamino-2,4,6-trinitrobenzene

Properties: bright yellow crystals

Uses: preferred in applications where safety is paramount, as in nuclear weapons; often used as the explosive ingredient in plastic-bonded explosives

Stability: insensitive to shock, friction, or impact, and is stable up to very high temperatures (> 662°F, 350°C); will not detonate accidentally even in a fire or an airplane crash

Detonation velocity: 4.7 miles per second (7,550 m/s)

Variants: the chemical structure of TATB is similar to the powerful experimental insensitive high explosive FOX-7 (1,1-diamino-2,2-dinitroethene, DADNE), first synthesized in 1998 in Sweden, with a detonation velocity of 5.2 miles per second (8,335 m/s)

TATP: *SEE* ACETONE PEROXIDE.

TCAP: *SEE* ACETONE PEROXIDE.

TETRAZENE

Raw materials: sodium nitrite and an aminoguanidine salt dissolved in acetic acid

Uses: sensitization of priming compositions; when ignited, produces large amounts of black smoke; used in airbags

Stability: high shock and friction sensitivity; slightly more impact-sensitive than mercury fulminate

Detonation velocity: approxmiately 2.5 miles per second (4,000 m/s)

Special attention: when pressed enough, its sensitivity is reduced or destroyed; this is known as dead pressing

TETRYL

Name: 2,4,6-trinitrophenylmethylnitramine, tetranitro-*n*-methylamine

Raw materials: dimethylaniline, nitric acid, sulfuric acid

Properties: yellow crystalline powder; not soluble in water, but soluble in solvents such as acetone and benzene; generally seen in the form of pressed pellets
Use: sensitive secondary high explosive used as a booster; used in both world wars; used in blasting caps in combination with mercury fulminate and potassium chlorate
Stability: safe to handle and very stable in storage
Detonation velocity: approximately 4.8 miles per second (7,770 m/s)
Variants: usually used on its own, though can sometimes be found in compositions such as tetrytol
Special attention: more powerful than TNT; may be detonated by flame, friction, shock, or sparks; no longer manufactured or used in the United States, but it can still be found in legacy munitions such as the M14 anti-personnel landmine

TETRYTOL

Raw materials: mixture of 65–80% tetryl and 35–20% TNT
Uses: military and demolition
Stability: more sensitive than tetryl and less sensitive than TNT; when stored below 149°F (65°C), does not change stability, acid content, sensitivity, or brisance
Detonation velocity: for a mixture of 70% tetryl to 30% TNT: 4.6 miles per second (7,370 m/s)

TNT

Other names: trotyl, 2,4,6-trinitrotoluene, trinitrotoluene, triton, tolite, trilite, tritol
Raw material: toluene and a mixture of sulfuric and nitric acids
Properties: tan-colored crystals; can be poured when in liquid form, which makes it a convenient explosive for filling shell casings; forms solid once in casing; releases black carbon smoke during explosion
Use: high explosive for military and construction; still widely used today in the United States and around the world
Stability: low sensitivity and high brisance; can be stored for long periods
Detonation velocity: 4.3 miles per second (6,900 m/s)
Variants: can be used in pure form or as an important part of other explosive mixtures

TORPEX

Name: from "**torp**edo **ex**plosive"
Raw materials: torpex 1: 45% RDX, 37% TNT, 18% aluminum powder, and 1% wax); torpex 2: 42% RDX, 40% TNT, 18% aluminum powder, and 1% wax; aluminum increases the destructive power underwater

Use: military explosive developed during World War II to be used mainly in underwater ordnance such as mines, torpedo warheads, and depth bombs
Stability: more sensitive than TNT; bullet impact and drop test sensitivities are similar to tetryl
Detonation velocity: torpex 2: approximately 4.6 miles per second (7,440 m/s)
Special attention: stable in storage, although it produces gas, which causes pressure in the case

TRICYCLOACETON PEROXIDE: *SEE* ACETONE PEROXIDE.

TROTYL: *SEE* TNT.

WATER-GEL EXPLOSIVES

Other name: slurries
Raw materials: fuel-sensitized explosive mixtures with an aqueous ammonium nitrate solution as an oxidizer; blasting agents contain fuels such as carbon, sulfur, or aluminum, and contain sensitive ingredients such as TNT, ammonium nitrate, calcium nitrate, aluminum, and ethylene glycol
Properties: jelly-like consistency; packaged in sausage-like packages stapled shut on both sides
Use: have displaced dynamite as the most-used civil blasting agents; often used in the mining industry
Stability: are thickened and gelled with a gum, such as guar gum, to give considerable water resistance; are relatively safe and easy to transport and store
Detonation velocity: between 2.3 and 3.4 miles per second (3,660 and 5,480 m/s), depending on ingredients, charge diameter, degree of confinement, and density
Variants: aluminized water-gel explosives give good results in extremely hard rock

WETTER ENERGIT

Name: Wetter is a German prefix given to all trade names for "permitted explosives," and *Wetter* is used in jargon to describe the gas mixture of air in underground coal mines (which usually consists of carbon dioxide, carbon monoxide, methane, hydrogen sulfide, and oxygen—the levels and combinations of these gases determine the level of danger)
Raw materials: 85% ammonium chloride and sodium nitrate with 11% blasting oil (mostly a mixture of nitroglycerin and nitroglycol); nitroglycerin is rarely used alone because it freezes around 50°F (10°C), which would render it ineffective in the cool temperatures in underground mines
Use: in coal mines because it has a short detonation flame and does not ignite the methane–air mixture or coal dust–air mixture found in underground mines

Detonation velocity: approximately 1.1 miles per second (1,700 m/s)
Variants: Wetter Energit is the trade name of a white powdered permitted explosive produced by the Orica company. Another popular product is Wetter-Roburit, which is made of 55–88% ammonium nitrate, 0.5% potassium permanganate, 7% dinitrobenzene or 12% TNT, dinitrochloronaphthalene, and other organic components.

WHITE POWDER: *SEE* POUDRE B.

Figure 11.6 A US soldier prepares to mark a UXO found during a training exercise.

Bibliography

Aragon, Carlos L., Erik H. Hofmeister, and Steven C. Budsberg. "Systematic Review of Clinical Trials of Treatments for Osteoarthritis in Dogs." *Journal of the American Veterinary Medical Association* 230, no. 4 (February 15, 2007): 514–21. https://doi.org/10.2460/javma.230.4.514.

B.B.C. News "Q&A: Air Freight Bomb Plot." (October 30, 2010). http://www.bbc.com/news/11658452.

Bennett, Brian. "PETN: The Explosive that Airport Security Is Targeting," *Los Angeles Times* (originally from the Tribune Washington Bureau). (November 24, 2010). http://articles.latimes.com/2010/nov/24/nation/la-na-petn-20101124.

Bright, Paula D. *USAF Military Dog Training Aids: Toxicity and Treatment*, (November 1989), AFOEHL Report 89-130EHO100LOC.

Cooper, Paul W. *Explosives Engineering*. New York: Wiley-VCH, 1996.

Everest, Dave. The Velocity of Detonation of High Explosives. Issue 3, (April 19, 2007). www.users.on.net/~kamel/files/VelofDet.doc.

Ewing, Robert G., Melanie J. Waltman, David A. Atkinson, et al. "The Vapor Pressures of Explosives." *Trends in Analytical Chemistry* 42 (January 2013): 35–48. https://doi.org/10.1016/j.trac.2012.09.010 http://www.sciencedirect.com/science/article/pii/S0165993612002828.

Fjellanger, Rune. "Remote Explosive Scent Tracing: A Method for Detection of Explosive and Chemical Substances." In *Vapour and Trace Detection of Explosives for Anti-Terrorism Purposes*, Michael Krausa, ed. NATO Science Series, Springer, 167 (2004): 63–68. http://link.springer.com/chapter/10.1007/978-1-4020-2716-1_8. https://doi.org/10.1007/978-1-4020-2716-1_8.

Furton, Kenneth G., and Lawrence J. Myers. "The Scientific Foundation and Efficacy of the Use of Canines as Chemical Detectors for Explosives." *Talanta* 54, no. 3 (May 10, 2001): 487–500. https://doi.org/10.1016/S0039-9140(00)00546-4 http://www.sciencedirect.com/science/article/pii/S0039914000005464.

Gazit, Irit, and Joseph Terkel. "Explosives Detection by Sniffer Dogs Following Strenuous Physical Activity." *Applied Animal Behaviour Science* 81, no. 2 (2003): 149–61. https://doi.org/10.1016/S0168-1591(02)00274-5.

Geneva International Centre for Humanitarian Demining. "Designer Dogs: Improving the Quality of Mine Detection Dogs." Geneva International Centre for Humanitarian Demining: Geneva, Switzerland, (December 2001). http://www.gichd.org/fileadmin/GICHD-resources/rec-documents/Catalogue_Designer_Dogs.pdf.

Grandjean, Dominique, J.P. Valette, M. Jougln, C. Gabillard, H. Barque, M. Bene, and J.P. Guillaud. "Use of a Nutritional Supplement with L-carnitine, Vitamin C and Vitamin B12 in Sporting Dogs." *Recueil de Médecine Vétérinaire* 169 (1993): 543–551.

Greenemeier, Larry. "Exposing the Weakest Link: As Airline Passenger Security Tightens, Bombers Target Cargo Holds." *Scientific American* (November 2, 2010). https://www.scientificamerican.com/article/aircraft-cargo-bomb-security/.

Harper, Ross J., José R. Almirall, and Kenneth G. Furton. "Identification of Dominant Odor Chemicals Emanating from Explosives for Use in Developing Optimal Training Aid Combinations and Mimics for Canine Detection." *Talanta* 67, no. 2 (August 15, 2005): 313–27. https://doi.org/10.1016/j.talanta.2005.05.019 http://www.sciencedirect.com/science/article/pii/S0039914005003188.

Hondebrink, Henk. Personal communication, 2000–2017.

Hondebrink, Henk, and Claudia Boomaars. *Opleiding Speurhondengeleider Narcotica*. Oosterhout: Dog Training Center Oosterhout, 2015.

Johnston, Jim M. "Enhanced Canine Explosives Detection." Ft. Washington, MD: Office of Special Technology, 1997. DTIC AD# B234756.

Johnston, Jim M. "Canine Detection Capabilities: Operational Implications of Recent R&D Findings." Institute for Biological Detection Systems, Auburn University, June 1999. http://www.barksar.org/K-9_Detection_Capabilities.pdf.

"Marvels of Mini-Weather." *The Sciences* 5, no. 2 (July 1965): 1–4. https://doi.org/10.1002/j.2326-1951.1965.tb00178.x. http://onlinelibrary.wiley.com/doi/10.1002/j.2326-1951.1965.tb00178.x/abstract.

Maslow, Abraham H. *The Psychology of Science: A Reconnaissance*. New York: Harper & Row, 1966.

Matyáš, Robert and Jiří Pachman. *Primary Explosives*. Berlin, Heidelberg: Springer-Verlag, 2013. https://doi.org/10.1007/978-3-642-28436-6.

Miklósi, Ádam, R. Polgárdi, J. Topál, et al. "Use of Experimenter-Given Cues in Dogs." *Animal Cognition* 1, no. 2 (1998): 113–21. https://doi.org/10.1007/s100710050016.

Mistafa, Ron. *K9 Explosive Detection*. Calgary, AB: Detselig Enterprises, 1998.

McLean, Ian G. *Designer Dogs: Improving the Quality of Mine Detection Dogs*, GICHD, Geneva, Geneva International Centre for Humanitarian Demining (GICHD), 2001.

McLean, Ian G. *Mine Detection Dogs: Training, Operations and Odour Detection*, Geneva, Geneva International Centre for Humanitarian Demining (GICHD), 2003.

Nolan, R.V., and D.L. Gravitte. "Mine-Detecting Canines: Summary Report 1975–1976," Army Mobility Equipment Research and Development Command, Fort Belvoir, VA, September 1977.

Östmark, Henric, Sara Wallin, and How Gee Ang. "Vapor Pressure of Explosives: A Critical Review." *Propellants, Explosives, Pyrotechnics* 37, no. 1 (February 2012): 12–23. https://doi.org/10.1002/prep.201100083 http://onlinelibrary.wiley.com/doi/10.1002/prep.201100083/full.

Pelletier, Bruno. "L-carnitine or Vitamin B6 of Interest in the Dog." *Action Veterinaire* 1210 (1992): 19.

Pfungst, Oskar. *Clever Hans (The Horse of Mr. Von Osten): A Contribution to Experimental Animal and Human Psychology*. New York: Holt, Rinehart & Winston, 1911. https://doi.org/10.5962/bhl.title.56164.

Pongrácz, Péter, A. Miklósi, E. Kubinyi, et al. "Social Learning in Dogs: The Effect of a Human Demonstrator on the Performance of Dogs in a Detour Task." *Animal Behaviour* 62, no. 6 (2001): 1109–17. https://doi.org/10.1006/anbe.2001.1866.

Powell, William. *The Anarchist Cookbook*. New York: Lyle Stuart, 1971.

Ram, Nico. Personal communication, 1980–1990.

Rhykerd, Charles L. "Guide for the Selection of Commercial Explosives Detection Systems for Law Enforcement Applications." In *NIJ Guide* 100–99. National Institute of Justice. Washington, DC: US Department of Justice, 1999. http://www.worldcat.org/title/guide-for-the-selection-of-commercial-explosives-detection-systems-for-law-enforcement-applications/oclc/42951142.

Snoek, Gerrit Michiel, Personal communication, 1980–1990.

Soproni, Krisztina, Á. Miklósi, J. Topál, et al. "Dogs' (*Canis familiaris*) Responsiveness to Human Pointing Gestures." *Journal of Comparative Psychology (Washington, D.C.)* 116, no. 1 (2002): 27–34. https://doi.org/10.1037/0735-7036.116.1.27.

Urška, Tomšic. "Detection of Explosives: Dogs vs. CMOS Capacitive Sensors." University of Ljubljana, Faculty of Mathematics and Physics, (March 2013). http://mafija.fmf.uni-lj.si/seminar/files/2012_2013/DETECTION_OF_EXPLOSIVES_-_Dogs_vs._CMOS_Capacitive_Sensors.pdf.

Wikipedia. "Explosive Material." Accessed February 2017: http://en.wikipedia.org/wiki/Explosive_material.

Yinon, Jehuda. *Modern Methods and Applications in Analysis of Explosives*. New York: Wiley, 1993.

Yinon, Jehuda. *Forensic and Environmental Detection of Explosives*. Chichester: John Wiley & Sons, 1999.

Photo Credits

Listed by figure number: *Department of Defence of the Netherlands*: 1.1–1.4, 1.9, 2.2–2.5, 2.10, 4.1, 4.2, 5.4, 6.3, 6.4, 6.12, 8.10, 8.20, 8.21, 8.26, 9.1–9.4, 11.3–11.5. *Dog Training Center Oosterhout*: 1.6, 1.7, 3.1–3.3, 3.5, 3.7, 3.8, 4.19, 5.1, 5.2, 5.5–5.14, 6.5–6.11, 7.1–7.5, 7.11, 8.12, 8.14, 8.15, 8.18, 10.1, 10.2, 10.5–10.7. *Shutterstock*: 2.8 (taviphoto); 2.9, 2.14 (Militarist); 2.12 (FabrikaSimf); 2.22 (GongTo); 2.23 (Vova Shevchuk); 2.24 (Fer Gregory); 2.25 (jannoon028); 2.28 (Boonroong); 2.29 (Levent Konuk); 4.22, 9.7 (Milan Tomazin); 7.6, 7.7, 8.7, 8.24 (NEstudio); 8.1 (Ernie); 8.2 (David Orcea); 8.3, 8.6, 8.23 (Vadim Ivanov); 8.4 (Sergei Prokhorov); 8.5 (Jakkrit Saelao); 8.8, 8.22 (szabozoltan); 8.11 (horkins); 8.16 (symbiot); 8.25, 11.2 (Sudtawee Thepsuponkul); 11.1 (molekuul_be). *Other*: 1.5 (US Marine Corps photo by Cpl. Reece Lodder/Public domain); 1.8 (Wikimedia/Hexogen); 1.10, 6.13 (US Marine Corps photos by Cpl. Alejandro Pena/Released); 1.11, 7.4 (US Army photo by Sgt. Kimberly Bratic/Public domain); 2.1 (US Dept of Defence photo by SPC Wayne Becton/Public domain); 2.6, 3.4, 11.6 (US Army photos by Sgt. Cody Quinn/Released); 2.20, 8.9 (US Dept of Defence photo by Ed Drohan, CJTF Paladin Public Affairs); 2.18, 2.21 (US Army Alaska, Fort Richardson); 4.3 (US Marine Corps photo by Cpl. Johnny Merkley/Public domain); 5.3 (US Marine Corps photo by

Lance Cpl. Cesar N. Contreras/Released); 6.1 (US Army photo by 2nd Lt. Sgt. Gene Arnold/Public domain); 6.2 (US Marine Corps photo by Lance Cpl. Zachary B. Martin/Released); 7.8 (US Marine Corps photo by Lance Cpl. Drew Tech/Released); 7.10 (US Dept of Defence photo by Cpl. Zachary J. Nola); 9.5 (Belgian federal police: www.polfed-fedpol.be); 9.6 (Bundeswehr/Bienert at Wikimedia Commons); 8.27 left, 8.28 (APOPO); 8.27 right (US Navy photo by Photographer's Mate 1st Class Brien Aho/Public domain); 10.4 (US Dept of Defence photo by Sgt. David Turner/Public domain).

About the Authors

Ruud Haak is the author of more than 30 dog books in Dutch and German. Since 1979 he has been the editor-in-chief of the biggest Dutch dog magazine, *Onze Hond* (*Our Dog*). He was born in 1947 in Amsterdam, the Netherlands. At the age of 13, he was training police dogs at his uncle's security dog training center, and when he was 15, he worked after school with his patrol dog (which he trained himself) at the Amsterdam harbor. He later started training his dogs in Schutzhund and IPO, and he successfully bred and showed German shepherds and Saint Bernards.

Ruud worked as a social therapist in a government clinic for criminal psychopaths. From his studies in psychology, he became interested in dog behavior and training methods for nose work, especially the tracking dog and the search-and-rescue dog. More recently he has trained drug- and explosive-detector dogs for the Dutch police and the Royal Dutch Airforce. He is also a visiting lecturer at Dutch, German, and Austrian police-dog schools.

In the 1970s, Ruud and his wife, Dr. Resi Gerritsen, a psychologist and jurist, attended many courses and symposia for Schutzhund, tracking, and search-and-rescue dog training in Switzerland, Germany, and Austria. In 1979, they started the Dutch Rescue Dog Organization in the Netherlands. With that unit, they attended many operations responding to earthquakes, gas explosions, and lost persons in wooded or wilderness areas. In 1990, Ruud and Resi

Ruud Haak with his German shepherd Yes van Sulieseraad and Malinois Google van het Eldenseveld.

Resi Gerritsen with her Malinois Halusetha's All Power and Malinois Google van het Eldensveld.

moved to Austria, where they were asked by the Austrian Red Cross to select and train operational rescue and avalanche dogs. They lived for three years at a height of 6,000 feet (1,800 m) in the Alps and worked with their dogs in search missions after avalanches.

With their Austrian colleagues, Ruud and Resi developed a new method for training search-and-rescue dogs. This way of training showed the best results after a major earthquake in Armenia (1988), an earthquake in Japan (1995), two major earthquakes in Turkey (1999), and big earthquakes in Algeria and Iran (2003). Ruud and Resi have also demonstrated the success of their unique training methods for tracking dogs as well as search-and-rescue dogs at the Austrian, Czech, Hungarian, and World Championships, where both were several times the leading champions.

Resi and Ruud have held many symposia and master classes all over the world on their unique training methods, which are featured in their books:

- *K9 Drug Detection: A Manual for Training and Operations*
- *K9 Complete Care: A Manual for Physically and Mentally Healthy Working Dogs*
- *K9 Investigation Errors and How to Avoid Them*
- *K9 Personal Protection: A Manual for Training Reliable Protection Dogs*
- *K9 Professional Tracking: A Complete Manual for Theory and Training*
- *K9 Scent Training: A Manual for Training Your Identification, Tracking, and Detection Dog*
- *K9 Schutzhund: A Manual for IPO Training through Positive Reinforcement*
- *K9 Search and Rescue: A Manual for Training the Natural Way*
- *K9 Working Breeds: Characteristics and Capabilities*

With Simon Prins they wrote *K9 Behavior Basics: A Manual for Proven Success in Operational Service Dog Training*; and with Dr. Adee Schoon, Ruud wrote *K9 Suspect Discrimination: Training and Practicing Scent Identification Line-Ups.* All of these books were published by Detselig Enterprises Ltd., Calgary, Canada (now Brush Education Inc./Dog Training Press).

Ruud and Resi now live in the Netherlands. They are training directors and international judges for the International Rescue Dog Organisation (IRO) and the Fédération Cynologique Internationale (FCI). Ruud and Resi are still successfully training their dogs as detector dogs for search and rescue, drugs, explosives, and IPO Schutzhund. You can contact the authors by e-mail at resigerritsen@gmail.com.

K9 Professional Training Series

See the complete list at
dogtrainingpress.com